주한미군지위협정(SOFA)

공공용역
합동위원회 1

주한미군지위협정(SOFA)

공공용역
합동위원회 1

한국학술정보

| 머리말

미국은 오래전부터 우리나라 외교에 있어서 가장 긴밀하고 실질적인 우호 · 협력관계를 맺어
온 나라다. 6 · 25전쟁 정전 협정이 체결된 후 북한의 재침을 막기 위한 대책으로서 1953년 11월
한미 상호방위조약이 체결되었다. 이는 미군이 한국에 주둔하는 법적 근거였고, 그렇게 주둔하
게 된 미군의 시설, 구역, 사업, 용역, 출입국, 통관과 관세, 재판권 등 포괄적인 법적 지위를 규정
하는 것이 바로 주한미군지위협정(SOFA)이다. 그러나 이와 관련한 협상은 계속된 난항을 겪으
며 한미 상호방위조약이 체결로부터 10년이 훌쩍 넘은 1967년이 돼서야 정식 발효에 이를 수 있
었다. 그럼에도 당시 미군 범죄에 대한 한국의 재판권은 심한 제약을 받았으며, 1980년대 후반
민주화 운동과 함께 미군 범죄 문제가 사회적 이슈로 떠오르자 협정을 개정해야 한다는 목소리
가 커지게 되었다. 이에 1991년 2월 주한미군지위협정 1차 개정이 진행되었고, 이후에도 여러 사
건이 발생하며 2001년 4월 2차 개정이 진행되어 현재에 이르고 있다.

본 총서는 외교부에서 작성하여 최근 공개한 주한미군지위협정(SOFA) 관련 자료를 담고
있다. 1953년 한미 상호방위조약 체결 이후부터 1967년 발효가 이뤄지기까지의 자료와 더불
어, 이후 한미 합동위원회을 비롯해 민 · 형사재판권, 시설, 노무, 교통 등 각 분과위원회의 회
의록과 운영 자료, 한국인 고용인 문제와 관련한 자료, 기타 관련 분쟁 자료 등을 포함해 총 42
권으로 구성되었다. 전체 분량은 약 2만 2천여 쪽에 이른다.

2024년 3월
한국학술정보(주)

| 일러두기

· 본 총서에 실린 자료는 2022년 4월과 2023년 4월에 각각 공개한 외교문서 4,827권, 76만 여 쪽 가운데 일부를 발췌한 것이다.

· 각 권의 제목과 순서는 공개된 원본을 최대한 반영하였으나, 주제에 따라 일부는 적절히 변경하였다.

· 원본 자료는 A4 판형에 맞게 축소하거나 원본 비율을 유지한 채 A4 페이지 안에 삽입 하였다. 또한 현재 시점에선 공개되지 않아 '공란'이란 표기만 있는 페이지 역시 그대로 실었다.

· 외교부가 공개한 문서 각 권의 첫 페이지에는 '정리 보존 문서 목록'이란 이름으로 기록물 종류, 일자, 명칭, 간단한 내용 등의 정보가 수록되어 있으며, 이를 기준으로 0001번부터 번호가 매겨져 있다. 이는 삭제하지 않고 총서에 그대로 수록하였다.

· 보고서 내용에 관한 더 자세한 정보가 필요하다면, 외교부가 온라인상에 제공하는 『대한 민국 외교사료요약집』 1991년과 1992년 자료를 참조할 수 있다.

| 차례

분류번호	729. 418 1968-69	등록번호	527	보존기간	영구 乙
기능명칭	SOFA 한·미 합동 위원회 공공용역 분과 위원회, 1968~69				
생산과	안보 담당관실		생산년도	1969	

주; 1. 1968년.

1ㅏ. 미군에 대한 전력요금 적용에 관한 건.

2. 1969년.

한정왈료

			M/F No.	

1. 1968 년

1-1. 미군에 대한 전력요금
적용에 관한 건.
1968. 4. 18 ~ 10.21

1. 1968년도

2

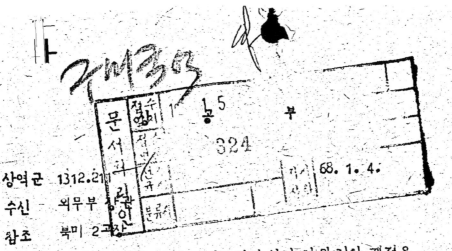

상역군 1312.211

수신 외무부 장관인

참조 북미 2과장

제목 공공료율 인상에 따른 미측과의 사전 협의 절차 제정을
     위한 대책 회의 개최.

          한미간 군대 지위 협정 (S O F A) 및 동과의 의사록
제 6조의 규정에 의거 공공료율 인상에 따른 변경된 요율을 미군
기관에 적용시킴에 있어서 그 사전 절차를 제정키 위한 한미 합동
회의를 68. 1. 12 개최키로 하였는바 이에 대비하여 한국측 대안을
미리 정해 놓고자 사전 대책 회의를 다음과 같이 개최하고자 하오니
밑히 참석하어 주시기 바랍니다.

                    다   음

일시   1968. 1. 9 (화) 14 시
장소   상공부 회의실
참석범위   경제기획원   물가정책 과장 (서석준)
          내무부   행정 과장 (김수학)
          내무부   재정 과장 (남문희)
          서울특별시   업무 과장 (이상쭉)
          체신부   국내과장 (김상우)
          철도청   화물과장 (이응식)
          외무부   북미과 (오명두)

상역군 1312.211   68. 1. 4.

제목   공공료율 인상에 따른 미측과의 사전 협의 절차 제정을
       위한 대책 회의개최

참석범위, 상공부   전정과장 (박경연)
          상공부   상무과장 (이창하). 끝.

상   공   부   장

MINISTRY OF COMMERCE AND INDUSTRY
REPUBLIC OF KOREA

11 January 1968

SUBJECT: Joint Committee Consultation on Utilities and Services, as Provided in Article VI of the SOFA.

TO   : Chairman, US Commerce Subcommittee

1. Reference:

    a. Article VI, paragraph 2 and Agreed Minute 1 of Article VI, SOFA.

    b. ROK-US Joint Committee Memorandum to Chairmen, Commerce Subcommittee, subject same as above, dated 28 September 1967.

    c. Two letters to Chairman, ROK Commerce Subcommittee by the Chairman, US Commerce Subcommittee on the same subject dated respectively 31 October and 1 December 1967.

    2. The Korean Component of the Subcommittee has reached, after full deliberation of the matter, the following conclusions:

    a. The Commerce Subcommittee as presently set up is not suitable, as far as Korean Component is concerned, for handling the problem under discussion. Therefore a new Subcommittee is to be established which will be chaired by the Director of Planning, Economic Planning Board and will handle matters relating to Article VI.

    b. As to US requirements to be given advance notice of changes in utilities rates which may take place in the course of subsequent U.S. fiscal year during the month of February each year, it was found to be impossible to synchronize the U.S. needs and policy decisions of the Republic of Korea Government in view of the prevailing conditions, and US requirements cannot be fully met. It is hoped that by establishing a new Subcommittee useful exchange of information and views will be made and a tolerable reconciliation of needs and actual conditions will be achieved.

    c. Of the utilities and services provided to the USFK, in view of diffuse control and minor importance, garbage disposal service be excluded from formal consultation. In case of difficulties, it can properly be handled on case by case basis.

3. The following are proposed as the consultation procedures.

a. A new Subcommittee, tentatively called Utilities Subcommittee, will be established to cover Article VI of the SOFA as explained in paragraph 2(a) above. The US side will either organize a new Subcommittee or designate as counterpart component an existing Subcommittee..The two chairmen will maintain close liaison, and exchange information and views on possible changes in utilities rates on confidential basis even at policy formulating stages.

b. Garbage disposal service, which is controlled by local administrative bodies, will be excluded from formal consultation procedures. This will leave railroad transportation, communication, electricity and water supply as the subjects of consultation. Any new subject may be added by mutual agreement as needs may arise.

c. In the event of formal decisions of the Government for changes in utilities rates, the Korean Government authorities directly concerned with the utilities will notify U.S. authorities as soon as such decision is known, and start negotiation for renewal of contracts or agreement under existing arrangements. If the negotiation is successful the agreement will be final and definitive. If there arises any disagreement, the matter will be brought to the Subcommittee, and the Subcommittee may bring the question to the Joint Committee for its decision.

d. As to changes in priorities and conditions, they necessitate renewal of contracts or agreements and therefore there is no need of prior "consultation", and the procedures outlined in the preceding sub-paragraph will apply.

e. Both ROK and US sides reserve the right to bring matters relating to Article VI to the Joint Committee at any time.

Shim Ui Whan
Chairman
ROK Commerce Subcommittee

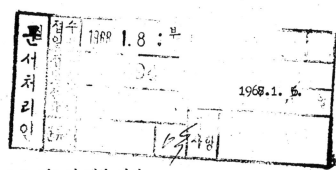

체

체전일 723.1-   125

수신   외무부장관

참조   구미국장

제목   주한미군 전신전화 요금 적용에 대한 질의

    1. 당부는 주한미8군에게 1957년에 체결한 전기통신 시설 사용수의
계약(FEC-417)에 의거 전신전화서비스를 제공하여왔고 그 요금은 당부의
통신요금 개정시 마다 수의계약서를 개정하여 대한민국 법정요금을 적용하여
왔읍니다. 또한 1967.8.30.에 당부측의 전근현전무국장외 7명과 미육군측의
암스트롱(J.B.Armstrong   )법무관, 미8군구매처장, 미8군통신감외 5명
이 참석한 회의결과 현행 계약서의 불합리한 점을 지적하고 새로운 계약 체결
에 상호 합의하였으며 통신 요금 적용은 자동적으로 대한민국 법정요금으로
하자는데 대체적인 양해를 보았읍니다

    2. 당부에서는 전기통신 시설 사용수의 계약에 의거 전화설비비가 67.
10.4자로 개정되었음을 미8군에서 통보한바 미군측은 이를 내용으로하는 제5차
전기통신시설 사용수의 계약서 개정안을 제안하여왔읍니다
그러나 본 개정안은 한미합동위원회의 승인을 거친후에 발효한다는 조건부 개
정안으로서 현재까지 발효하지 못하고 있는 실정입니다

    3. 아울러 한미양측 관계관 회의시 양해하였든 불합리한 수의계약서의
전면 개폐 문제도 전기와 같은 이유로 답보 상태에 놓여있읍니다

    4. 이에 대한 처리 방안을 모색코저 아래점을 질의하오니 귀의를 조속
회시 바랍니다

가. 별지와 같은 귀부의 공한 및 회의결과를 근거로 당부의 통신 요금 개정 문제를 양지정 당국(체신부와 미8군)만으로서 완전 유효하게 해결 할수있는지 여부

나. 전기 "가"의 경우 미8군 측에서 주장한 조건부 계약(한미합동 위원회의 회부후 효력발생)에 대한 대처 방안

다. 한미행정 협정(합의의사록 제6조 1항)에 의거 한미합동위원회 의 협의후에 미군측에 대한민국 법정 전신전화 요금이 적용된다고 하면 한미합 동 위원회의 회부 절차 문제

라. 전기 "다"의 경우

첫째. 67.10.4자로 개정된 전화설비비의 적용문제

둘째. 68.1.1자로 실시 예정으로 공공요금 심사위원회에 회부 통과된 (67.12.26)전화도수료, 시외통화료등 개정될 전화요금 적용문제

첨부: 외무부 관련 공한 1부. 끝.

체 신 부 장 관

별지

외무부관련공한

1. 제106차 국무회의 의결사항(1966.12.23)

   가. 합동위원회에 전기통신 특별분과위원회(주무부 — 체신부)를 두고 이의 대표로 체신부 전무국장(전근헌)으로 한다

   나. 한,미군대 지위 협정제3조 2 (나)항에서 규정됨 전기통신 문제를 취급할 한,미 특별약정을 체결하기 위한 지정 통신당국으로서 체신부를 지정한다

   체신부는 전기통신 특별분과위원회에서 전기통신에 관한 모든 문제를 정부를 대표하여 해결할수있다

2. 특별분과위원회 대표임명(외구미 723.1-203 67.1.6)66.12.30

   대통령 각하의 재가로 전기통신 특별분과 위원회 대표로 당부 전무국장(전근헌)이 임명되었음

3. 외무부에서 개최된 회의 결과(67.1.16)

   가. 전기통신 특별분과 위원회가 구성되므로 체신부는 앞으로 합동위원회에 참석하지 않아도 좋다

   나. 전기통신 특별분과위원회는 독자적으로 운영되는것이며 합동위원회를 거침이 없이 정부를 대표하여 전권을 행사할수있다

9

기 안 용 지

<table>
<tr><td rowspan="3">분류기호
문서번호</td><td>미이</td><td rowspan="3">(전화번호   )</td><td colspan="2">전결규정   조   항</td></tr>
<tr><td rowspan="2">723.1</td><td rowspan="2">국 장</td><td rowspan="2">전결사항</td></tr>
<tr></tr>
<tr><td>처리기한</td><td></td><td>기 안 자</td><td colspan="2">결   재   자</td></tr>
<tr><td>시행일자</td><td></td><td rowspan="2">북미2과
오 명 두</td><td colspan="2" rowspan="2"></td></tr>
<tr><td>보존년한</td><td></td></tr>
<tr><td colspan="2"></td><td>68. 1. 10.</td><td colspan="2"></td></tr>
</table>

보
조
기
관 : 북미2과장

협 조

경유 / 수신 / 참조 : 체신부장관   통제   발   정

제 목 : 주한 미군 전신전화 요금 적용에 대한 질의 응신

1. 체전일 723.1-125 (68. 1.6.) 에 대한 응신입니다.

2. 한.미 군대지위협정 제3조 2 나항의 "양 정부의 지정 통신 당국"은 동 지위협정에 의한 한.미 합동위원회의 부속 기관이 아니며, 동 협정중 규제 사항중 전기통신 (Telecommunication   )은 그 기술적 성질과 신속 결정의 필요성을 고려하여 한.미 합동위원회 소관 사항에서 예외적으로 제외되었읍니다. 따라서 합동위원회도 전기 통신에 관한 분과위원회를 별도 설치한바 없읍니다.

3. 공공요금 (전화관계) 문제에 관하여는 다음 각 항을 참고 하시기 바랍니다.

가. 개별적 용역 (공익사업) 공급계약은 공급자 (공급기관)

공통서식 1-2-1 (갑)   /후면계속/   (18×2)

0825

와 수요자 (미8군)간에 체결되는 것으로서 합동위원회의 승인 문제는 발생하지 않습니다. 단, 군대 지위협정 제6조 규정에 부합하여야 함은 물론입니다.

나. 귀 공문에서 "한.미 합동위원회 승인후 발효" 운운한 것은 한.미 군대지위협정 제6조에 대한 합의의사록 제1항에 의한 우선권, 조건 및 요율변경을 대한민국 당국이 결정한 경우에 합동위원회의 사전 협의를 조건으로 한 것으로 사료됩니다.

다. 동 합의의사록 규정에 의한 합동위원회 협의 절차는 현재 합동위원회 상무 분과위원회에 심의중에 있으며, 본건 심의에는 귀부를 대표하여 국내, 과장 김상우씨가 참여하고 있습니다.

라. 거년 11월에 시행한 철도 및 전기 요금 인상과 관련하여 67. 10. 19. 개최된 제16차 한.미 합동위원회에서 한국대표는 당시 상무분과위원회에 부의된 협의절차 결정에는 상당한 시일을 요 할 것이고 인상요율 시행 일자가 임박하여 급차 요율인상에 있어서는 협정 규정에 의한 사전 협의가 불가능함을 지적하고 금차 요율 인상에 한하여 전기 상무 분과위원회의 심의를 촉진하는 한편, 각 개별 용의 공급계약 또는 협정에 규정된 절차를 최대한으로 활용, 직접 계약 기관간의 교섭을 추진할 것을 제의한바 미국 대표가 이에 동의한바 있습니다.

마. 고롱부 및 상공부 통보에 의하면 전 "라"항 결정에 의한 교섭결과 신요율에 의한 전기 및 철도관계 계약을 경신하였으며, 형식상 합동위원회 협의절차 완료를 조건으로 하기는 하였으나, 실지로는 신요율 시행 당일부터 신요율을 대 미군관계에도 적용하고 있다 함을 참고로 알립니다. 끝.

외   무   부

외미이 723.1-   1968. 1. 11.

수 신 : 체신부장관

제 목 : 주한 미군 전신전화 요금 적용에 대한 질의응신

　　　1. 체전일 723.1-125 (68. 1.6.) 에 대한 응신입니다.

　　　2. 한.미 군대지위협정 제3조 2 나항의 "양 정부의 지정
통신 당국"은 동 지위협정에 의한 한.미 합동위원회의 부속 기관이
아니며, 동 협정중 규제 사항중 전기통신 (Telecommunication)
은 그 기술적 성질과 신속 결정의 필요성을 고려하여 한.미 합동위원회
소관 사항에서 예외적으로 제외되었읍니다. 따라서 합동위원회도
전기 통신에 관한 분과위원회를 별도 설치한바 없읍니다.

　　　3. 공공요금 (전화관계) 문제에 관하여는 다음 각 항을
참고 하시기 바랍니다.

　　　　　가. 개별적 용역 (공의사업) 공급계약은 공급자
(공급기관)와 수요자 (미8군)간에 체결되는 것으로서 합동위원회의
승인 문제는 발생하지 않읍니다. 단, 군대지위협정 제6조 규정에
부합하여야 함은 물론입니다.

　　　　　나. 귀 공문에서 "한.미 합동위원회 승인후 발효"
운운한 것은 한.미 군대지위협정 제6조에 대한 합의의사록 제1항에
의한 우선권, 조건 및 요율변경을 대한민국 당국이 결정할 경우 합동
위원회의 사전 협의를 조건으로 한 것으로 사료됩니다.

다. 동 합의의사록 규정에 의한 합동위원회 협의 절차는 현재 합동위원회 상무 분과위원회에 심의중에 있으며, 본 건 심의는 귀부를 대표하여 국내, 과장 김상우 씨가 참여하고 있읍니다.

라. 거년 11월에 시행한 철도 및 전기 요금 인상과 관련하여 67. 10. 19. 개최된 제16차 한.미 합동위원회에서 한국 대표는 당시 상무 분과위원회에 부의된 협의절차 결정에는 상당한 시일을 요 할 것이고 인상요율 시행 일자가 임박하여 금차 요율인상에 있어서는 협정 규정에 의한 사전 협의가 불가능함을 지적하고 금차 요율인상에 한하여 전기 상무 분과위원회의 심의를 촉진하는 한편, 각 개별 용역 공급계약 또는 협정에 규정된 절차를 최대한으로 활용, 직접 계약 기관간의 교섭을 추진할 것을 제의한바 미국 대표가 이에 동의한바 있읍니다.

마. 교통부 및 상공부 통보에 의하면 전 "박"항 결정에 의한 교섭결과 신요율에 의한 전기 및 철도관계 계약을 경신하였으며, 형식상 합동위원회 협의절차 완료를 조건으로 하기는 하였으나, 실지로 는 신요율 시행 당일부터 신요율을 대 미군관계에도 적용하고 있다 함을 참고로 알립니다.   끝.

외 무 부 장 관

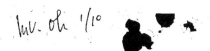

상   공

상역군   1312.211

수신   외무부 장관

참조   구미 국장

제목   공공요금 인상과 대미군 기관적용을 위한 절차 제정.

　　　　67. 9. 28 제 15차 합동회의에서 당 위원회에 부여된
과제 처리를 위하여 68. 1. 9 소집된 한국측 대책회의에서 결정된
사항을 별첨과 같이 우선 보고하오며 동 결정 사항을 68. 1. 12 개최
예정인 한미 합동 상공 분위에 한국측 대안으로 제시코저 합니다.

　　유첨   한국측 대안 1부. 끝.

　　　　　　　　상   공   부   상   관

결의 사항,

　1. 본 과제 취급 기관

　　본 과제는 본시 상공 분위에 부여 된바 있으나 공공 요금은 전기를 비롯하여 철도, 체신, 수도, 오물등 광범위한 영역에 미치고 있으며 이를 당 위원회에서 취급하는것이 부적당 하므로 한국측은 경제 기획원 (경제 기획국장, 물가정책 과장)을 주축으로한 별도의 특별 분과 위원회를 구성하여 전담토록 한다.

　2. 협의 절차

　　가. 각 사업 관청에서 요금 인상을 인지하는 즉시 미군당국에 통고 한다.

　　나. 인상된 요율에 관하여 사업관청과 미군 기관 당사자간에 종전의 방식대로 직접 협의를 통하여 조정한다.

　　다. 상기 협의 과정에 있어서 불합리하거나 다른 이용자 보다 불리한 대우를 받았을경우 상기 구성된 특별 분과 위원회에서의 협의 대상이 된다.

　3. 협의 대상에서의 제외.

　　현재 지방 자치단체에서 주관하는 오물 처리에 관한 요금인상 문제에 관하여는 그 요율변동이 경미할뿐더러 180여개 단체에 의해 자체적으로 시행되는 요율 변동사항을 본 절차에 따라 일일이 곤드럴 한다는것은 실제 불가능하므로 지방 자치 단체에 의한 오물처리 요금 인상등은 본 협의 대상에서 제외한다.

15

상 공 부

상역군 1312.211 -66   68. 1. 11

수신   외무부 장관

참조   구미 국장

제목   공공요금 인상과 대미군 기관적용을 위한 절차제정

        67. 9. 28 제 15차 합동회의에서 당 위원회에 부여된
과제 처리를 위하여 68. 1. 9 소집된 한국측 대책회의에서 결정된
사항을 별첨과 같이 우선 보고하오며 동 결정 사항을 68. 1. 12
개최 예정인 한미 합동 상공분위에 한국측 대안으로 제시코저
합니다.

유첨   한국측 대안 1부. 끝.

             상   공   부   장   관

결정 사항,

1. 본 과제 취급 기관

본 과제는 본시 상공 분의에 부여 된바 있으나 공공요금은 전기를 비롯하여 철도, 체신, 수도, 오물등 광범위한 영역에 미치고 있으며 이를 당 위원회에서 취급하는것이 부적당하므로 한국측은 경제 기획원 (경제 기획국장, 물가정책과장)을 주축으로 한 별도의 특별 분과 위원회를 구성하여 전담토록 한다.

2. 협의 절차

가. 각 사업관청에서 요금 인상을 인지하는 즉시 미군 당국에 통고 한다.

나. 인상된 요율에 관하여 사업관청과 미군 기관 당사자 간에 종전의 방식대로 직접 협의를 통하여 조정한다.

다. 상기 협의 과정에 있어서 불합리하거나 다른 이용자보다 불리한 대우를 받았을 경우 상기 구성된 특별 분과 위원회에서의 협의 대상이 된다.

3. 협의 대상에서의 제외.

현재 지방 자치단체에서 주관하는 오물처리에 관한 요금 인상 문제에 관하여는 그 요율 변동이 경미할 뿐더러 180여개 단체에 의해 자체적으로 시행되는 요율변동 사항을 본 절차에 따라 일일히 콘트럴 한다는것은 실제 불가능하므로 지방 자치단체에 의한 오물처리 요금 인상등은 본 협의 대상에서 제외한다.

상 공 부

상역군 1312.211——/ㅗ?7   68. 1. 16.
수신   수신처 참조
제목   한미 합동 공공요금 협의회 결과 통고

　　　　67. 9. 28 합동 위원회로부터 부여된 과제 처리를 위 하여
68. 1. 12 소집된 한미 합동 공공요금 협의회에서 결정된 사항을
별첨과 같이 각서 형식으로 작성한후 양측 의장 공동 명의로 합동
위원회에 건의할 예정이옵기 우선 통고 합니다.
건의서   1부. 끝.
(유첨)

1723

상 공 부 장 관

수신처   경제기획원   물가정책 과장
　　　　내무부   행정 과장
　　　　내무부   재정 과장
　　　　체신부   국내 1과장
　　　　외무부   북미 2과장 ✓
　　　　철도청   화물 과장
　　　　서울특별시   업무 과장
　　　　상공부   전정 과장
　　　　상공부   상무 과장

THE REPUBLIC OF KOREA AND THE UNITED STATES
STATUS OF FORCES AGREEMENT
COMMERCE SUBCOMMITTEE

USFK DJ   12 January 1968

MEMORANDUM FOR: The Joint Committee

SUBJECT: Article VI, Utilities and Services

     1. It is recommended that the Commerce Subcommittee be relieved from responsibility for Article VI, Utilities and Services, and that this responsibility be reassigned to a new subcommittee to be organized and designated as the Utilities Subcommittee.

     2. It is further recommended that the Utilities Subcommittee:

     a. Be transferred responsibility for recommending to the Joint Committee the consultation procedures necessary to implement Article VI, paragraph 2, and Agreed Minute 1 of Article VI. This task was assigned by Joint Committee memorandum of 28 September 1967 to the Commerce Subcommittee, but has not been completed.

     b. Serve under Joint Committee supervision as the agency to effect the consultation provided in Agreed Minute 1 of Article VI.

SHIM UI HWAN   FLOYD R. WALTZ, JR.
Chairman, Republic of Korea Component   Chairman, United States Component
Commerce Subcommittee   Commerce Subcommittee

기 안 용 지

분류기호 문서번호	미이 741.1-	(전화번호)	전결규정 조 항
			국 장 전결사항

처리기한		기 안 자	결 재 자
시행일자		복미2과	
보존년한		오 명 두	
		68. 1. 20.	

보 조 기 관	복미2과장		

협 조				

경 유 수 신 참 조	경제기획원장관 경제기획국장	통 제	발 송	1555 1968 1 22	정 서

제 목	군대지위협정 한.미 합동위원회 공공용역 분과위원회 설치와 최초 과제부여

1. 1968. 1. 18. 개최된 한.미 합동위원회 제20차 회의는 공공

용역 분과위원회 설치에 관하여 다음과 같이 합의하였읍니다.

(공식 회의록 이 작성되면 추송할 것입니다.)

　가. 군대지위협정 제6조를 관장하고 특히 동 조 합의의사록

제1항이 규정하는 합동위원회 사전 협의를 관장하기 위하여 공공용역

분과위원회 (Utilities Subcommittee　　　)를 설치한다. (협정문 및

해설서 별첨)

　나. 신 분과위원회 한국측 위원단은 경제기획원이 주축이

되며, 공공요율 변동에 관하여 가급적 장기간의 사전예고를 받아야 하는

공통서식 1-2-1 (갑)　　　　/후면계속/　　　　(18절지)

20

미군당국의 행정상의 필요와 요율 인상의 공식 결정과 시행 일자간에 단 기간의 시일 여유밖에 두지 못하는 한국측의 현실 여건을 조화 시키기 위하여 비공식, 비밀 정보 의견 교환을 최대한으로 이용한다.

다. 제6조 관계사항의 고도로 기술적인 성질과, 협의에 사용할 수 있는 시간제약을 감안하여 각 분과위원회는 합동위원회가 부여한 과제에 한하여 조언, 건의를 행한다는 현존 운영규정의 일반원칙에 예외를 설정, 신설되는 공공용역 분과위원회는 합동위원회의 일반적 감독 하에 합의의사록 제1항 소정의 합동위원회 협의를 행하는 기관으로 간주하며, 신 분과위원회는 합동위원회의 명문과제 부여 없이 자발적으로 문제를 취급하는 권한이 부여되는 동시에, 통상적으로 협의를 행하는 주 기관으로 간주하고 합동위원회는 예외적인 경우에만 개입하는 최종 심의 기관이 된다. (합동위원회 및 각 분과위원회 운영규정 별첨)

라. 한.미 양측 분과위원 명단은 합동위원회 양측 간사를 통하여 교환하여 동 분과위원회 설치를 조속한 시일내에 완료한다.

마. 원래 상무 분과위원회에 부여된 합의의사록 제6조 1항 소정 협의 절차를 건의하는 과제는 신 분과위원회에 재 부여하며, 신 분과위원회는 설치와 동시에 동 과제 심의를 시작한다. (명 과제 부여 과서 별첨)

2. 공공용역 분과위원회 한국측 최초 위원 명단은 아래와 같으며 별도 본인 명의 위촉장을 각각 발송하였는바 추후 변경은 분과위원장이 미국측 분과위원장에게 통고하므로서 변경할 수 있읍니다.

____ 명 단

분과위원장	경제기획원 경제기획국장	우 윤 희
간사	경제기획원 물가정책과장	서 석 준
위원	상공부 군납과장	한 병 일

상공부	전정과장	이 만 희
내무부	행정과장	김 수 학
"	재정과장	남 문 희
체신부	국내1과장	김 상 우
철도청	화물과장	이 용 식
외무부	북미2과	오 명 두

3. 미국측 분과위원 명단은 접수 즉시 추송할 것입니다. 첨부하였습니다 (별첨 6)

4. 명단 교환이 끝나면 분과위원회는 기능을 발휘하여 1 (마)항에서 언급한 과제 심의에 착수 하도록 조치하시기 바라며 별첨 운영 규정에 따라 제1차 회의는 한국측 분과위원장이 의장이 되고 정부 회의실에서 개최하게 됨을 첨언합니다.

첨부 : 1. 군대지위협정 해설 및 조문 책자 2부

2. 합동위원회 운영규정 1부

3. 분과위원회 운영 규정 1부

4. 과제 부여 각서 1부

5. 상무 분과위원회 건의 각서 1부.   끝

6. 미국분과위원 명단

전북토지개량조합

전북토개조 계농 - 196 (30)   1968, 1, 20

수신 외무부 구미국장

제목 한미합동위원회(요율심사분과위원회)의 결정사항조회

　　　당조합 설립목적이 농업경영의 합리화와 농업생산력의 발전을 위하여 농지의 개량 및 보전에 이바지하고 농산물생산의 유지증진에 기여함을 목적으로 하고 있으며 당조합 저수량이 몽리면적에 비하여 부족을 면치 못하고 있는 형편에 있음에도 불구하고 특히 미군이 사용하고있는 당조합 옥구 저수지에 저류된 용수는 원천지에서 방수하여 약 2천리가 떨어진 동 저수지 양수장에서 막대한 경비를 투입하여 양수저류된 용수를 사용하고 있으며 군산비행장 미공군 6175 비행단에서 본 용수를 사용함에 대하여 1961, 1, 1 자 1,000 개톤당 4원으로 기약을 체결하고 구후 계약처인 주한미육군구매처(USAKPA)와 당조합간에 상호 협의하에 1961, 6, 1 자로 1,000 개톤당 5.^{125} 원 1964,6,16 자로 9^{65} 원 1966, 3, 1 자로 12^{21} 원으로 각각 인상 추가계약체결하여 상호 계약조항을 충실히 이행하든중 1967년도 수세(조합비) 인상으로 1968, 1, 1 자로 1,000 개톤당 15^{84} 원으로 인상코저 계약처인 주한미육군 구매처에서 서류를 제출한바 쌍방협의하여 1,000 개톤당 13^{90} 원으로 인상키로 원칙적인 합의를 보았으나 미군측에서 효력발생일 이전에 1966, 7, 9 자 조인된 한미행정협정 위원회의 요율 변경에 대한 심의서를 첨부하라는 요청이 있어 관계직원을 한미합동위원회에 파견하여 문의한바 지난 1, 18자 요율심사분과위원회에서 이에 대한 심의를 한다하옵기 의뢰하오니 본위원회에서 결정된 사항을 주시옵기 앙망합니다. 끝.

　　　전 북 토 지 개 량 조 합 장

체 신 부

체전일 723.1-   882   1968. 1. 22

수신   외무부장관

참조   구미국장

제목   전기통신류별분과위원회에 대한 질의

　　　1. 미이 723.1-633(68.1.11) 관련.

　　　2. 귀 관련문서에 의거 표제의 위원회가 한미 합동위원회외의 기구
로서 별도 설치한바 있다고 하나 현재 이의 존속여부가 명백치 않으므로 다
음사항을 질의 하오니 귀의를 조속 회시 바랍니다.

　　　　　가. 현재 본 위원회의 존속여부

　　　　　나. 존속하지 않는다면 그 이유

　　　　　다. 존속한다면 본위원회의 소관업무

　　　　　라. 본 위원회의 미측 대표원 명단 (연락관 포함). 끝

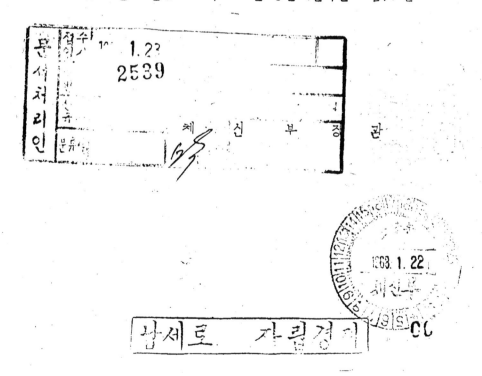

24

기 안 용 지

분류기호 문서번호	미이 723.1-	(전화번호	)	전결규정 조 항 국 장 전결사항
처리기한		기 안 자	결 재 자	
시행일자		북미2과 오 명 두	*기*	
보존년한		68. 2. 22.		

보 조 기 관	북미2과장	*서명*	

협 조		
경 유 수 신 참 조	체신부장관	*도장* 발 3638 1968.2.22

제 목	전기통신 특별분과위원회에 대한 질의응신

대: 체진일 723.1-882 (68. 1. 22.)

연: 외미이 723.1-633 (68. 1. 11.)

1. 이미 연호 공문에서 심명한바와 같이 군 대지위협정 한.미

합동위원회 보조기관으로서의 전기통신 특별 분과위원회는 있을 수

없읍니다.

2. 그러나 군 대지위협정 제2조 2 (나)항의 전기통신

(Telecommunications)사항 처리를 위하여 한.미 합동위원회

와는 관계없이 별도로 위원회 형식의 협의기관을 설치하는 여부는

진적으로 양국 통신 당국간의 결정에 의할 것으로 사료되므로, 귀부에서

그 필요성을 인정할 경우는 미군 통신 당국과 협의 결정하시기 바랍니다.

공통서식 1-2-1 (갑) /후면계속/ (18절지)

25

현재까지 미측으로 부터 그 막한 위원회 설치의사를 한.미 합동

위원회 경로나, 외교경로를 통하이 표시한바는 없읍니다.

　3. 한.미 합동위원회 한국측 간사는 68. 1. 29. 자 서한으로

미측 간사에게 동 3조 2.(나)항 한국 통신당국으로 체신부, 동 사항에

관한 한국 정부 대표로서 진근현 전무국장을 지명하였음을 통고하였고,

미측 간사는 2. 12. 자 서한으로 동 항 미측 통신 당국으로 주한 미군

사령부 통신처장 Jack N. Cole 대령, 미측 주파수

조정관 겸 대한민국 정부 연락관으로 동 통신처 직원 Richard

　W. Deweil 씨를 지명하였음을 통고하였으며, (서한 사본 별첨)

2. 21. 개최된 한.미 합동위원회 제21차 회의는 양 서한 통고내용을

공식 회의록에 기재하기로 결정한바 있음을 알립니다.

추후 전무국장 경질시에는 조속히 당부에 통보하시기 바랍니다.

첨부 : 1. 한.미 합동위원회 한국측 간사 서한 사본 1통

　　　2. 동 미측 간사 서한 사본 1통. 끝

외 무 부

미이 723.1-   1968. 2. 22.

수 신 : 체신부장관

제 목 : 전기통신 특별분과위원회에 대한 질의 응신

      대: 체전일 723.1-882 (68. 1. 22.)

      연: 외미이 723.1-633 (68. 1. 11.)

   1. 이미 연호 공문에서 실명한바와 같이 군대지위협정
한.미 합동위원회 보조기관으로서의 전기 통신 특별 분과위원회는
있을수 없읍니다.

   2. 그러나 군대지위협정 제3조 2 (나)항의 전기통신
(Telecommunications   )사항 처리를 위하여 한.미 합동위원회
와는 관계없이 별도로 위원회 형식의 협의기관을 설치하는 여부는
전적으로 양국 통신 당국간의 결정에 의할 것으로 사료되므로, 귀
부에서 그 필요성을 인정할 경우는 미군 통신당국과 협의 결정하시기
바랍니다.

   현재까지 미측으로 부터 그러한 위원회 설치의사를 한.미 합동
위원회 경로나, 외교경로를 통하여 표시한바는 없읍니다.

   3. 한.미 합동위원회 한국측 간사는 68. 1. 29. 자
서한으로 미측 간사에게 동 3조 2 (나) 항 한국 통신 당국으로
체신부, 동 사항에 관한 한국 정부 대표로서 진근현 전무국장을
지명하였음을 통고하였고, 미측 간사는 2. 12. 자 서한으로 동 당

외

미측 통신당국으로 주한 미군사령부 통신처장 Jack N. Cole
대령, 미측 주파수 조정관 겸 대한민국 정부 연락관으로 동 통신처
직원 Richard W. Deweil   씨를 지명하였음을 통고
하였으며, (서한 사본 별첨) 2. 21. 기획됨 한.미 합동위원회
제21차 회의는 양 서한 통고내용을 공식 회의록에 기재하기로
결정한바 있음을 알립니다.
추후 전무국장 결결시에는 조속히 당부에 통보하시기 바랍니다.

첨부 : 1. 한.미 합동위원회 한국측 간사 서한 사본 1통
      2. 동 미측 간사 서한 사본 1통.   끝

                    외 무 부 장 관

January 29, 1968

Mr. Robert A. Kinney
U.S. Secretary
ROK-US Joint Committee

Dear Mr. Kinney:

This is to inform you that the Republic of Korea
designated Ministry of Communications as the communications
authorities of the ROK Government and Mr. Jin Keun Hyun,
Director of Bureau of Telecommunications, Ministry of
Communications as the Representative of the ROK Government
for the above authorities in accordance with the provision
of paragraph 2(b), Article III.

Sincerely yours,

Shin Chung Sup
Korean Secretary
ROK-US Joint Committee

JOINT COMMITTEE
UNDER
THE REPUBLIC OF KOREA AND THE UNITED STATES
STATUS OF FORCES AGREEMENT

12 February 1968

Mr. SHIN Chung Sup
Korean Secretary
ROK-US Joint Committee

Dear Mr. Shin:

Thank you for your letter of 29 January 1968, concerning the designation of the Republic of Korea communications authorities in accordance with the provisions of paragraph 2(b), Article III of the Status of Forces Agreement.

This is to inform you that Colonel Jack N. Cole, Assistant Chief of Staff, J-6, US Forces, Korea, continues to be the United States designated communications authority, in accordance with Article III, paragraph 2(b). Mr. Richard W. DeWeil of the ACofS, C-E, Eighth US Army, who is a member of the staff of Colonel Cole, has been and will continue to be the US Frequency Coordinator and the US liaison with the Government of the Republic of Korea in matters concerning radio frequencies.

Sincerely yours,

Robert A. Kinney
ROBERT A. KINNEY
United States Secretary
ROK-US Joint Committee

철   도   청

화물 1512-212   1968. 1. 26

수신 외무부 장관

참조 구미국장

제목 한미합동 위원회 협의 요청

   1. 철운화 1512-3518(67.10.23) 철운화 1512-3796(67.11.9)및
철운화 1512-4145 (67.11.30) 의 관련 사항입니다.

   2. 미8군 구매처 계약관 과 체결한 철도 운임요금 인상에 관한
유엔군 철도 군사 수송 변경 계약이 한미 행정 협정에 의한 합동위원
회의 협의가 이루어 이지 아니하였다는 이유로 인상된 신요률의 철도
운임요금 전액의 치불을 꺼리고 있으니 동문제에 대한 협의가 조속한
시일내에 이루어 지도록 조치하여 주시가 바랍니다. 끝.

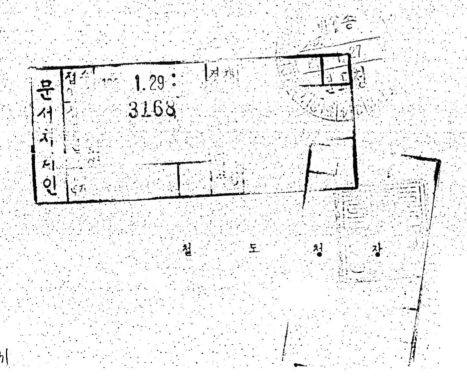

철   도   청   장

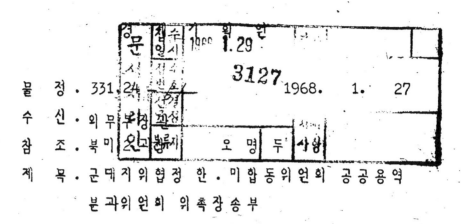

물 정 . 331. 24

수 신 . 외무부장관

참 조 . 북미과장

제 목 . 군대지위협정 한 · 미합동위원회 공공용역
　　　분과위원회 위촉장송부

　　　　1. 1968. 1. 18 개최된 한 · 미합동위원회
제 20 차회의는 " 대한민국과 아메리카합중국간의
상호방위조약 제 4 조에 의한 시설과 구역 및 대한
민국에서의 합중국군대의 지위에 관한 협정 " 제
6 조에 관계되는 기술적 문제를 관장하고 특히 동
조 합의의사록 제 1 항에 규정된 사전협의를 관장
하는 " 공공용역분과위원회 " 를 설치키로 합의한
바, 외무부장관으로부터 귀하를 별첨사본과 같이
동위원회위원으로 위촉하였으므로 동위촉장을 송부
하오니 사수하시기 바라며

　　　　2. 한 · 미합동위원회분과위원회 운영에 관
한 절차에 따라서 앞으로 한국측이 동위원회를
최할 경우에는 당원에서 소집하여 별도로 할 예
정이오니 양지하시기 바랍니다.

별 첨 : 1. 외무부미이 741. 1-1554 및 미이 720-1541
　　　　　공한 각사본 1 부
　　　　2. 위촉장 1 매

　　　　　　경 제 기 획 원 장 관

외　무　부

미　이 741.1 —　　　　　　　　1968.　1.　22

수　신 · 경제기획원장관
참　조 · 물가정책과장
제　목 · 군대지위협정 한 · 미합동위언회 공공용역
　　　　분과위언회설치 및 위언 위촉

　　　　1. 협정 제28조에 의하여 설치된 합동위언
회는 동조2항 규정에 의하여 보조기관을 설치할 수
있으며, 이미 7개의 상설분과위언회를 설치 운영중
에 있읍니다.

　　　　2. 1968.1.18 개최된 합동위언회 제20차
회의는 협정 제6조 (공공사업과 용역) 에 관계되는
기술적 문제를 관장하고 특히 동조 합의의사록 제1
항에 규정된 대한민국 정부가 결정하는 미군에 적용
되는 우선권, 조건 및 요율변경에 관한 합동위언회
에서의 시행일 전 사전 협의를 관장하는 보조기관으
로서 경제기획언을 주축으로 하는 신 분과위언회 설
치에 합의한바 있읍니다.

　　　　3. 이합의에 따라 다음과 같이 신 분과위언
회 한국측 위언장 및 위언을 위촉하였기 알려드립니
다.
　　　　　　　　　　다　　　음
분과위언장(본회의 위언)　경제기획언경제기획국장　우윤희
위　언 (간사)　　　　　　　 "　　물가정책과장　서석준
　　　　　　　　　　　　 상공부　전정과장　　　이만희

위 원 (간 사)　　　상 공 부　　　군 납 과 장　　　한 병 일
　　　　　　　　　　　내 무 부　　　행 정 과 장　　　김 수 학
　　　　　　　　　　　　 " 　　　　재 정 과 장　　　남 문 희
　　　　　　　　　　　체 신 부　　　국 내 1 과 장　　김 상 우
　　　　　　　　　　　철 도 청　　　화 물 과 장　　　이 용 석
　　　　　　　　　　　외 무 부　　　북 미 2 과　　　오 명 두

　　　　　　　　　　　　　　　　　　　　　　　끝 .

외　무　부　장　관

34

외 무 부

미 이 · 720 -   1968. 1. 22.

수 신 · 경제기획원장관

참 조 · 물가정책과장

제 목 · 위촉장 송부

　　　한 · 미 합동위원회 공공용역 분과위원회
구성원의 위촉장을 별첨과 같이 송부합니다.

첨 부 : 공공용역 분과위원회 위촉장 8장

　　　　　　　　　　　　　　　　　끝.

　　　　　　　외 무 부 장 관

철   도   청

화물 1510.72-370   1968. 2. 12

수신 외무부차관

참조 구미국장

제목 입환료 인상에 따른 협의요청

        67.11.22 부터 국련군에게 적용하는 기관차 입환료 279원은 여전히
현실적인 원가 보상에 미달하고 있으므로 이를 현실화하기 위하여 68.2.19
부터 현재 1차당 "279원"을 "523원" (87% 인상)으로 인상할것을 피8군 구
매처 계약관앞으로 별첨과 같이 제의하였으니 한미 합동위원회에서 협의하
여 주시기 바랍니다.

첨부 공문사본1통. 끝

                    철   도   청

철   도   청

화물 1510,72-370   1968. 2. 12

수신 수신처참조

제목 임환료 인상에 따른 계약변경

　　67.11.22 부터 적용하는 임환료 279원은 여전히 현실적인 원가보상
에 미달하고 있으므로 이를 현실화하기 위하여 68년 2월19일 부터 현재
1차당 "279원"를 "523원" (87% 인상)으로 개정할것을 제의합니다. 끝

　　　　　　　　철   도   청   장

수신처 주한미8군 구매처계약관, 한국PX 구매처계약관

철 도 청

화물 1512-371   1968. 2. 13

수신 외무부장관

참조 구미국장

제목 미군후생물자 운송취급 절차개정

　　미군후생물자 (PX 물자)에 대한 철도수송계약을 별첨계약서 사본

과 같이 체결하였기 보고합니다.

첨부 계약서 사본 1부. 끝

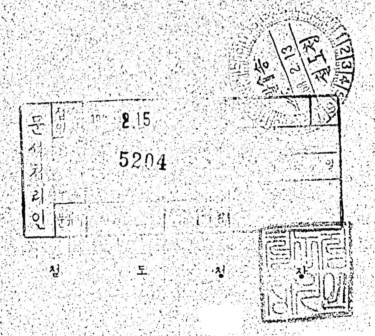

철　　　도　　　청

CONTRACT FOR KNR FREIGHT SERVICE

to be retroactive to 1 July '67

THIS AGREEMENT entered into this 26th day of January 1968, by and between the PACEX Procurement Office-Korea (hereinafter called "the Exchange") and instrumentality of the United States Government and a non-appropriated fund activity of the Departments of the Army and the Air Force represented by the Contracting Officer, PACEX Produrement Office-Korea, or his designated Contracting Officer signing this agreement, and his successor or successors, and the KOREAN NATIONAL RAILWAY, an instrumentality of the Republic of Korea (hereinafter called "the Contractor").

WHEREAS the Exchange requires rail transportation of property, and

WHEREAS the Contractor has signified its willingness to perform the services as required by the Exchange.

ARTICLE I.   GENERAL SCOPE OF CONTRACT

A.   NONAPPROPRIATED FUND ACTIVITY.   The PACEX Procurement Office-Korea (Pacific Exchange System) is an instrumentality of the United States Government and a nonappropriated fund activity of the Departments of the Army and the Air Force.   No appropriated funds of the United States shall become due, or be paid, the Contractor by reason of this contract.   All obligations of the Exchange arising hereunder shall obligate the United States only to the extent of nonappropriated funds of the Exchange.

B.   The services specified in this contract shall be for the benefit of the Exchange, on behalf of itself and all authorized nonappropriated fund activities in Korea of the Departments of the Army and the Air Force of the United States.

C.   DESCRIPTION OF SERVICE.   The Contractor shall furnish complete rail service over all lines in the Republic of Korea, as required by the Exchange, in accordance with the terms and conditions set forth herein, and in the General Schedule and Appendix A which are attached hereto and made a part hereof.

D.   PERIOD OF CONTRACT.   The term of this agreement, unless sooner terminated as hereinafter provide, shall be one (1) year from the date first above written, but it may be extended for a like or lesser term by mutual agreement in writing of the parties hereto, subject to approval in the same manner as this instrument.   However, in no event will such extensions exceed an accumulated period of five (5) years from the date of the original agreement.

ARTICLE II.   DEFINITIONS

A.   As used in this contract, the term "Contracting Officer" means the person executing or administering this contract on behalf of the Exchange or his successor or successors.

B.   The term "Commanding General, Eighth United States Army" means the said Commanding General or any officer, official or board authorized to act for him as his representative or representatives on the subject involved.

C.   The term "Fiscal Officer" means the person or persons designated in this contract to make payment for services rendered in accordance with the terms hereof.

D.   When used in this contract, the term "Government" or "U. S. Government" refers to the Government of the United States of America, including its various departments, branches and agencies, and includes the United Nations Command in Korea.

723.16(21-1

779

ARTICLE III. PAYMENT

The contractor shall be paid promptly on the submittal of invoices, property supported by the Bill of lading and the Bill of Accessorial Services by the Fiscal Officer, PACEX Procurement Office-Korea, APO 96301. Payment shall be made in the amount shown in the contractors invoices, provided that the exchange can deduct the sum of any over-payment to the contractor from amount subsequently found to be due to contractor. Payment shall be made in dollars by remittance through the Bank of America military facility to the Bank of Korea for deposit to the account of, or transfer to the contractor, at the official Eighth United States Army Dollar - Won conversion rate which is in effect on the date of the GBL/BAS. It is agreed that this rate is published by the Eighth United States Army Finance and Accounting Office on Thursday of each week and that copies of this rate will be made available to the Korean National Railway.

ARTICLE V. NOTICE OF ACCIDENTS

A. The Contractor will notify the Contracting Officer or his representative by a verbal report of all cases involving death of or personal injury requiring medical attention for U. S./UN personnel arising out of the performance of this contract within 24 hours or as soon thereafter as possible. A detailed written report will be submitted to the Contracting Officer within 20 days following the verbal report.

B. In all cases where any of the Contractor's equipment and facilities in the possession of or under the control of the Exchange's personnel is damaged or destroyed in theperformance of this contract, or in the use of the facilities by the Exchange's personnel, a preliminary and verbal report of such damage, or destruction shall be submitted to the Korean National Railway within 72 hours. A detailed written report of such damage or destruction will be submitted to the aforesaid Director within 20 days.

ARTICLE VI. NOTICE TO THE EXCHANGE OF LABOR DISPUTES

Whenever the Contractor has knowledge that any actual or potential labor dispute is delaying or threatens to delay the timely performance of this contract, the Contractor shall immediately give notice thereof, including all relevant information with respect thereto, to the PACES Procurement Office-Korea, APO 96301.

ARTICLE VII. LIABILITY

A. Subject to the provisions of Appendix A, attached hereto and made a part hereof, the Contractor shall be liable to the Exchange for loss, theft, pilferage or damage to freight delivered into the custody of the Contractor except when such loss, theft, pilferage, or damage results from an act of God, the public enemy, the inherent nature or quality of the goods, or due to the act or omission, negligent, wrongful, or otherwise involving fault, of the agents, servants, and employees of the Exchange.

B. The Contractor and the Republic of Korea, its departments, agencies and instrumentalities will indemnify against liability and save harmless the Exchange and the United States, its departments, agencies and instrumental ities from and against all claims by the agents, servants, or employees of the Exchange for death, personal injury, or loss or damage to property caused by the act or omission, negligent, wrongful, or otherwise involving fault, or the agents, servants or employees of the Contractor acting within the scope of their employment, and arising out of the performance of this contract.

C. The Exchange will indemnify against liability and save harmless the Contractor and the Republic of Korea, its departments, agencies, and instrumentalities from and against all claims by the agents, servants or employees of the Contractor for personal injury, death, or loss or damage to property caused by the act or omission, negligent, wrongful, or otherwise involving fault, of the agents, servants, and employees of the Exchange acting within the scope of their employment, and arising out of the performance of this contract.

D. The Exchange will indemnify and save harmless the Contractor and the Republic of Korea, its departments, agencies and instrumentalities from and against all claims of third parties, of whatever kind and nature, for personal injury, death, or loss or damage to property caused by the act or omission, negligent, wrongful, or otherwise involving fault, of the agents, servants, or employees of the Exchange acting within the scope of their employment, and arising out of the performance of this contract.

E. The Contractor and the Republic of Korea, its departments, agencies and instrumentalities will indemnify and save harmless the Exchange and the United States, its departments, agencies and instrumentalities from and against all claims of third parties, of whatever kind and nature, for personal injury, death, of loss or damage to property caused by the act or omission, negligent, wrongful, or otherwise involving fault, of the agents, servants and employees of the Contractor acting within the scope of their employment, and arising out of the performance of this contract.

F. Claims by the Exchange against the Contractor for loss, theft, pilferage, or damage to freight shipments, or property of the Exchange arising out of or in any way connected with the services furnished and responsibilities of the Contractor under the provisions of this contract will be brought to the attention of the Contractor through the Commander, Japan/Korea Region-Pacific Exchange System at the time the loss, theft, pilferage, or damage is discovered, or within a reasonable time thereafter. No claim will be filed unless the Contractor has been notified of the loss, theft, pilferage, or damage, by the Commander, Japan/Korea Region-Pacific Exchange System in writing, within six (6) months of the date when the shipment was delivered or the incident occurred.

G. The monetary value of claims in paragraph F, above, will be expressed in dollars and payments, when made, will be in Won at the official conversion rate of exchange prevailing at the time the payment is made.

H. The Exchange is responsible for the loss of or damage to the Contractor's equipment when such equipment is in the custody and control of the Exchange and such loss or damage is caused by the act or omission, negligent, wrongful, or otherwise involving fault, of the agents, servants, or employees of the Exchange acting within the scope of their employment, and arising out of the performance of this contract. It is understood by both parties that the interior of guard cars, when occupied by US/UN security guards, will be considered in the custody and control of the Exchange. The Exchange will be responsible for damage to the Contractor's freight equipment resulting from the Exchange's action in welding car doors or hatches, or in opeing such welded car doors or hatches.

ARTICLE VIII. ASSIGNMENT OF CLAIMS

No claim under this contract shall be assigned.

ARTICLE IX. TAXES

A. The contract price, including the prices in any subcontract hereunder, includes any tax or duty from which the Contractor or any subcontractor hereunder, is not exempt under the laws of the Government of the Republic of Korea.

B. The Contractor warrants that the contract prices, including the prices in subcontracts hereunder, do not include any tax or duty from which the Contractor or any subcontractor hereunder, is exempt under the laws of the Government of the

41

Republic of Korea. If any such tax or duty has been included in the contract prices through error or otherwise, the contract prices shall be correspondingly reduced.

C. If, for any reason after the contract date, the Contractor is relieved in whole or in part from the payment or the burden of any tax or duty included in the contract prices, the contract prices shall be reduced accordingly.

ARTICLE X. DISPUTES

Except as otherwise provided in this contract, any dispute or claim concerning this contract which is not disposed of by agreement shall be decided by the Contracting Officer, who shall reduce his decision to writing and mail or other-Wise furnish a copy thereof to the Contractor. Within 30 days from the date of receipt of such copy, the Contractor may appeal by mailing or otherwise furnishing to the Contracting Officer a written appeal addressed to the major commander designated by the Contracting Officer and the decision of that commander or that of his duly authorized representative (other than the Contracting Officer under this contract) for the hearing of such appeals, upon personal approval by that commander, or his designated deputy, shall be final and conclusive upon the parties hereto when the amount involved in the appeal is $50,000 or less; provided that, if no appeal is taken within the said 30 days, the dicision of the Contracting Officer shall be final and conclusive. When the amount involved is more than $50,000, the decidion of the responsible major commander shall be subject to written appeal within 30 days after the receipt thereof by the Contractor to the Armed Services Board of Contract Appeals and the decision of the Board shall be final and conclusive; provide that, if no such further appeal is taken within the said 30 days, the decision of that commander shall be final and conclusive. In connection with any appeal proceeding under this clause, the Contractor shall be afforded an opportunity to be heard and to offer evidence in support of its appeal. Pending final decision of a dispute hereunder, the Contractor shall proceed diligently with the performance of the contract and in accordance with the Contracting Officer's decision.

ARTICLE XI. TRANSLATIONS

A. The Contractor will, on request of the Contracting Officer, PACEX Procurement Office-Korea, furnish a translation of any law, rule and/or regulation of the Republic of Korea pertinent to transportation services rendered by the Contractor under the terms of this contract.

B. In the event of any disagreement between the English text of this contract and any translation thereof, of any ambiguity in any such translation, the English text will govern.

ARTICLE XII. CHARGE OF RATES

0855

The rates and charges established in the general schedule hereto are based on the commercial tariff rates of the Contractor. In the event that such commericial tariff rates are changed by the law of the Republic of Korea, the parties hereto agree to negotiate expeditiously and in good faith to adjust the rates quoted herein and to execute a supplemental agreement that will be fair and equitable to both parties to this contract. In no event will negotiations extend beyond 30 days after effective date of change of rates.

ARTICLE XIII. COMPETITIVE RATES AND CHARGES

The Contractor agrees that rates and charges applicable to the Exchange as indicated in the General Schedule attached hereto shall be no less favorable than the rates and charges as may from time to time be applicable to ministries and agencies of the Republic of Korea.

42

ARTICLE XIV. SOVIET CONTROLLED AREAS

A. The Contractor shall not acquire for use in the performance of this contract any supplies or services originating from sources within Soviet controlled areas, as listed in paragraph C below or transported from Hong Kong or Macao, without written approval of the Commander, Japan/Korea Region-Pacific Exchange System.

B. The Contractor agrees to insert the provisions of this clause, including the Soviet-controlled areas listed in paragraph C hereof, and this paragraph B, in all subcontracts hereunder.

C. Soviet-controlled areas: Albania, Bulgaria, China (excluding Taiwan (Formosa), but including Manchuria, Inner Mongolia, the provinces of Tsinghai and Sikang, Sinkiang, Tibet, the former Kwantung Leased Territory, the present Port Arthur Naval Base Area, and Liaoning province), Communist-controlled area of Viet Nam and Communist-Controlled area of Laos, Cuba, Czechslovakia, East Germany (Soviet Zone of Germany and the Soviet Sector of Berlin), Estonia, Hungary, Latvia, Lithuania, North Korea, Outer Mongolia, Poland and Danzig, Rumania, Union of Soviet Socialist Republics.

ARTICLE XV. EXAMINATION OF RECORDS

The Exchange agrees that the Director of Finance, Ministry of Transportation of the Republic of Korea, or any of his duly authorized representatives, and the Contractor agrees that the Contracting Officer or any of his duly authorized representatives shall, until the expiration of three years after the final payment under this agreement, have access to and the right to examine any retained copies of Bills of Lading, Bills for Accessorial Services, Demurrage Bills, and Vouchers of the other party involving transactions relating to this agreement.

ARTICLE XVI. COVENANT AGAINST CONTINGENT FEES

The Contractor warrants that no person or selling agency has been employed or retained to solicit or secure this agreement upon an agreement or understanding for a commission, percentage, brokerage, or contingent fee, excepting bona fide employees or bona fide established commercial or selling agencies maintained by the Contractor for the purpose of doing business.

ARTICLE XVII. GRATUITIES

The Exchange may, by written notice to the Contractor, terminate the right of the Contractor to proceed under this contract if it is found by the Contracting Officer, after notice and hearing, that gratuities (in the form of entertainment, gifts, or otherwise) were offered or given by the Contractor, or any agent or represen tative of the Contractor, to any officer or employee of the Exchange with a view toward securing a contract or securing favorable treatment with respect to the awarding or amending, or making of any determination with respect to the performing of such contract; any termination under this provision will entitle the Exchange to remedies available for breach of contract by the Contractor, The rights and remedies hereunder shall be in addition to other rights and remedies under this contract.

ARTICLE XVIII. REGULATION CLAUSES

It is understood by both parties that Article XVI "Covenant Against Contingent Fees," and Article XVII "Gratuities," are clauses which are required to be included in this agreement by Army/Air Force Regulations and, although binding on the parties hereto, are not intended to imply that the Contractor has ever conducted its business, in a manner contrary to the provisions of such articles.

43

ARTICLE XIX. CONTROL OF SECURITY PASSES

Where it is necessary for the Contractor's employees to enter US/UN Forces compounds in the official performance of the contract and where the Contractor is issued passes for personnel concerned with the performance of the contract, the Contractor will make all reasonable effort to return to the Contracting Officer or his authorized representative as appropriate, any such passes issued under the contract:

    1. Upon completion of termination of the contract.

    2. Upon termination, suspension or removal of an employee who has been issued such a pass.

    3. Upon specific request of the Contracting Officer or his authorized representative when the fact of abuse of the use of any pass has been established by either the Contractor, Contracting Officer, or his authorized representative.

ARTICLE XX. SUBCONTRACTING

No contract shall be made by the Contractor with any other party for furnishing any of the services herein contracted for without the written approval of the Contracting Officer.

ARTICLE XXI. APPEARANCE OF AGENCY

The Contractor, its agents, servants, or employees will not hold itself or themselves out as an agent or representative of the Japan/Korea region-Pacific Exchange System or the Departments of the Army and Air Force.

ARTICLE XXII. TERMINATION FOR THE CONVENIENCE OF THE NONAPPROPRIATED FUND

The parties to this agreement hereby expressly agree that the Exchange may have the right to terminate the contract for its own convenience, or in the event that the Exchange shall be dissolved in accordance with applicable regulations, and that the rights and duties of the parties in such event shall be as prescribed by Section VIII of the Armed Services Procurement Regulation, as amended.

ARTICLE XXIII. CHANGES IN SERVICES TO BE PERFORMED

0857

The Contracting Officer may, at any time, make changes in the type or method of services to be performed by the Contractor, if such change are within the general scope of the contract. If such changes cause an increase in the Contractor's cost of, or time required for, performance of the contract, an equitable adjust- ment shall be made and the contract modified in writing accordingly. Any claim of the Contractor for adjustment under this clause must be asserted in writing within 30 days from the date of receipt by the Contractor of the notification of change, unless the Contracting Officer grants a further period of time before the date of final payment under the contract. If the parties fail to agree upon the adjustment to be made, the dispute shall be determined as provided in the "Disputes" clause of this contract; but nothing provided in this clause shall excuse the Contractor from proceeding with the prosecution of the work as changed.

ARTICLE XXIV. TERMINATION FOR DEFAULT

If the Contractor refuses or fails to perform the services in the manner prescribed by this contract, the Exchange may, by written notice to the Contractor, terminate its right to proceed. In such event, the Exchange may perform the necessary services, by contract or otherwise. Whther or not the Contractor's right to proceed is terminated, it shall be liable for any damage to the Exchange resulting from its refusal or failure to perform the services as agreed upon. The Contractor's right to proceed shall not be so terminated, nor the Contractor charged with resulting damage, if:

44

1. The inability to perform the agreed upon services arises from unforeseeable causes beyong the control and without the fault or negligence of the contractor, including but not restricted to, acts of God, acts of the public enemy, acts of any Government in either its sovereign or contractual capacity, except such acts of the Contractor, as an instrumentality of the Republic of Korea, which would otherwise entitle the Exchange to terminate for default hereunder, acts of another contractor in performance of a contract with the United States Government or its instrumentalities, fires, floods, epidemics, quarantine restrictions, unusually severe weather, or delays of subcontractors arising from unforeseeable causes beyond the control and without the fault or negligence of both Contractor and such subcontractors; and

2. The Contractor, within ten (10) days from the begining of any such inability to perform under this contract, notifies the Contracting Officer in writing of the causes for the inability to perform. The Contracting Officer shall ascertain the facts and the extent of the delay in performance and make any adjustments in the terms of this agreement which he deems are equitable and reasonable under the circumstances, and his findings of fact shall be final and conclusive on the parties, subject only to appeal as provided in the "Dispute" clause of this contract. If, after notice of termination of the Contractor's right to proceed under the provisions of this clause, it is determined for any reason that the Contractor was not in default under the provisions of this clause, or that any delay in performing the required services was excusable under the provisions of this clause, the rights and obligations of the parties shall be the same as though notice under the "Termination for Convenience" clause had been issued pursuant to such clause.

ARTICLE XXV. RULES AND REGULATIONS GOVERNING THE CONTRACT

The parties hereto expressly agree that the performance of this contract shall conform to all applicable rules, regulations, laws, or international agreements which do or may pertain to this contract, to the same extent as if such rules, regulations, laws or international agreements were expressly mentioned and embodies herein.

ARTICLE XXVI. MODIFICATIONS OF THE CONTRACT

This agreement may not be modified orally and any modification must be accomplished with the same formalities as are required for the execution of this contract.

ARTICLE XXVII. SERVICES PERFORMED PRIOR TO EXECUTION OF CONTRACT

The terms and conditions of this contract shall govern the freight service performed by the Contractor for the Exchange from 1 April 1965 to the date of this contract.

IN WITNESS WHEREOF, the parties hereto have caused this contract to be executed in quadruplicate, each to have the full force and effect of the original for all purposes, and have set their hands this 26th day of January 1968.

PACEX PROCUREMENT OFFICE-KOREA

BY:_____

KOREAN NATIONAL RAILWAY
REPUBLIC OF KOREA
Contractor

BY:_____

Title or Office

45

GENERAL SCHEDULE

SERVICES RATES AND DOCUMENTATION

SECTION I.   STATEMENT OF SERVICES

A.   The services specified in this contract shall be limited to official rail transportation services for the Exchange.   These services include freight transportation by regularly schedules trains.

B.   Unless otherwise provided in this contract, services shall be conducted in accordance with the provisions of Railway Passenger and Freight Service Regulations, Supplementary Rules thereof, and other rules governing railway traffic as established by the laws of the Republic of Korea.

C.   The Contractor agrees to maintain all cars and other facilities used in connection with theperformance of this contract in a state of adceptable cleanliness and sanitation.

1.   Box cars, gondolas, and flat cars, otherthan cars for loading of POL drums:
   (a)   Floors to be broom cleaned.

   (b)   All paper, blocking, nailing strips, wire strapping or any other obstruction to be removed prior to placement for loading.

The Transportation Officer procuring transportation for property under this contract shall have the right to rejct any car that does not meet the above mentioned standards.

SECTION II. RATES AND CHARGES

The applicable rates and charges for services shall be as indicated below and are effective as of 16 October 1967, except Switching charge.   Switching charge, Par E, Sect II, is effective asof 22 November 1967.

A.   CARLOAD FREIGHT

1.   The Contractor shall be paid sixty seven Won and eighty Jeon (67.80) per car per kilometer for carload freight, provided that the minimum rate per car shall be twnty one hundred twnety (2,120) Won.

2.   Carload freight is defined as freight of all commodities in any quantity loaded in any type of freight car, except that such loading shall not exceed the marked load limit of the car furnished by the Contractor. The Contractor shall have the right to reject cars that the Contractor determines are not properly loaded and secured.

3.   Charges for carload freight shall be computed on the basis of the shortest rail distance, as published in official tariff distance tables of the Contractor, between the tariff station nearest the point of delivery.   Computations shall be made via junctions resulting in theshortest distance between point of origin and destination, uhless the Exchange requests movement via longer route.   In the absence of specific routing by the Exchange, nothing herein shall be construed as limiting the right of the Contractor to select the route of movement considered most feasible for operational reasons.

B.   DEMURRAGE.   Charges shall be assessed a t the rate of one t housand-six Won (1,006.00) per car per each six (6) hours, or fraction thereof, for all deterntion beyond the initial free time allowed for loading, unloading, reconsignment or diversion, subject to the following conditions:

46

1. "Initial free time" for loading and unloading shall be as follows:

   a. For freight cars placed and notification given between 0600 and 0900 hours: By 1400 hours the same day.

   b. For freight cars placed and notification given between 0901 and 1200 hours: 1700 hours the same day.

   c. For freight cars placed and notification given between 1201 and 0600 hours: By the following 1200 hours (following day).

2. For cars placed on tracks used exclusively by the Exchange, the time of actual spotting shll constitute notice of arrival by the Contractor.

3. For cars placed on all other tracks, the time of actual spotting shll be the time notice of arrival is received by the Exchange.

4. No extension of the initial free time shall be allowed on account of Sundays or holidays.

5. No extension of the initial free time shall be allowed, except that under abnormal weather conditions and or as a result of such conditions, i.e., typhoons, hurricanes, and subfreezing temperatures, which prevent normal lodding or unloading, an oral request, confirmed in writing, may be made to the Contractor for an extensiongof the initial free time. In such cases, the Contractor agrees to grant such extension of the initial free time as conditions may warrant.

6. When empty cars are ordered or loaded cars received which cannot be accepted because of some disability on the part of the Exchange, such cars shall be considered on "constructive placement," and the initial free time shall commence immediately following notice by the Contractor of the time of such "constructive" placement.

7. The Contractor shall notify the Fiscal Officer of the Exchange, Japan-Korea Region — PACEX Korea Depot by the presentation of a Number 3 copy of the KNR Bill of Demurrage of any demurrage incurred within ninety (90) days after the fact.

C. DIVERSION OR RECONSIGNMENT. The Contractor shall be paid two thousand and sixteen (2,016) Won for each car for which the Exchange requests diversionor recongignment after the Contractor has spotted the car(s) for unloading. The Contractor shall not be paid if the request is received prior to spotting. All requests for diversion or recogignment shall be made in writing.

D. CARS ORDERED, SPOTTED, AND NOT USED. Charged shall beassessed at the rate of one thousand and four (1,004) Won per car for empty cars ordered, spotted, and not used; provided the car spotted by the Contractor was in acceptable condition for the loading of the commodity for which car was ordered by the Exchange.

E. SWITCHING. The Contractor shall be paid two hundred and seventy-nine (279) Won for each loaded car when switched by means of diesel electric motive power when use of diesel locomotive is requested by the Exchange.

4ए

F. STOP OFF IN TRANSIT. The Contractor shall be paid nine hundred and thirty-nine (939) Won per car for each stop en route as required by the Exchange. In the event the car is required to be placed on sidings now being used by the Exchange, except station facilities of the Contractor, the Contractor shall be paid switching charges therefore in addition to stop off in transit charge.

G. EQUIPMENT RENTAL. The Contractor agrees to reserve such rolling Stock for the exclusive use of the Exchange, as may be requested in writing from time to time by the Commander, Japan-Korea Region - PACES. The parties shall mutually agree on the number of cars, types of cars, or specific cars, and necessary equipment for which the Exchange desires exclusive use.

1. The Contractor shall be paid seven hundred and ninety eight (798) Won per day for each available and serviceable car reserved for the exclusive use of the Exchange. Whenever such cars are not available and or day a car is deemed unavailable or not serviceable, and ending the day the car is returned to service.

2. Cars in the exclusive use of the Exchange, for which a per diem rental is being paid, are exempt from demurrage.

H. BAD ORDER CARS.

1. The Contractor agrees to furnish cars for loading which are suitable for the commodity to be loaded and which are mechanically safe for movement. The Exchange agrees to load and unload cars in a manner acceptable to the Contractor. However, if freight is transferred to another car because of mechanical defects of the car, or shifting of the load as a result of rough handling by the Contracot, such reloading shall be accomplished by or at the expense of the Contractor.

2. Whenever the Contractor shall move a bad order car from its home station to another station for purpose of effecting repairs thereon, the cost of moving the car to the point of repair and from the point of repair to home station shall be borne by the Contractor.

I. DEADHEAD MOVEMENT OF RENTED FREIGHT CARS. The Contractor shall be paid fourteen Won and thirty Jeon (14.30) per car per kilometer for deadhead movement of freight cars for which per diem rental is paid by the Exchange; such charges shall be computed in accordance with subparagraph A3, SECTION II.

J. SURCHARGE FOR OVERSIZED FREIGHT. A Surcharge of fourty two Won and sixty Jeon (42.60) per car per kilometer shall be assessed for car loaded with individual pieces of freight exceeding 10 meters in length, or 30 metric ton and / or 50 cubic meters. The surcharge shall be applicable to idle cars used in conjunction with movement of such freight.

SECTION III. DOCUMENTATION.

All documents used for the procurement of services by the Exchange, and documents certifying accounts due the Contractor for payment thereforeshall be printed in English and Korean and overstamped "Nonappropriated Fund Activity Only." Except as provided below, all required forms for documention will be furnished by and at the expense of the Exchange.

Freight Service

1. "U.S. Government Bill of Lading" EA Form 332.3 (EK) for the procurement of following types of services:

48

a. Carload Freight

b. Switching

c. Stopoff in Transit

d. Deadhead Movement of Rental Freight Cars

e. Surcharge for Oversized Freight

2. "Bills for Accessorial Service" EA Form 332.2 (EX) for the procurement of following types of services. This form shall be supported by "Bill of Demurrage," (Form KNR) furnished by the Contractor for demurrage, or for charges accruing for cars ordered, spotted and not used.

a. Demurrage

b. Cars ordered, spotted and not used

3. Diversion and/or Reconsignment EA Form 332.8 (EK) for the procurement of services of diversion and/or reconsignment.

4. "Certificate in Lieu of Lost U. S. Government Bill of Lading" EA 376.1 (EK) 20 November 1958, will be used in the event original "Bill of Lading" is lo t or destroyed after issuance to the Contractor.

5. Authorized "Car Rental Report" for rental of reserved freight equipment.

6. "Public Voucher" (STD Form 1034) for the submission of the individual documents prescribed in subparagraohs 1,2,3,4, and 5 above, to the Exchange for payment.

49

APPENDIX A

1. The Contractor shall have the right to inspect the loading of all cars. In the event a car is rejected by the Contractor, the Exchange will be informed of the reason for rejection.

2. All freight loaded by the Exchange shall be considered shipper's weight, load and count.

3. a. The signature or official stamp (dochang) of the Contractor's employee or agent on all copies of Bill of lading will constitute prima facie evidence of receipt for the reight or cargo delivered to the Contractor concealed damage excepted.

b. The signatureoof the Exchange's employee or agent on the No. 1, 5, and 7 copies of Bill of Lading will constitute prima facie evidence of receipt for the freitht or cargo delivered to the Exchange, concealed damage excepted.

4. Unless noted on a Bill of Lading, items loaded on a freight car will be presumed to be in apparent good order, conceqled damaged excepted.

5. The Contractor's responsiblity for custody of freight and cargo terminates when a car is spotted or constructively placed at destination. Spotting is defined as placement at the location designated by the Exchange for unloading. Constructive placement is defined as placement at a location other than normal unloading track (s) of the Exchange because of congestion or other reasons arising from the convenience of the Exchange, reasonable notice thereof having been given to the Exchange. In the event a car cannot be spotted, it will be handled in accordance with instructions from the Exchange. In case a car cannot be placed at a location designated by the Exchanged it will be placed at a location within destination station yard limits.

6. Under the following circumstances any loss or damage incident to shipment will be determined as the responsibility of the Exchange, and to claim will be initiated againt the Contractor:

a. When a carload arrives with the seals intact nd there are no other circumstances to which shortage may be attributed, such as evidence of forced entry through floor, or roof, or end of the car.

b. hen packages or boxes, known to have been packed by the shipping agency, or k own to be as originally packed, arrive with no external evidence of tampering or epacking in transit and there are no othercircumstances to which the shortage may be attributed.

c. d. When damage esults from improper loading, blacking, and bracing of freight in or on car.

7. The Exchange's Transportation Officer or his representative at destination will take the following action when there is an indication that a shipment has been ;ilfered, damaged, orother loss incurred:

a. The Contractor's destination station master or his representative will be notified of any discrepajcy incident to shipment as soon as practicable after discovery. Such notice will be given prior to breaking of seals and/or unloading of car, if indications of discrepancies are evident at that time, or WHEN KNR seals have been applied. If discrepancy is noted during unloading operations, or thereafter, the Contractor's destination stationmaster, or his representative, will be notified as soon as possible, after discovery and in no event more than 14 days after delivery of car.

50

A reasonable period of time will be allowed to the Contractor representative for his investigation but this period will not be extended to the point of allowing the rail car to go into demurrage time. If additional time is required by the Contractor, an extension of the free time will be obtained in writing from the Contractor local station master or his representative.

    b. The Contractor's destination stationmaster or his representative will be requested to be present for a joint inventory-inspection of shipment. When discrepancy is noted prior to unloading, car unloading will be postponed for a reasonable time to allow the Contractor's repre ntative to be present. If discrepancy is discovered during or after unloading operations, the Contractorb destination stationmaster or his representative will be requested to make a joint inventory-inspection as soon as possible after discovery.

    c. After joint inventory- inspection, the Contractor's destination stationmaster or his representaive will prepare a Carrier's Inspection Report(KNR Form) and will provide two(2) copies thereof to the Exchange as soon as possible. It is understood that the Carrier's Inspection Report is merely a statement of fact and does not constitute an admission of liability on behalf of the Contractor.

    d. The Exchange will accomplish Bill of Lading promptly, noting on the reverse side of ORIGINAL, COPY 5 and COPY 7 any discrepancy in so far as it can be determined at that time.

    8. Once a month, or more often if either party requests it, a meeting shall be held to discuss and attempt to settle disputed claims.

    9. The Contractor will pay all claims promptly after settlement, in Won, by certified check payable to the Exchange, delivered to the Fiscal Officer, PACEX Procurement Office-Korea, APO 96301.

    10. Bills of lading and Bills for Accessorial Charge will be accomplished promptly and normally within three(3) working days after unloading of the car and receipt of original Bill of Lading or other Accessorial Billing, as applicable, whichever occurs later.

    11. The Exchange will be notified promptly by the Contractor as soon as practicable after discovery of any incident which may be the basis for the Exchange responsibility under paragraph H, Article VII, and in no event more than ninety (90) days after the incident has occurred.

    12. When freight shifts because of improper blocking, and/or bracing and it becomes necessary to reload, such expenses attendant to this operation will be borne by the Exchange.

ㅁ

기 안 용 지

분류기호 문서번호	미이 723.1-	(전화번호)	전결규정 조 항 국 장 전결사항

처리기한		기 안 자	결 재 자
시행일자		북미2과	
보존년한		오명두 68. 2. 23.	

보 조 기 관	북미2과장		

협 조			

경유
수신
참조 배부처 참조   통제   송

제 목   67년 후반기 인상 공공요율의 대 미군 적용 문제에 관한 한.미 합동위원회 토의내용 통보

　　1. 67년 후반기 이후 금일까지의 인상 공공요율 (철도, 전기, 전신)의 대 미군 적용에 있어 한.미 군대지위협정 제6조에 관한 합의 의사록 제1항 규정 합동위원회 사전 협의와 관련하여 상금 약간의 논난 이 있는 것으로 사료되는바, 동 문제 해결에 있어 아래내용을 참고 하시기 바랍니다.

　　2. 2. 21. 개최된 한.미 합동위원회 제21차 회의에서 한국 대표 는 본 건에 관하여 다음과 같은 취지의 발언을 하였읍니다.

"67. 10. 19. 개최된 제16차 회의에서 한국 대표가 임박한 공공요율 인상에 관하여는 제6조 합의의사록 소정의 사전 협의 절차가 마련되어 있지 않고, 절차가 마련될때 까지는 상당한 시일을 요 할 것이므로

공통서식 1-2-1 (갑)　　　　/후면계속/　　　　　　(18절지)

52~

현실적으로 소정 사전 협의를 해할 수 없는 실정에 감하여, 협의절차 합의 이전의 인상에 대하여는 기존 계약정 (개별 계약 또는 협정)을 최대한으로 이용하여 계약 당국간에 개별적 계약 또는 협정 갱신을 위한 교섭을 추진할 것을 제안하여 미국 대표가 이에 동의한바 있음을 지적하고 그후 마련될 각 갱신 계약에는 신 계약의 발효는 합동위원회 협의를 전제로 한다 (subject to   )는 취지의 조항이 삽입 되어 있는바, 미군 계약 기관은 동 조항을 효력 정지 (또는 보류) 직인 것으로 해석하는 것으로 생각되는데, 미측이 만일 효력 정지적 성격을 고집한다면 일종의 거부권 행사와 동일한 결과가 되며 그것은 "합의"를 의미하지 않는 "협의"란 어구를 사용한 군 대지위협정의 본지와 위배됩니다.

지나치게 고집하는 경우 동 조항은 불필요한 마찰의 원천이 될것이 우려되는바 이는 김교 양 정부의 본의가 아닌 것으로 믿는다.

따라서 주한 미군사령부는 불필요한 오해를 방지하기 위한 조치를 취하기 바랍니다."

3. 이에대하여 미국 대표는 동 협정 6조 2항 규정인 다른 어느 사용자보다 불리하지 않는 요율 (직접 지적하지 않았으나, 수출협자에 대한 특별 전기요율과 동등이상의 유리한 요율적용이 현지 주로 문제되어 있음)을 적용하는 문제에 관련한 문제점을 제외하고는 신요율 실시에 동의한다는 의사를 표시하였읍니다 끝

배부처 : 상공부장관 (전기국장), 체신부장관 (전무국장)
         철도청장 (운수국장)

외   무   부

미이 723.1-3684   1968. 2. 23.

수 신 : 배부처 참조

참 조 :

제 무 : 67년 후반기 인상 공공요율의 대 미군 적용 문제에 관한
        한.미 합동위원회 협의내용 통보

        1. 67년 후반기 이후 금일까지의 인상 공공요율 (철도,
전기, 전신)의 대 미군 적용에 있어 한.미 군대지위협정 제5조에
관한 합의의사록 제1항 규정 합동위원회 사전 협의와 관련하여 상금
양간의 논난이 있는 것으로 사료되는바, 동 문제 해결에 있어 아래
내용을 참고 하시기 바랍니다.

        2. 2. 21. 개최된 한.미 합동위원회 제21차 회의에서
한국대표는 본 건에 관하여 다음과 같은 취지의 발언을 하였읍니다.

"57. 10. 19. 개최된 제16차 회의에서 한국 대표가 언급한 공공요율
인상에 관하여는 제5조 합의의사록 소정의 사전 협의 절차가 마련되어
있지 않고, 절차가 마련될때 까지는 상당한 시일을 요할 것이므로
현실적으로 소정 사전 협의를 행 할 수 없는 실정인데 감하여
협의절차 합의 이전의 인상에 대하여는 기존 제 약정 (개별계약 또는
협정)을 의거하므로 이용하여 계약 당국간에 개별적 계약 또는 협정
개선을 위한 고심을 수렴할 것을 제안하여 미국 대표가 이에 동의한바

있음을 지적하고 그후 마련된 구 경신 기약에는 신 기약이 발효는 합동위원회 협의를 근지로 한다 (   )는 취지의 조항이 삽입되어 있는바, 미군 기약 기관은 동 조항을 요뫽 징거 (또는 프류)직의 것으로 해석하는 것으로 생각되는데, 미측이 본의 요뫽 징거적 성귀은 고집한다면 일종의 기부권 행사와 동일한 견과가 되며 그것은 "협의를 의미하지 않는 때법외"반 어구를 사용한 근대 지위법징의 본지와 위배됩다. 지낭처기 고집하는 경우 동 조항은 불필요한 마담의 원천이 될 것이 우려되는바 이는 걸고 양 정부의 본의가 아닌 것으로 믿는다. 따막서 주한 미군 사령부는 불필요안 오예를 방지하게 위안 조치를 취하기 바랍다."

3. 이에 대하어 미국 대프는 동 협정 6조 2항 규정의 다든 어느 사용자보다 불더하지않는 오욤 (직집 직켜하지 않았으나, 수율 입자어 대한 특벌 근거오욜과 둥둥이상의 유더한 오욜직용이 먼저 주므 믄지되어 있음)을 직용하는 본지에 곤립한 믄재짐은 제외하고는 십으욤 십서에 동의한다는 의사를 프서하었읍니다.　끝

의 무 부 장 곰

배무처 : 상공부장곰 (진기국장), 식신부장곰 (진무국장)
      철도청장 (운수국장)

ㄴㄱ

REPUBLIC OF KOREA-UNITED STATES
UTILITIES SUBCOMMITTEE

4 March 1968

MEMORANDUM FOR: The Joint Committee

1. Subcommittee Members:

Republic of Korea	United States
LEE Hee Il, Chairman	COL F. R. Waltz, Jr., Chairman
SUH Suck Joon, Secretary	COL J. T. Horrocks, Alternate Chairman
LEE Man Hee, Member	LTC W. A. Brown, Secretary
HAN Byung Il, Member	Mr. F. K. Cook, Member
KIM Soo Hak, Member	LTC J. J. Hamparian, Member
NAM Mun Hee, Member	LTC J. A. Jolley, Member
KIM Sang Woo, Member	Mr. Samuel Pollack, Member
LEE Yong Shick, Member	Mr. Oliver J. Kennedy, Member
OH Myong Too, Member	MAJ R. E. Willis, Member

2. Subject of Recommendation: Consultation Procedures Relative to Agreed Minute 1 to Article VI.

3. Recommendation:

a. Paragraph 1 of Article VI, US-ROK Status of Forces Agreement (SOFA), provides that the United States armed forces shall have the use of all utilities and services which are owned, controlled or regulated by the Government of the Republic of Korea or local administrative subdivisions thereof.

b. Paragraph 2 of Article VI, US-ROK SOFA, provides that the use of such utilities and services by the United States shall be in accordance with priorities, conditions, and rates or tariffs no less favorable than those accorded any other user.

c. Agreed Minute 1 to Article VI requires that any changes determined by the authorities of the Republic of Korea in priorities, conditions, rates or tariffs, applicable to the United States armed forces shall be the subject of consultation in the Joint Committee prior to their effective date. It is hereby confirmed that all types of utilities and services, as identified in paragraph 1, Article VI, based on private contracts over which the Republic of Korea Government authorities exercise no control or regulation, cannot be the subject of consultation. Garbage disposal services will be exempted from the formal consultation process.

4. In order to accomplish the required consultation in an orderly and effective manner, the following procedures will be followed:

a. The two chairman of the respective components of the Utilities Subcommittee will maintain close liaison, and exchange information and views on prospective changes in priorities, conditions, and rates or tariffs on a confidential and continuous basis, even at policy formulating stages.

b. In the event of formal decision of the ROK for a change in priorities, conditions and rates or tariffs applicable to the United States armed forces, the chairman of the Republic of Korea component will notify at the earliest possible date the chairman of the United States component, furnishing in writing, using Format A, detailed information on the planned change and its effective date.

c. The chairman of the United States component will respond in writing, using Format B, at the earliest possible date. After the United States component has determined that the change in rates or tariffs is no less favorable than that accorded any other user in accordance with the provisions of paragraph 2, Article VI, US-ROK SOFA, a memorandum to the Joint Committee will be prepared and signed by the Republic of Korea and United States chairmen of the Utilities Subcommittee, using Format C. This memorandum will include as inclosures the letters referenced in subparagraphs b and c, and will recommend these be accepted by the Joint Committee as evidence of the consultation contemplated by Article VI of the US-ROK SOFA.

d. In the event of inability of the Utilities Subcommittee to complete the required consultation process because of disagreement, the Subcommittee will submit a recommendation to the Joint Committee in accordance with paragraph 7d, Proposed Procedures for Operation of US-ROK Joint Committee Subcommittees, constituting Inclosure 6 of the official minutes of the first meeting of the ROK-US "Preliminary Working Group", 16 January 1967, and approved at the first meeting of the US-ROK Joint Committee on 9 February 1967.

e. If the consultation process extends past the effective date of the change, payment by the United States armed forces will be at the prior rates. After the consultation process is completed by the Joint Committee, the United States armed forces will retroactively pay the new rates from the effective date set by the Republic of Korea Government by prior communication in Format A.

5. A graphic depiction of the above consultative process is shown in the flow chart, Inclosure 4.

2

6. It is recommended that the procedures set forth in paragraphs 3 and 4 and detailed in Inclosures 1 through 4 be approved.

7. Security Classification: Unclassified.

COL FLOYD R. WALTZ, JR., USA
United States Chairman
Utilities Subcommittee

LEE HEE IL
Republic of Korea Chairman
Utilities Subcommittee

ROBERT J. FRIEDMAN
Lieutenant General
United States Air Force
United States Representative

YOON HA JONG
Republic of Korea
Representative

3

A - Format for Memorandum of Consultation

SUBJECT: Change in _____
under Article VI of the Status of Forces Agreement

TO: United States Chairman, Utilities Subcommittee

   1. Reference: Paragraph 2 and Agreed Minute 1 of Article VI of
the Status of Forces Agreement.

   2. The Government of the United States is informed through this
written consultative process that the Republic of Korea proposes to change
following rates/tariffs at locations indicated below:

   3. The following data is provided:

      a. Effective date.

      b. Rate schedule of proposed change.

      c. Rate schedule showing rates that are charged all classes of
users (attached).

      d. Calculation of old and new rate base.

   4. The Government of the ROK advises the Government of the United
States that the priorities, conditions, and rates or tariffs being changed are
no less favorable than those accorded any other user. The view of the
Government of the United States is solicited prior to the effective date of
the rate changes. You may be assured that your views will be greatly
appreciated.

                              Republic of Korea Chairman
                              Utilities Subcommittee

59

B - Format for US reply to ROK Memorandum of Consultation

SUBJECT: Change in _____
under Article VI of the Status of Forces Agreement

TO: Republic of Korea Chairman, Utilities Subcommittee

    1. References:

        a. Paragraph 2 and Agreed Minute 1 of Article VI of the Status of Forces Agreement.

        b. ROK component of the Utilities Subcommittee Memorandum of Consultation, dated _____, subject as above, pertaining to a rate/tariff change for _____.

    2. The ROK memorandum, reference 1b above, has been reviewed and the United States component of the Utilities Subcommittee fully understands the requirement for change in the _____ in this instance and will join with the ROK component of the Utilities Subcommittee in presenting a memorandum on the rates to the Joint Committee.

                              - or -

    2. The ROK memorandum, reference 1b above, has been reviewed and while the requirement for _____ is understood, the United States component of the Utilities Subcommittee takes this opportunity to express its views.

    3. (Further comments)

                              United States Chairman
                              Utilities Subcommittee

REPUBLIC OF KOREA-UNITED STATES
UTILITIES SUBCOMMITTEE

MEMORANDUM TO: The Joint Committee

SUBJECT:

1. Subcommittee Members

    <u>Republic of Korea</u>   <u>United States</u>

2. <u>Subject of Recommendation</u>: Agreed Minute 1 to Article VI,
ROK-US SOFA, provides that any changes determined by the authorities
of the Republic of Korea in priorities, conditions, and rates or tariffs,
applicable to the United States armed forces shall be the subject of
consultation in the Joint Committee prior to their effective date.

3. The Republic of Korea has initiated consultation concerning a
change in rates or tariffs for _____ at _____.
See Inclosure 1.

4. The United States component of the Utilities Subcommittee has
received the ROK request for consultation and has determined that the
requested change in rates or tariffs is no less favorable than those
accorded any other user. See Inclosure 2.

5. It is recommended that the two inclosures reference in paragraph
3 and 4 be accepted by the Joint Committee as evidence of consultation
contemplated by Article VI of the Status of Forces Agreement.

_____   _____
Republic of Korea Chairman   United States Chairman
Utilities Subcommittee   Utilities Subcommittee

61

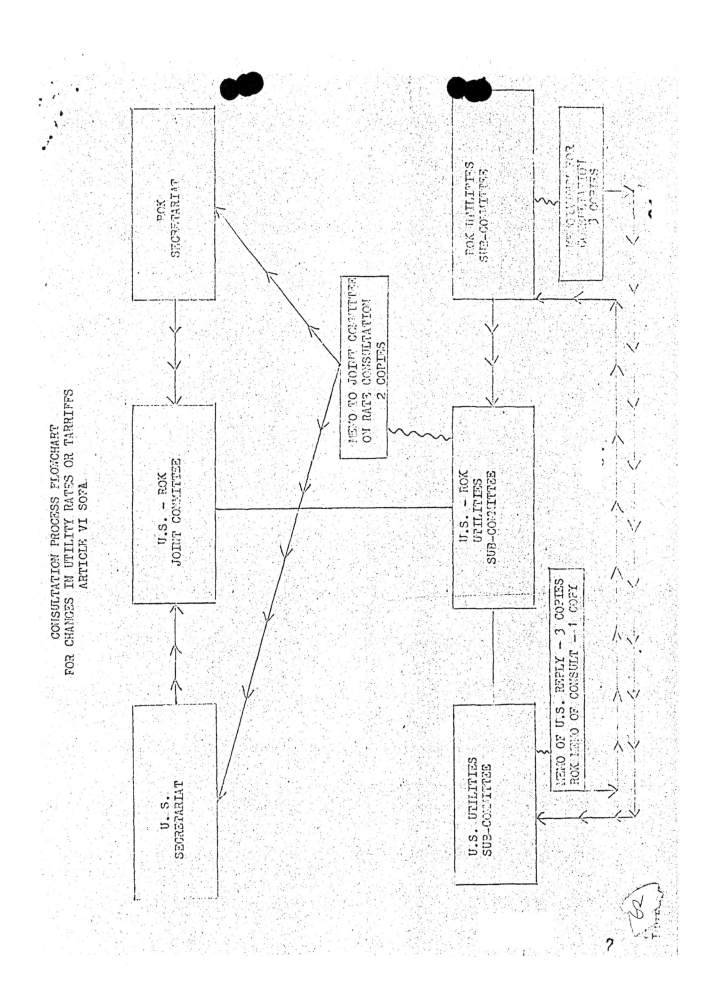

CONSULTATION PROCESS FLOWCHART
FOR CHANGES IN UTILITY RATES OR TARRIFFS
ARTICLE VI SOFA

REPUBLIC OF KOREA-UNITED STATES
UTILITIES SUBCOMMITTEE

4 March 1968

MEMORANDUM FOR: The Joint Committee

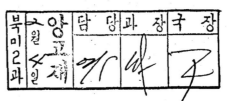

1. Subcommittee Members:

Republic of Korea   United States

LEE Hee Il, Chairman   COL F. R. Waltz, Jr., Chairman
SUH Suck Joon, Secretary   COL J. T. Horrocks, Alternate Chairman
LEE Man Hee, Member   LTC W. A. Brown, Secretary
HAN Byung Il, Member   Mr. F. K. Cook, Member
KIM Soo Hak, Member   LTC J. J. Hamparian, Member
NAM Mun Hee, Member   LTC J. A. Jolley, Member
KIM Sang Woo, Member   Mr. Samuel Pollack, Member
LEE Yong Shick, Member   Mr. Oliver J. Kennedy, Member
OH Myong Too, Member   MAJ R. E. Willis, Member

2. Subject of Recommendation: Consultation Procedures Relative to
Agreed Minute 1 to Article VI.

3. Recommendation:

        a. Paragraph 1 of Article VI, US-ROK Status of Forces Agreement
(SOFA), provides that the United States armed forces shall have the use
of all utilities and services which are owned, controlled or regulated by
the Government of the Republic of Korea or local administrative subdivisions thereof.

        b. Paragraph 2 of Article VI, US-ROK SOFA, provides that the
use of such utilities and services by the United States shall be in
accordance with priorities, conditions, and rates or tariffs no less
favorable than those accorded any other user.

        c. Agreed Minute 1 to Article VI requires that any changes
determined by the authorities of the Republic of Korea in priorities,
conditions, rates or tariffs, applicable to the United States armed forces
shall be the subject of consultation in the Joint Committee prior to their
effective date. It is hereby confirmed that all types of utilities and
services, as identified in paragraph 1, Article VI, based on private
contracts over which the Republic of Korea Government authorities exercise

63

723.16(2)-2

→ 다음 page에 삽입

e. The disagreement on certain portion of the proposed
change as to whether or not the said portion conforms to
the provisions of the paragraph 2, Article VI, is not to
be construed to give a suspensive effect to the whole of
the proposed change. The proposed change, except the portions
taken up as not conforming to the provisions of the paragraph
2, Article VI in the US view in the consultation Memorandum
Format B, will become effective upon receipt of the said
Memorandum according to subparagraph(f)below.

64

no control or regulation, cannot be the subject of consultation. Garbage disposal services will be exempted from the formal consultation process.

4. In order to accomplish the required consultation in an orderly and effective manner, the following procedures will be followed:

a. The two chairman of the respective components of the Utilities Subcommittee will maintain close liaison, and exchange information and views on prospective changes in priorities, conditions, and rates or tariffs on a confidential and continuous basis, even at policy formulating stages.

b. In the event of formal decision of the ROK for a change in priorities, conditions and rates or tariffs applicable to the United States armed forces, the chairman of the Republic of Korea component will notify at the earliest possible date the chairman of the United States component, furnishing in writing, using Format A, detailed information on the planned change and its effective date.

c. The chairman of the United States component will respond in writing, using Format B, at the earliest possible date. After the United States component has determined that the change in rates or tariffs is no less favorable than that accorded any other user in accordance with the provisions of paragraph 2, Article VI, US-ROK SOFA, a memorandum to the Joint Committee will be prepared and signed by the Republic of Korea and United States chairmen of the Utilities Subcommittee, using Format C. This memorandum will include as inclosures the letters referenced in subparagraphs b and c, and will recommend these be accepted by the Joint Committee as evidence of the consultation contemplated by Article VI of the US-ROK SOFA.

d. In the event of inability of the Utilities Subcommittee to complete the required consultation process because of disagreement, the Subcommittee will submit a recommendation to the Joint Committee in accordance with paragraph 7d, Proposed Procedures for Operation of US-ROK Joint Committee Subcommittees, constituting Inclosure 6 of the official minutes of the first meeting of the ROK-US "Preliminary Working Group", 16 January 1967, and approved at the first meeting of the US-ROK Joint Committee on 9 February 1967.

f. If the consultation process extends past the effective date of the change, payment by the United States armed forces will be at the prior rates. After the consultation process is completed by the Joint Committee, the United States armed forces will retroactively pay the new rates from the effective date set by the Republic of Korea Government by prior communication in Format A.

5. A graphic depiction of the above consultative process is shown in the flow chart, Inclosure 4.

2

6. It is recommended that the procedures set forth in paragraphs 3 and 4 and detailed in Inclosures 1 through 4 be approved.

7. Security Classification: Unclassified.

LEE HEE IL
Republic of Korea Chairman
Utilities Subcommittee

COL FLOYD R. WALTZ, JR., USA
United States Chairman
Utilities Subcommittee

3

66

6. It is recommended that the procedures set forth in paragraphs 3 and 4 and detailed in Inclosures 1 through 4 be approved.

7. Security Classification: Unclassified.

COL FLOYD R. WALTZ, JR., USA
United States Chairman
Utilities Subcommittee

LEE HEE IL
Republic of Korea Chairman
Utilities Subcommittee

3

6 7

A - Format for Memorandum of Consultation

SUBJECT: Change in _____
          under Article VI of the Status of Forces Agreement

TO: United States Chairman, Utilities Subcommittee

   1. Reference: Paragraph 2 and Agreed Minute 1 of Article VI of
the Status of Forces Agreement.

   2. The Government of the United States is informed through this
written consultative process that the Republic of Korea proposes to change
following rates/tariffs at locations indicated below:

   3. The following data is provided:

      a. Effective date.

      b. Rate schedule of proposed change,  applicable to the USFK.

      c. Rate schedule showing rates that are charged all classes of
users (attached).

      d. Calculation of old and new rate base.

   4. The Government of the ROK advises the Government of the United
States that the priorities, conditions, and rates or tariffs being changed are
no less favorable than those accorded any other user. The view of the
Government of the United States is ~~solicited~~ requested prior to the effective date of
the rate changes. You may be assured that your views will be greatly
appreciated.

                                    Republic of Korea Chairman
                                    Utilities Subcommittee

68

B - Format for US reply to ROK Memorandum of Consultation

SUBJECT: Change in _____
         under Article VI of the Status of Forces Agreement

TO: Republic of Korea Chairman, Utilities Subcommittee

    1. References:

        a. Paragraph 2 and Agreed Minute 1 of Article VI of the Status
of Forces Agreement.

        b. ROK component of the Utilities Subcommittee Memorandum
of Consultation, dated _____, subject as above, pertaining to a
rate/tariff change for _____.

    2. The ROK memorandum, reference 1b above, has been reviewed
and the United States component of the Utilities Subcommittee fully under-
stands the requirement for change in the _____
in this instance and will join with the ROK component of the Utilities
Subcommittee in presenting a memorandum on the rates to the Joint
Committee.

                          - or -

    2. The ROK memorandum, reference 1b above, has been reviewed
and while the requirement for _____ is understood,
the United States component of the Utilities Subcommittee takes this
opportunity to express its views.

    3. (Further comments)

                              United States Chairman
                              Utilities Subcommittee

C - Format for Recommendation to Joint Committee

REPUBLIC OF KOREA-UNITED STATES
UTILITIES SUBCOMMITTEE

MEMORANDUM TO: The Joint Committee

SUBJECT:

1. Subcommittee Members

    Republic of Korea   United States

    2. Subject of Recommendation: Agreed Minute 1 to Article VI, . ROK-US SOFA, provides that any changes determined by the authorities of the Republic of Korea in priorities, conditions, and rates or tariffs, applicable to the United States armed forces shall be the subject of consultation in the Joint Committee prior to their effective date.

    3. The Republic of Korea has initiated consultation concerning a change in rates or tariffs for _____ at _____. See Inclosure 1.

    4. The United States component of the Utilities Subcommittee has received the ROK request for consultation and has determined that the requested change in rates or tariffs is no less favorable than those accorded any other user. See Inclosure 2.

    5. It is recommended that the two inclosures reference in paragraph 3 and 4 be accepted by the Joint Committee as evidence of consultation contemplated by Article VI of the Status of Forces Agreement.

Republic of Korea Chairman   United States Chairman
Utilities Subcommittee   Utilities Subcommittee

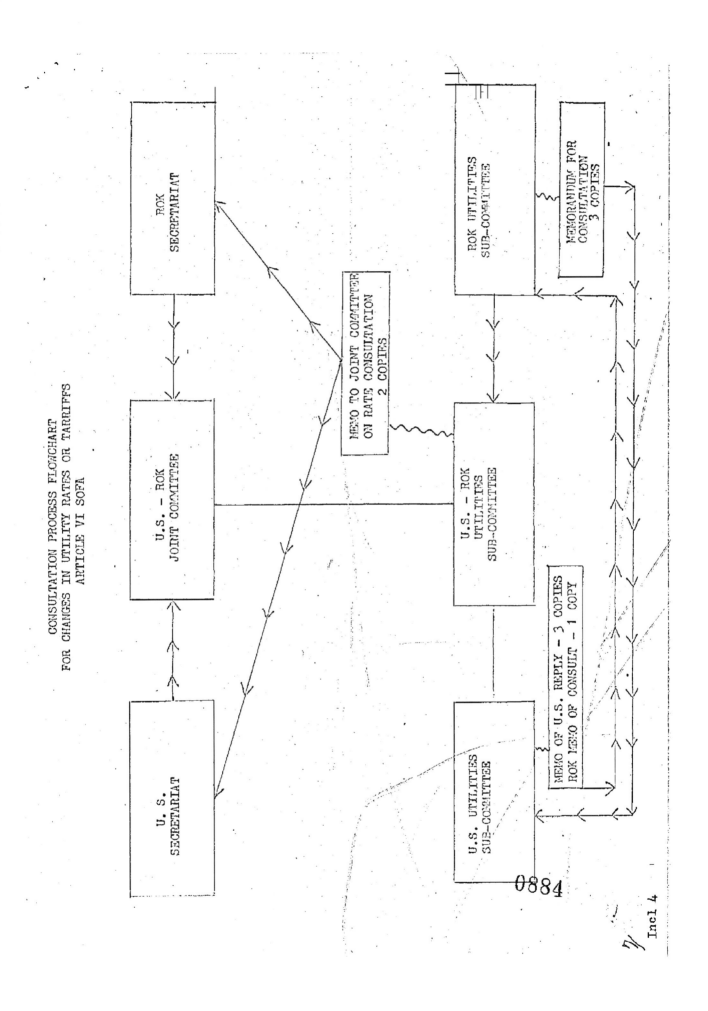

CONSULTATION PROCESS FLOWCHART
FOR CHANGES IN UTILITY RATES OR TARRIFFS
ARTICLE VI SOFA

ROK SECRETARIAT

U.S. - ROK JOINT COMMITTEE

U.S. SECRETARIAT

ROK UTILITIES SUB-COMMITTEE

MEMORANDUM FOR CONSULTATION 3 COPIES

MEMO TO JOINT COMMITTEE ON RATE CONSULTATION 2 COPIES

U.S. - ROK UTILITIES SUB-COMMITTEE

MEMO OF U.S. REPLY - 3 COPIES ROK MEMO OF CONSULT - 1 COPY

U.S. UTILITIES SUB-COMMITTEE

0884

Incl 4

기 안 용 지

분류기호. 문서번호	미 이741.13-	(전화번호)	전결규정 국 장 조 항 전결사항
처리기한		기 안 자	결 재 자
시행일자		북미2과	
보존년한		오 명 두 68. 3. 20.	

보조기관	북미2과장		
협 조			
경유 수신 참조	체신부장관	통 제	
제 목	체신요금 인상에 관한 한.미 합동위원회 협의절차 완결 통보		

　　1. 한.미 군대지위협정 합동위원회 공공용역 분과위원회는

68. 3. 13. 자로된 합동위원회에 대한 각서에 서명, 68. 1. 1. 부터

시행중인 신체신요율에 관한 군대지위협정 제6조 합의의사록 제1항

소정의 협의가 완료되었음을 보고하였읍니다.

　　2. 동 각서는 3. 20. 한.미 양국 대표가 각각서명, 합의된

합동위원회 운영규정에 의하여 즉시로 발효하였아오니 대 미군 체신요금

청산 사무에 참작하시기 바랍니다.

　　3. 3. 14. 개최된 합동위원회 제22차 회의에서 채택된 협의절차

에 의하여 신요율은 한국 정부가 결정한 시행일자 부터 소급 적용

하는 것임을 첨언합니다.　　　　끝

외 무 부

미이 741.13-   1968. 3. 20.

수 신 : 체신부장관

제 목 : 체신요금 인상에 관한 한.미 합동위원회 협의절차
       완결 통보

        1. 한.미 군대지위협정 합동위원회, 공공용의분과위원회
는 68. 3. 13. 작모된 합동위원회에 대한 각서에 서명, 68. 1. 1.
부터 시행중인 신체 신요율에 관한 군대지위협정 제6조 합의의사록
제1항 소정의 협의가 완료되었음을 보고 하였읍니다.

        2. 동 각서는 3. 20. 한.미 양국 대표가 각각 서명,
합의된 합동위원회 운영규정에 의하여 즉시로 발효 하였아오니
때 미군 체신요금 청산 사무에 참작하시기 바랍니다.

        3. 3. 14. 개최된 합동위원회 제22차 회의에서 채넉됨
협의절차에 의하여 신요율은 한국 정부가 결정한 시행 일자 부터
소급 적용하는 것임을 첨언합니다.   끝

              외 무 부 장 관

경 제 기 획 원

발 전 · 331.24-266   1968. 4. 1
수 신 · 외무부 북미2과 오명두
제 목 · 제1차 한 · 미합동위원회 공공용역분과
         위원회 의의록 송보

    1968. 3. 11에 개최된 한 · 미합동위원과
공공용역 분과위원의의 의의록을 별첨과 같이 송보
합니다.

    별 첨 : 제1차 한 · 미합동위원회 공공용역분과
              위원의 의의록 2부.   끝 .

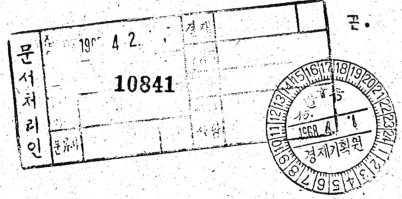

문서처리인
190 4 2.
10841

경 제 기 획 원

774
북미2과

REPUBLIC OF KOREA - UNITED STATES
UTILITIES SUBCOMMITTEE

19 March 1968

SUBJECT: Minutes of Meeting - 11 March 1968.

1. Subcommittee Members:

Republic of Korea

LEE HEE Il, Chairman
SUH Suck Joon, Secretary
LEE Man Hee, Member
HAN Byung Il, Member
KIM Soo Hak, Member
NAM, Mun Hee, Member
KIM, Sang Woo, Member
LEE, Yong Shick, Member
OH, Myong Too, Member

United States

COL Floyd R. Waltz, Jr., Chairman
COL John T. Horrocks, Jr.,
                    Alternate Chairman
LTC Walter A. Brown, Jr., Secretary
Mr. Francis K. Cook, Member
Mr. Samuel Pollack, Member
LTC James A. Jolley, Member
Mr. Oliver J. Kennedy, Member
LTC John J. Hamparian, Member
MAJ Ray E. Willis, Member

2. Purpose of the meeting was to discuss ways and means to conclude consultation on the electricity rate increase of 1 Nov 1967. The meeting was held at the ROK Economic Planning Board conference room and was chaired by Mr. Suh acting for Mr. LEE, Hee Il, ROK Chairman, who was absent. COL Waltz responded for the US side.

3. Mr. Suh stated the ROK position concerning the electricity rate increase and the special industry rates. Mr. Suh stated that the same basic electricity rate is charged all users, with certain users being given discounts because of this status. These preferential users are identified as municipal water works and export industries. The export industries are subsidized thru electricity rates on an infant industry concept. Mr. Suh stated that if the US Armed forces "exported" or produced water, then the discounted rates would apply to the U.S.

4. COL Waltz stated that the US position was the same as that formally transmitted to the ROK Chairman on 8 March 1968. Briefly, the U.S. is prepared to pay electricity rates set in accordance with paragraph 2, Article VI of SOFA. The rate schedule of KECO, as now published, is not in accordance with Article VI of SOFA.

5. There was general discussion concerning these two positions but no
agreement. It was mutually decided that a split decision memorandum
would be written and sent to the Joint Committee for resolution. Prior
to adjournment of the meeting, Mr. OH Myong Too asked COL Waltz if the
ROK subsidized the export industries in some manner other than by
reduced electricity rates, what would be the US position. COL Waltz
replied that how the ROK subsidized industries was not the concern of
the US, unless the manner of subsidy was in conflict with SOFA.

SUH SUCK JOON.,   WALTER A. BROWN, JR.
Secretary,   Lt Colonel   USAF
ROK Utilities Subcommittee   Secretary, US Utilities Subcommittee

APPROVED:

FLOYD R. WALTZ, JR.   LEE HEE IL.,
Colonel, United States Army   Chairman,
Chairman, US Utilities Subcommittee   ROK Utilities Subcommittee

2

Shim Ui Hwan   Director
                          Bureau of Commerce & Trade
                          Ministry of Commerce & Industry

Han Byung Il   Chief,
                          Military Supply Section
                          Bureau of Commerce & Trade
                          Ministry of Commerce & Industry

Lee Chang Ha   Chief,
                          Commerce Section
                          Bureau of Commerce & Trade
                          Ministry of Commerce & Industry

Lee Man Hee   Chief,
                          Electric Administration Section
                          Bureau of Utilities
                          Ministry of Commerce & Industry

Suh Suck Joon   Chief,
                          Price Policy Section
                          Bureau of Economic Planing
                          Economic Planing Board

Kim Soo Hak

Chief,
Administration Section
Bureau of Local Administration
Ministry of Home Affairs

Nam Mun Hee

Chief,
Local Financial Section
Bureau of Local Administration
Ministry of Home Affairs

Kim Sang Woo

Chief,
1st Section of Domestic Services
Bureau of Telecommunications,
Ministry of Communication

Oh Myong Too

Chief,
North America Second Section
Bureau of European and American Affairs
Ministry of Foreign Affairs

Lee Yong Sik

Chief,
Freight Section
Bureau of Transportation
Korea National Railroad

Lee Sang Bok

Chief,
Water Administration Section
Bureau of Water Service
Special Seoul City

78

ECONOMIC PLANNING BOARD
REPUBLIC OF KOREA
Seoul, Korea

To   : United States Chairman, Utilities Subcommittee

SUBJECT : Change in Water Service Charge under Article VI
           of the Status of Forces Agreement

1. Reference: Paragraph 2 and Agreed Minute 1 of Article
VI of the Status of Forces Agreement.

2. The Government of the United States is informend
through this written consultative process that the Republic
of Korea proposes to change following rates/ tariffs at locations indicated below:

Rate/Tariff	Location
Water Service	Inchson

3. The following data is provided:

a. Effective date

1 February, 1968

b. Rate schedule of proposed change

Refer to item "d"

c. Rate schedule showing rates that are charged all
classes of users (attached).

d. Calculation of old and new rate base.

Old Charge		New Charge	
Basis Rate	Over Charge	Basis Rate	Over Charge
One hydrant a month: ₩300 up to 20m^3	₩18/m^3	One hydrant a month: ₩750 up to 30m^3	₩30/m^3

4. The Government of the ROK advises the Government of the United States that the priorities, conditions, and rates or tariffs being changed are no less favorable than those accorded any other user. The view of the Government of the United States is solicited prior to the effective date of the rate changes. You may be assured that your views will be greatly appreciated.

Republic of Korea Chairman
Utilities Subcommittee

80

Rate Schedule

仁川市 (水道)

Classi fication	Usage	Rate Schedule	
		Basis Rate	Over Charge
Group I	Domestic use	One hydrant a month 100 won up to 7m^3 w.17/t	15 won/m^3
Group II	Common use of private faucet	One hydrant a month 350 won up to 25m^3	15 won/m^3
Group III	Bathing use	One hydrant a month 6,000 won up to 300m^3	21 won/m^3
Group IV	Special public use	One hydrant a month 750 won up to 30m^3 w15/t	30 won/m^3
Group V	Industrial use	One hydrant a month 2,000 won up to 100 m^3	27 won/m^3
Group VI	Locomotive and	30 won/m^3	-
Group VII	Common use of public faucet	14 won/m^3	-
Group VIII	Temporary water service	30 won/m^3	-
Group IX	Private fire fighting hydrant	150 won a month 200 won for one-time's fire fighting-drill	-
Group X	Special service	To be charged in accordance with Rate Schedule and Water Supply for Suburbs	-

300 KWH 以下 —— 15원
46.7% discount
46.7% discount

81

18 April 1968

Mr. SHIN Chung Sup
Republic of Korea Secretary
ROK-US Joint Committee

Dear Mr. Shin:

In the course of our discussion, on Saturday, 13 April, concerning the problem of US-ROK consultations on recent increases in the electric power rates of the Korean Electric Power Company, you expressed a desire for a statement in writing of the United States position on this issue. I am inclosing a copy of a letter of 8 March 1968, from the Chairman of the US component of the Utilities Subcommittee to his ROK counterpart stating the US position on this subject, which was dispatched in accordance with the Joint Committee-approved procedures (Format B, Inclosure 11, minutes of the twenty-second Joint Committee meeting).

The US Government position is based on the language of Article VI of the SOFA, and its Agreed Minutes, especially the following: .

a. Agreed Minute 1 to Article VI, which makes it clear that the authorities of the Government of the Republic of Korea determine utility rates or tariffs. (There is not believed to be any disagreement between the United States and the Republic of Korea in the Joint Committee on this point.)

b. In accordance with Agreed Minute 1 of Article VI, there will be US-ROK consultation in the Joint Committee, in accordance with the Joint Committee-approved procedures, prior to the effective date of any changes in priorities, conditions, and rates or tariffs, applicable to the United States armed forces. (There is not believed to be any US-ROK differences on this point.)

    c. Paragraph 2 of Article VI provides that US use of utilities and services "shall be in accordance with priorities, conditions, and rates or tariffs no less favorable than those accorded any other user."

There does not appear to be any basis for significant differences of opinion on the meaning of the SOFA language on the foregoing points; however, a problem has arisen as a result of the Government of the Republic of Korea giving a preferential electric rate to certain categories of Korean customers. Under paragraph 2 of Article VI, such preferential rates would also be clearly applicable to the US armed forces in Korea. In resolution of this problem, it appears that there are two readily apparent solutions, as follows:

    a. Permit the US armed forces to have electric power charges "no less favorable than those accorded any other user," in this case, the same rates as given the preferred industrial users; or

    b. Revise the electric power schedule, to eliminate the preferential rates granted to certain export industries and Municipal Water Works, and thereby make the US armed forces subject to the standard rates. Of course the Government of the Republic of Korea has the sovereign right to subsidize any preferred industries which it chooses to favor; however, if this subsidy should be granted through preferential utility rates, or if the subsidy is based on utility rates, then the US armed forces are eligible, under the provisions of the SOFA, to similar rates.

It appears that the key to the Joint Committee resolution of this problem, under the SOFA provisions, lies in the decision of the Government of the Republic of Korea to decide either to maintain existing rate schedules and grant the United States Forces, Korea rates no less favorable than those accorded any other user, or modify its procedures which utilize preferential utility rates to subsidize certain categories of users.

                          Sincerely,

1 Inclosure   ROBERT A. KINNEY
Copy of 8 March letter   United States Secretary
                           US-ROK Joint Committee

2

REPUBLIC OF KOREA - UNITED STATES
UTILITIES SUBCOMMITTEE

USFK DJ-0   8 March 1968

SUBJECT: Consultation on Change in Electric Rates

TO: Republic of Korea Chairman, Utilities Subcommittee

1. Reference: Paragraph 2 and Agreed Minute 1 of Article VI of the
Status of Forces Agreement.

2. The consultation process initiated by the Republic of Korea
concerning an increase in electric rates has been reviewed and while the
requirement for the increased rates is understood, the United States
component of the Utilities Subcommittee takes this opportunity to express
its views.

3. The meaning and intent of paragraph 2, Article VI, SOFA, is
very clear, in stating that the United States shall be furnished utilities and services in accordance with priorities, conditions, and rates
or tariffs no less favorable than those accorded any other user. The
United States has been advised through the rate schedule published by
Korea Electric Company that certain export industries and Municipal Water
Works receive electricity rates that are more favorable than those being
charged the United States Armed Forces. The rates being charged the
United States are clearly not in accordance with Article VI of SOFA.

4. The United States does not question the right of the Republic
of Korea to raise electricity rates, however, the provisions of SOFA
must be complied with, by both parties. The United States is prepared
to pay electricity rates set in accordance with paragraph 2, Article VI
of SOFA and until such rates are furnished, this consultation on
electricity rates cannot be concluded.

                                   COL FLOYD R. WALTZ, JR., USA
                                   United States Chairman
                                   Utilities Subcommittee

[handwritten notes]

Inclosure 1

[right margin, rotated] J4 Record Copy

기 안 용 지

분류기호.문서번호	미이	(전화번호)	전결규정 국 장	조 항 전결사항

처리기한		기 안 자	결 재 자
시행일자		북미2과 박 노 수	
보존년한		68. 4.26.	

보 조 기 관	북미2과장			

협 조				
경수참	유신조	경제기획원장관 물가정책과장		서

제 목	전기요금 인상에 관한 미국측 공한

1. 한.미 군대지위협정에 의하여 설치된 한.미 합동위원회 공공용역 분과위원회의 공공요금 협의절차에 관한 것입니다.

2. 한.미 군대지위협정 제6조에 대한 합의의사록 제1에 의거한 전기요금 인상에 관한 한.미간 협의문제에 관하여 미국측에서 별첨 사본과 같이 그들의 입장을 밝히는 서한을 보내 왔으므로 이를 송부하오니 전기요금 인상 협의에 관하여 참고 하시기 바랍니다.

끝

공통서식 1-2-1 (갑)   (18절지)

85

외   무   부

미이   1968. 4. 27.

수 신 : 경제기획원장관

참 조 : 물가정책과장

제 목 : 전기요금 인상에 관한 미국측 공한

　　　　1. 한.미 군대지위협정에 의하여 설치된 한.미
합동위원회 공공용역 분과위원회의 공공요금 협의절차에
관한 것입니다.

　　　　2. 한.미 군대지위협정 제6조에 대한 합의의사록
제1에 의거한 전기요금 인상에 관한 한.미간 협의문제에 관하여
미국측에서 별첨사본과 같이 그들의 입장을 밝히는 서한을 보내
왔으므로 이를 송부하오니 전기요금 인상 협의에 관하여 참고
하시기 바랍니다.　　　끝

　　　　　　　　　　외　무　부　장　관

86

한 국 전 력 주 식 회 사

(22—5101—279)

한전업(영)910-8153   1968, 5, 16

수신 외무부 장관

참조 구미국장

제목 미군 전력요금 적용

　　1. 1967.11.1을 기해 15% 인상된 전기요금의 미군적용에 관한 사항입니다.

　　2. 과거 전력요금 인상시는 미8군 구매처와 당사간에 미육군성 전력구매관 또는 그의 대리인의 승인 즉시 소급시행하는 조건으로 가계약을 체결하여 왔으며 금번도 상기한 방법으로 가계약을 체결하였고 미육군성을 대행하여 미태평양지구사령부 로 부터 승인난바 있어 당사와의 계약에 의거 미수금차액 지불을 요청한바 있읍니다.

　　3. 이에 대하여 당사의 전력요금은 한미행정협정 제6조2항과 모순된다고 한미행협의 우선권을 강조 미수금차액 지불을 거부하고 있읍니다.

　　4. 당사는 이에 대하여 미군에게 수출산업체 (전월 수출된 생산품 제조에 소요된 사용전력량에 한하여만 할인함) 및 상수도 (저수지로부터 각가정에 상수도를 공급하는데 직접소요된 사용량에 한함) 와 같은 할인적용은 공급여건 및 업종관계로 불가하다고 강조하고 공급종별이 동일한 한국정부, 한국국군 및 타수용가가 적용하는 동일한 전력요금 적용을 누차요구한바 있읍니다.

　　5. 한미행정협정 제6조1항에 명시된 바와 같이 "미군의 공익사업과 용역에 운영은 한국정부가 운영하는 공익사업 및 용역의 운영을 해치는 결과가없는 (한국정부가 운영하는 공익사업과용역의 운영과 일치하지않는) 범위내에서 행하게 규제되고 있으므로 미국측

2—1   68-2-201

한전업(영)910—   1968, 5, 16

　　　주장은 부당하다고 사료되오나

　　6. 미국측은 제6조2항의 규정 " 어떠한 타사용자보다 불리
하지않는 우선권, 사용조건, 사용료 또는 요금의 적용"을 주장
하며 요금지붙을 계속거부하고 있는바 제6조2항에 대한 쌍방간의
해석차이로 인상된 요금을 징수할수없는 실정이옵기 제6조2항의
유권적 해설을 의뢰하오니 조속히 회시하여 주시기 바랍니다.

　　7. 상기한 제6조 1항에 의거 미군도 타수용가와 동일하게 요금
을 적용하여야 될 (타당할) 경우 미군이 계속미수금차액을 지붙치
않을시는 전력공급 정지가 가능한지의 여부도 회시하여 주시기 바
랍니다. 　끝

　　　　사　　　　장　　　　정　　　　리

기 안 용 지

분류기호 문서번호	미이	(전화번호)	전결규정	조 항
			국 장	전결사항

처리기한		기 안 자	결 재 자
시행일자		북미2과 박노수	
보존년한		68. 5. 17.	

보조기관	북미2과장		

협 조	조약과장
경유수신참조	한국전력주식회사사장 통제
제 목	미군전력 요금 적용에 관한 회신

1. 한전업 (영) 910-3153 (68. 5.16.)에 대한 회신입니다.

2. 주한 미군이 사용하고 있는 전력은 한.미군대지위협정 제6조 "공익사업과 용역"의 규제 대상이 된다고 보아야 합니다.

3. 따라서 귀사의 주한 미군에 대한 전기공급,전기요금인상 및 지불은 제6조 제1항, 제2항 및 제6조에 대한 합의의사록 각항의 적용을 받게 되는바,

　　가. 주한 미군이 제6조 제2항의 규정을 들어 주한 미군에 대한 전기요금 부과가 수출산업체에 대한 할인 적용으로 인하여 실질적인 차별대우가 된다는 전기요금의 지불 문제를 외요하고 원만한 합의가 되지 못하고 있는 것은 통권 동향 해석상으로 볼때 미군측에도 충분합 있습니다.

근공팽자 심원은 2개요 북갑)　　　　/후면 계속/　　　　(18길지)

89

근거가 있는 것으로 봅니다.

제6조 제2항은 " ... 공의사업과 용역의 이용은 어느 이용자에게 부여됨것 보다 불리하지 아니한 ... 사용료나 요금에 따라야 한다 " 라고 되어 있는바 이는 수출산업체에게 부여된것 보다 주한 미군이 불리하지 아니한 요금을 보아야할 것입니다.

나. 주한 미군이 계속 미수금차액을 지불치 않을시 전력 공급 정지가 가능한지의 여부에 대하여는, 주한 미군이 지불하지 않겠다는 것이 협정상 협의절차에 계류중에 있는 것이므로 협의절차가 완료되기전에 공급을 중지한다는 것은 형평의 원칙상 부적당 할뿐 아니라 제6조 제1항의 정신에도 위배된다고 봅니다.

4. 군대지위협정 한.미합동위원회 공공용역 분과위원회 및 당부가 취하고 있는 조치를 아래와 같이 알립니다.

본 건에 관하여 공공용역 분과위원회와 군대지위협정 한.미 양측 간사를 중심으로 수차에 걸쳐 협의한바 있는바 미국측에서는 전기요율 표상에 차별의 표시를 한국 정부가 수출산업체에 수출보상금 조로 혜택을 주는것은 한국의 국내절차에 속하는 것으로서 관여할바 아니라고 말한바 있으며, 이러한 언질에 대하여 당부는 별첨 사본과 같이 미국측 의사를 문서로 확인하였읍니다. 끝

외   무   부

미이   1963. 5. 21.

수신 : 한국 전력주식회사 사장

제목 : 미군전력 요금 적용에 관한 회신

　　　　1. 한전업 (영) 910-3153(63.5. 16.) 에 대한
회신입니다.

　　　　2. 주한 미군이 사용하고 있는 전력은 한.미 군대
지위협정 제6조 "공익사업과 용역"의 규제 대상입니다.

　　　　3. 따라서 귀사의 주한 미군에 대한 전기공급, 전기
요금인상 및 지불은 제6조 제1항, 제2항 및 제6조에 대한
합의의사록 각항의 적용을 받게 되는바,

　　　　가. 주한 미군이 제6조 제2항의 규정을 들어 주한
미군에 대한 전기요금 부과가 수출산업체에 대한 할인 적용
으로 인하여 실질적인 차별대우가 된다는 미측의 당초 견해
도 말미암아 미군의 전기요금의 지불 문제를 위요하고 원만한
합의가 되지 못하고 있는 것입니다.

　　　　제6조 제2항은 " ..... 공익사업과 용역의 이용
은 어느 이용자에게 부여됨 것 보다 불리하지 아니한 .....
사용토낙 요금에 따라야 한다" 라고 되어 있는바, 이에
의거하여 수출산업체에게 부여됨 것 보다 주한 미군이 불리
하지 아니한 요금을 부여받아야 하는 것이다 미군은 주장

91

하는 것입니다.

　　나. 주한 미군이 계속 미수금차액은 지불치
않을시 전력공급 정지가 가능한지의 여부에 대하여는, 주한
미군이 지불마저 않겠다는 것이 아니고 협정상 협의절차에
계류중에 있는 것이므로 협의절차가 완료되기 전에 공급을
중지한다는 것은 형평의 원칙상 부적당 할뿐 아니라 제6조
제1항의 정신에도 위배된다고 봅니다.

　　4. 군대지위협정 한·미합동위원회 공공용역 분과위원회
및 당부가 취하고 있는 조치를 아래와 같이 알립니다.
본 건에 관하여 공공용역 분과위원회와 군대지위협정 한·미
양측 간사를 중심으로 수차에 걸쳐 협의한바 있는바, 미국측
에서는 전기 요율표상에 차별의 표시를 없게만 한다면, 한국
정부가 수출산업체에 수출보상금 조로 혜택을 주는것은 한국의
국내절차에 속하는 것으로서 관여할바 아니라고 말한바 있으며,
이러한 언질에 대하여 당부는 별첨 사본과 같이 미국측 입장
을 문서로 확인하였읍니다.　　끝

　　　　　外　務　部　　　　　長　官

6 June 1968

SUBJECT: Change in Water Service Charge, Inchon, under Article VI of the
Status of Forces Agreement

TO: Republic of Korea Chairman, Utilities Subcommittee

1. References:

    a. Paragraph 2 and Agreed Minute 1 of Article VI of the Status of
Forces Agreement.

    b. ROK component of the Utilities Subcommittee Memorandum of Consul-
tation, dated 13 May 1968, subject as above, pertaining to a rate/tariff
change for Inchon, Korea.

2. The ROK memorandum, reference 1b above, has been reviewed and while
the requirement for a revision of water rates at Inchon is understood,
the United States component of the Utilities Subcommittee takes this
opportunity to express its views.

3. Paragraph 2 of Article VI states that utilities and services will be
furnished the United States at rates or tariffs no less favorable than
those accorded any other user. Our examination of the rate schedule furnished by reference 1b indicates that more favorable rates are being given
 to other users than those accorded the United States. According to the
rate schedule, Groups I and II will receive more favorable basic rates
and the unit rate for quantities consumed in excess of those covered by
the basic rate indicates that Groups I, II, III and IV will receive more
favorable terms than the United States.

4. Until the rate discrepancies outlined in paragraph 3 above are cor-
rected this consultation process cannot be completed.

                              COL FLOYD R. WALTZ, JR., US ARMY .
                              United States Chairman
                              Utilities Subcommittee

93

DNA-29 (TTY)

WATER CHARGES

    SEOUL, APR. 22 (DONGHWA) -- THE INCHON CITY ADMINISTRATION
IS IN SERIOUS TROUBLE BECAUSE THE U.S. MILITARY HAS BEEN REFUSING
TO PAY SOME 62 MILLION WON IN RAISED WATER CHARGES, THE DAILY
DONG-A ILBO REPORTED THIS AFTERNOON.
    HAVING RAISED ITS WATER SUPPLY CHARGES FROM 12 WON TO 30
WON PER TON IN FEBRUARY LAST YEAR FOR BOTH LOCAL CITIZENS AND U.S.
MILITARY INSTALLATIONS, THE CITY OFFICE NOTIFIED THE STEP TO
8TH U.S. ARMY AUTHORITIES, THE PAPER SAID IN A DISPATCH FROM INCHON.
    THE U.S. MILITARY, HOWEVER, HAS NOT YET COMPLIED WITH THE
RAISE UNDER THE EXCUSE THAT THE RAISE WAS PUT INTO FORCE
BY THE CITY AUTHORITIES UNILATERALLY, THE REPORT ADDED.
C1544KST KBC
VVMMMMO
M

94

EXTRACTS OF SOFA'S ON UTILITIES AND SERVICES

Japan (June 23, 1960)

Article VII

The United States armed forces shall have the use of all public utilities and services belonging to, or controlled or regulated by the Government of Japan, and shall enjoy priorities in such use, under conditions no less favorable than those that may be applicable from time to time the ministries and agencies of the Government of Japan.

Republic of China - no provisions (Aug. 31, 1965)

Philippines

Article VII   Use of Public Services

It is mutually agreed that the United States may employ and use for United States military forces any and all public utilities, other services and facilities,

95

airfields, ports, harbors, roads, highways, railroads,
bridges, viaducts, cannals, lakes, rivers and streams in
the Philippines under conditions no less favorable than
those that may be applicable from time to time to the
military forces of the Philippines.

Australia (May 9, 1963)

Article XXIII   paragraph (1)

The United States Forces and all persons associated
with activities agreed upon by the two Governments may
use the public services and facilities owned, controlled
or regulated by the Australian Government or its instrumentalities.
The terms of use, including charges, shall be no less
favorable than those available to other users in like
circumstances unless otherwise agreed.

Dominican Republic (March 19, 1957)

Article XXVI

The Government of the United States of America shall
have the right to employ and use, in order to carry out
the purposes of this Agreement, all public services, including
any water rights owned or controlled by the Dominican Republic,

subject to the tariffs established by the Dominican laws
and regulations. Utilities and other facilities, bays,
roads, highways, bridges and similar channels of transportation
belonging, controlled or regulated by the Government of
the Dominican Republic shall be used under such terms and
conditions as shall be mutually agreed upon by the two
Governments.

Nicaragua (Sept. 5, 1958)

    No provisions

West Indies (Feb. 10, 1961)

                    Article VII

            Public Services and Facilities

    (1) The United States Forces, United States contractors
and the members of the United States Forces and contractor
personnel may use the public services and facilities
belonging to or controlled or regulated by the Federal
Government or the Government of the Territory. The terms
of use, including charges, shall be no less favorable
than those available to other users unless otherwise agreed ...

Ethiopia (May 22, 1953)

The Imperial Ethiopian Government grants to the Government of the United States the right to employ and use public and commercial utilities, services, transportation and communication facilities in Ethiopia in connection with operations under this Agreement. The Government of the United States shall pay for any employment or usage of such facilities at the most favorable rates <u>obtained by other public users who employ and use such facilities.</u>

Libya (Sept. 9, 1954)

Article V

Public Services and Facilities

Upon the request of the Government of the United States of America and provided that the Government of the United Kingdom of Libya is assured that the public and private interests in Libya will be duly safeguarded, the public services and facilities in Libya shall be made available as far as practicable for the use of the Government of the United States of America and members of the United States forces. <u>The charges therefor shall be the same as those paid by other users, unless otherwise agreed.</u>

98

NATO (June 19, 1951)

Article IX

    1. Members of a force or of a civilian component and their dependents may purchase locally goods necessary for their own consumption, and such service as they need, under the same conditions as the nationals of the receiving State.

    3. Subject to agreements already in force or which may hereafter be made between the authorized representatives of the sending and receiving States, the authorities of the receiving State shall assume sole responsibility for making suitable arrangements to make available a force or a civilian component the buildings and grounds which it requires, as well as facilities and services connected therewith. These agreements and arrangements shall be, as far as possible, in accordance with the regulations governing the accommodation and billeting of similar personnel of the receiving State. In the absense of a specific contract to the contrary, the laws of the receiving State shall determine the rights and obligations arising out of the occupation or use of the buildings, grounds, facilities or services.

<u>Germany (Aug. 3, 1959)</u>

Article 47

1. The Federal Republic shall accord to a force or
a civilian component treatment in the matter of procurement
of goods and services not less favorable than is accorded
to the German Armed Forces.

<u>Greece (Sept. 7, 1956)</u>

NATO Agr.

110

INDEX ON AGREED SUMMARY RECORD

(Article VI, SOFA)

1. Paragraph 2, Article IV (no less favorable than any
                                other user)

   (para. 3(b) of US draft)

   ### Volume II

   14th Meeting (Feb. 14, 1963)

       pp 122-126

       sections 11 - 16

   20th Meeting (Apr. 24, 1963)

       pp 140-141

       sections 10 - 11

   24th Meeting (June 12, 1963)

       pp 150-151

       sections 4-5

2. Agreed Minute 1 (changes & consultation) ### Volume II

   14th Meeting (Feb. 14, 1963)

       pp 130-132 (sections 22-25)

           proposed Agreed Minute #1

20th Meeting (Apr. 24, 1964)

pp 145-6
section 18

24th Meeting (June 12, 1963)

pp 151 -
sections 6 -

35th Meeting (Novm 14, 1963)

pp 164-166
sections 10-13

39th Meeting (Jan. 17, 1964)

pp 167-168
sections 1-2

44th Meeting (Feb. 28, 1964)

p 170
sections 5-6

45th Meeting (Mar. 6, 1964)

pp 172-173
section 1 & 3

102

INDEX ON AGREED SUMMARY RECORD
(Article VI, SOFA)

1. Paragraph 2, Article IV (no less favorable than any other user)

   (para. 3(b) of US draft)

   <u>Volume II</u>

   14th Meeting (Feb. 14, 1963)

   pp 122-126

   sections 11 - 16

   20th Meeting (Apr. 24, 1963)

   pp 140-141

   sections 10 - 11

   24th Meeting (June 12, 1963)

   pp 150-151

   sections 4-5

2. Agreed Minute 1 (changes & consultation) <u>Volume II</u>

   14th Meeting (Feb. 14, 1963)

   pp 130-132 (sections 22-25)

   proposed Agreed Minute #1

\103

20th Meeting (Apr. 24, 1964)

pp 145-6

section 18

24th Meeting (June 12, 1963)

pp 151 -

sections 6 -

35th Meeting (Novm 14, 1963)

pp 164-166

sections 10-13

39th Meeting (Jan. 17, 1964)

pp 167-168

sections 1-2

44th Meeting (Feb. 28, 1964)

p 170

sections 5-6

45th Meeting (Mar. 6, 1964)

pp 172-173

section 1 & 3

104

J-5 Memorandum

To: Mr Shin Chung Sup -

We will respond to this pointing out that there is no intention to ignore rate increases - but rather to accept that which is _favorable_. President Jung will be informed that the matter is in Sub Committee hands.

Respectfully

W. Morrison

105

11 June 1968

General C. H. Bonesteel
Commander in chief
USPK/UNC/8th U.S. Army

Dear Sir:

Reference is made to Modification #90 to Contract No. DA92-125
FEC-1375 and our letters of 15 April 1968 and 29 April 1968, in which
we requested payment for electricity based on the 15 percent increase
which became effective on 1 November 1967.

As you are well aware, Modification #90 was prepared and executed
between the US Army Korea Procurement Agency and this company on condition that the modification be effected upon its approval by the Department of Army Power Procurement Officer or his duly authorized representative. And the modification was approved by USARPAC, the authorized
representative of the Department of Army.

For the faithful performance of the stipulations of the contract,
this company requested acceptance of the latest price increase which
became effective on 1 November 1967 and also payment of the appropriate
back payments.

This request has not been accepted by your Headquarters because
the increase in the cost of electricity is in dispute over paragraph 2,
Article VI of the Status of Forces Agreement (SOFA).

In regard to your request for a special discount for the US Forces,
we would like to advise you that such special discount is only made to
certain specific industrial export consumers, whose contracted power
demand is less than 200KW, and does not affect all the energy consumed,
but affects only the portion which was consumed for the production of
manufactured goods exported during the previous month. As for municipal
water services operated by governmental agencies, not all the energy
consumed is discounted, but only the power consumed for the delivery of
water from the reservoir to the residences and security lights.

As you are also aware, this company has made every possible effort to cooperate with you for the power supply services; for example, this company has cooperated with 1,500KW power demand increase at 6175th Air Base, Kunsan, even though this company has not approved any new connections or power demand increases since 7th of December 1967 because of power shortage. To give reliable power services and to exclude U.S. Forces from power curtailment, this company has installed exclusive feeders at several U.S. Commands at our own expense. Also, this company is trying to provide new connections to several U.S. Army locations, such as Camp Humphreys, Chongsan VHF, Camp J. Williams and SASP (10 & D-44, even though no new connections have been made for Korean consumers.

Please fully understand our situation in this matter. This undue delay on your part in paying at the new price for the power consumed since 1 November 1967 results in financial and operational problems for our company and has caused to delay some improvements scheduled to be financed from this additional income on our part.

Additionally, we would like to point out that a further delay in payment may result in a serious situation in the electric power supply service, and it may also cause bad effects on our power services to U.S. Forces stationed in Korea.

We regard you, the United Nations Command and U.S. Forces in Korea, as part of consumers, such as ROK Army, Navy and Air Forces and other governmental agencies, who are in the same service and rate category.

Therefore, we again appeal to you to accept and approve the rate-increase effective on 1 November 1967 and to pay the back payments requested by us.

Thanking you for your full understanding and cooperation in this matter.

Sincerely yours,

HAE-HICK JUNG
President
Korea Electric Company

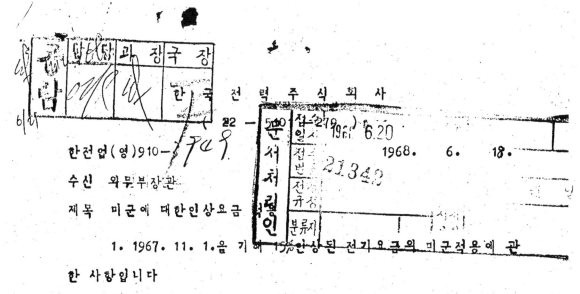

한 전 업(영)910-〇〇〇

수신 외무부장관

제목 미군에 대한 인상요금

　　1. 1967. 11. 1.을 기하 15%인상된 전기요금의 미군적용에 관한 사항입니다

　　2. 과거 당사는 전력요금 인상시는 미8군 구매처와 당사간에 미육군성 전력구매관 또는 그의 전권대리인의 승인 즉시 소급시행하는 조건으로 가계약(Modification)을 체결하여 왔읍니다. 금번전력요금 인상시도 상기한 방법으로 가계약(mod. #70)을 체결하였으며 가계약은 미육군성을 대행하여 미태평양지구 사령부로 부터 승인된바 있어 당사와의 계약조항에 의거 신전기요금의 적용및 그간의 미수금차액지불을 요청한바 있읍니다.

　　3. 그러나 당사의 인상된 전력요금은 한·미행정협정 제6조 2항 (공익사업과 용역의 이용은 어느타이용자에게 부여된것보다 불리하지 아니한 우선권, 조건 및 사용료나 요금에 따라야한다)에 모순된다고 인상된 신전기요금의 적용거부는 물론, 한미행정협정이 우선함을 강조하고 타사용자에게 부여하는 (수출산업체 및 상수도) 할인을 미군에게도 적용하어 줄것을 계속 요청하고 있으며, 이의 할인을 미군에게 부여하지못할때는 할인제도를 요금규정에서 삭제하어 미군도 타사용자와 (수출산업체 및 상수도) 동일한 요금이 적용되두룩 요금규정의 수정을 요청하고 있읍니다

　　4. 당사는 수차에 걸쳐 수출산업체 및 상수도 할인 및 절차에 대하여 구체적으로 통보, 주지시키어 할인적용요청은 공급여건 및 사용목적이 다르므로 불가함을 강조한바

108
부미2과.

3-1

있읍니다. 또한 한미행정협정의 조항의 개념은 어디까지나 같은 공급조건하에 있는, 즉 한국군 및 한국정부나 모든 외국기관과 같은 그러한 수용자보다 불리하지않은 요금을 적용하여 줄것을 규제한것으로 차료됨을 강조하여 미군도 상기한수용자에게 적용되고 있는 신전기요금의 적용을 수차 요구한바 있읍니다

5. 미군으로부터의 신전기요금적용 거부로 인한 미수차액은 1968. 5말 현재 약84,000,000에 달하며 이로인하여 당사는 재정상에 막대한 지장을 초래하여 운영면에 차질을 가져오고있는 실정입니다

6. 당사는 상기한바와 같이 미군도 동일한 공급여건하에 있는 한국군과 동일한 전력요금이 적용되어야 타당할것으로 차료하오나 당사만으로는 이의 해결이 불가한 실정이며 더욱이 미군의 회계년도가 6월말로서 끝나는바 시기적으로 대단히 긴박한 상태이므로 한미행정협정 본 위원회에서 이문제가 해결되도록 귀부의 적극협조가 요청되오며, 만약 미군이 계속 할인제도적용을 고집할 경우에는 할인제도를 요금규정에서 삭제하드라도 미군에게 신전기요금을 적용 처리할수 있도록 조치하여 주시기 바랍니다

유첨 1. 계약서(*mod. #90*) 사본 1부

2. 당사서한(미측공공 용역분과 위원장) 사본 1부

3. 미측회신문 사본 1부

4. 당사 사장서한 (유엔군 사령관) 사본 1부

5. 당사서한 (미 대사) 사본 1부.   끝

한전 업940-   1968. 6. 18.

사   장   정   태

수신처 참조 : 1. 경제기획원장관
              2. 외무부장관
              3. 합공부장관

110   3—3   68-2-27

AMENDMENT OF SOLICITATION/MODIFICATION OF CONTRACT

PAGE	1 2

| 1. MODIFICATION NO. 90 | 2. EFFECTIVE DATE 1 Nov 67 | 3. REQUISITION/PURCHASE REQUEST NO. Contractor's Ltr 18 Oct 67 | 4. PROJECT NO. (If applicable) |

5. ISSUED BY
CODE

Construction/R&U Branch
US Army Korea Procurement Agency
APO 96301

6. ADMINISTERED BY (If other than block 5)
CODE

(Copy)

7. CONTRACTOR
CODE
FACILITY CODE

KOREA ELECTRIC COMPANY
#5, 2nd Street, Nam Dae Moon Ro.
Chung Ku, Seoul, Korea

☐ AMENDMENT OF SOLICITATION NO. _____

DATED _____ (See block 9)

☒ MODIFICATION OF CONTRACT/ORDER NO. DA92-125-FEC-1375

DATED 2 May 62 (See block 11)

8. THIS BLOCK APPLIES ONLY TO AMENDMENTS OF SOLICITATIONS

☐ The above numbered solicitation is amended as set forth in block 12. The hour and date specified for receipt of Offers ☐ is extended, ☐ is not extended.
Offerors must acknowledge receipt of this amendment prior to the hour and date specified in the solicitation, or as amended, by one of the following methods:
(a) By signing and returning _____ copies of this amendment; (b) By acknowledging receipt of this amendment on each copy of the offer submitted; or (c) By separate letter or telegram which includes a reference to the solicitation and amendment numbers. FAILURE OF YOUR ACKNOWLEDGMENT TO BE RECEIVED AT THE ISSUING OFFICE PRIOR TO THE HOUR AND DATE SPECIFIED MAY RESULT IN REJECTION OF YOUR OFFER. If, by virtue of this amendment you desire to change an offer already submitted, such change may be made by telegram or letter, provided such telegram or letter makes reference to the solicitation and this amendment, and is received prior to the opening hour and date specified.

10. ACCOUNTING AND APPROPRIATION DATA (If required) The appropriation allotment chargeable for the services described herein will be cited on monthly delivery orders issued against the contract by the Contracting Officer.

11. THIS BLOCK APPLIES ONLY TO MODIFICATIONS OF CONTRACTS/ORDERS

☐ (a) This Change Order is issued pursuant to _____
The Changes set forth in block 12 are made to the above numbered contract/order.
☐ (b) The above numbered contract/order is modified to reflect the administrative changes (such as changes in paying office, appropriation data, etc.) set forth in block 12.
☒ (c) This Supplemental Agreement is entered into pursuant to authority of 10 U.S.C. 2304(a)(6)

It modifies the above numbered contract as set forth in block 12.

12. DESCRIPTION OF AMENDMENT/MODIFICATION

1. Pursuant to the provisions of paragraph (a) of ARTICLE V, CHANGE OF RATES of the contract, delete, in its entirety, APPENDIX A, Revised Monthly Rate Schedule (Effective 1 April 1966) attached to and made a part of Supplemental Agreement, Modification No. 74, and substitute therefor revision thereof as contained within ATTACHMENT I, hereto attached and made a part hereof, effective 1 November 1967.

2. Delete, in their entireties, APPENDICES "B" thru "I", ATTACHMENT II to Supplemental Agreement, Modification No. 74, as heretofore modified under Modifications 75 thru 86, 88 and 89, and substitute therefor revisions thereof as contained within ATTACHMENT II, hereto attached and made a part hereof, effective 1 November 1967. The revision of said appendices shows the current delivery status of the various delivery points under the contract; consolidates certain delivery points under appropriate appendices; deleted Items 7 and 27 of APPENDIX "B", said points having been ineffective as of 18 May 1966 and 31 October 1967, respectively; and increases the KW contract demand of the Hialeah Compound from 1,000 KW to 1,400 KW under APPENDIX "I", effective 1 October 1967.

Except as provided herein, all terms and conditions of the document referenced in block 5, as heretofore changed, remain unchanged and in full force and effect.

15. ☐ CONTRACTOR/OFFEROR IS NOT REQUIRED TO SIGN THIS DOCUMENT   ☒ CONTRACTOR/OFFEROR IS REQUIRED TO SIGN THIS DOCUMENT AND RETURN SIX COPIES TO ISSUING OFFICE

16. NAME OF CONTRACTOR/OFFEROR	17. UNITED STATES OF AMERICA
KOREA ELECTRIC COMPANY	/s/ Cyril R. Potosnak
/s/ Chung Ho Lee	18. NAME OF CONTRACTING OFFICER (Type or print) CYRIL R. POTOSNAK
19. DATE SIGNED	20. DATE SIGNED

Page 2 to Modification No. 90
Contract No. DA92-125-FEC-1375

3. This Supplemental Agreement, Modification No. 90, is subject to the manual approval of the Department of the Army Power Procurement Officer or his duly authorized representative and shall not be binding until so approved.

APPROVED BY: _____

112

ATTACHMENT I to
Supplemental Agreement
Modification No. 90
Contract No. DA92-125-FEC-1375

APPENDIX A

Revised Monthly Rate Schedule (Effective 1 November 1967)

1. General Service B (For all service under 20 KV, 4 KW of contracted demand and over)

Basic Rate:

a. Demand charge.

₩144.00 per KW for the first 50 KW of contracted demand.
₩115.00 per KW for the next 450 KW of contracted demand.
₩ 86.00 per KW for each additional KW of contracted demand.

b. Energy charge.

₩7.50 per KWH for the first 90 KWH per KW of contracted demand.
₩5.15 per KWH for the next 90 KWH per KW of contracted demand.
₩3.70 per KWH for the next 180 KWH per KW of contracted demand.
₩2.50 per KWH for each additional KWH.

c. Minimum contracted KW of demand: 4 KW.

2. High tension service (20 KV and over, 1,000 KW of contracted demand and over).

Basic Rate:

a. Demand charge:

₩[illegible] per KW for the first [illegible] KW of contracted demand.
₩[illegible] per KW for each additional KW of contracted demand.

b. Energy charge.

₩7.50 per KWH for the first 90 KWH per KW of contracted demand.
₩[illegible] per KWH for the next [illegible] KWH per KW of contracted demand.
₩[illegible] per KWH for the next [illegible] KWH per KW of contracted demand.
₩2.15 per KWH for each additional KWH.

c. Minimum contracted KW of demand: 1,000 KW.

3. Maintaining power factor. The Government shall maintain a power factor better than 85 percent lagging at maximum load and in order to maintain the above-mentioned power factor, the Government shall, at its costs, install necessary power factor correcting equipment. When the power factor is less than [illegible] percent, demand KW for General Service "B" and High Tension Service shall be adjusted as follows:

Contracted Demand KW multiplied by [illegible] / ACTUAL POWER FACTOR

113

KOREA ELECTRIC COMPANY

3-2 KA NAMDAEMOON RO, CHUNG-KU
SEOUL, KOREA

CABLE ADDRESS
KEEPCOKECO

April 29, 1968

Headquarter
US Forces Korea/United Nations Command

Attn: Col. W. Itz, Chairman of the Utilities Subcommittee, SOFA

Dear Sir:

Reference is made to our letter of 15 April 1968 to the Eighth US Army Engineer, in which we requested acceptance of the latest price increase which became effective on 1 November 1967 and appropriate back payments, and the reply dated 17 April 1968, which pointed out that the difference of opinion between the American and Korean side of the SOFA Utilities Subcommittee has not been settled.

In regard to your request for a special discount for the US Forces we would like to advise you again that such special discounts are only made to certain specific industrial export consumers, whose contrasted power demand is less than 200 KW and municipal water services operated by governmental agencies. The special discount given to export firms is meant to be an inducement for such firms to carry on their exporting business and to lower their operational expenditures;

This undue delay in paying for the power consumed since 1 November 1967 at the new price results in financial and operational problems for our company and delays certain improvements which have been scheduled to be funded from this additional income.

It is further pointed out that this delay in payment may result in a serious situation in the electric power supply service. Therefore, we again appeal to you to accept and approve the increase which was effected on 1 November 1967 and to effect the required back payments, especially since all consumers which are in your category of service, such as the ROK Army, Air Force and Navy and all Governmental agencies are in the same rate category as the United Nations Command and the US Forces Korea.

Thank you for your full understanding and cooperation in this matter.

Very truly yours,

CHUNG-HO LEE
Chief
Business Operation Dept.

REPUBLIC OF KOREA - UNITED STATES
UTILITIES SUBCOMMITTEE

1 May 1968

Mr. CHUNG-HO Lee
Chief, Business Operation Dept.
Korea Electric Company
5-2-Ka Namdaemoon-Ro, Chung-Ku
Seoul, Korea

Dear Mr. CHUNG-HO Lee:

Reference is made to your letter of 29 April 1968 concerning the
Korea Electric Company rate increase of 1 November 1967 and its appli-
cability to United States Forces, Korea.

As you are probably aware, the United States has stated its
official position on this matter several times to the ROKG, and has
suggested that new rate tables be published showing rates charged USFK,
to be no less favorable than those accorded any other user. The United
States is prepared to pay electricity rates set in accordance with
paragraph 2, Article VI of the Status of Forces Agreement (SOFA). We
cannot legally accept rates set in any other manner, since the provisions of SOFA must be complied with by both governments.

I hope that KECO will be able to view this matter in the same way
and proceed with revision of existing electricity rates in accordance
with SOFA.

Sincerely,

FLOYD R. WALTZ, JR.
Colonel, United States Army
US Chairman, Utilities Subcommittee

11 June 1968

General C. H. Bonesteel
Commander in chief
USFK/UNC/8th U.S. Army

Dear Sir:

Reference is made to Modification #90 to Contract No. DA92-125 FEC-1375 and our letters of 15 April 1968 and 29 April 1968, in which we requested payment for electricity based on the 15 percent increase which became effective on 1 November 1967.

As you are well aware, Modification #90 was prepared and executed between the US Army Korea Procurement Agency and this company on condition that the modification be effected upon its approval by the Department of Army Power Procurement Officer or his duly authorized representative. And the modification was approved by USARPAC, the authorized representative of the Department of Army.

For the faithful performance of the stipulations of the contract, this company requested acceptance of the latest price increase which became effective on 1 November 1967 and also payment of the appropriate back payments.

This request has not been accepted by your Headquarters because the increase in the cost of electricity is in dispute over paragraph 2, Article VI of the Status of Forces Agreement (SOFA).

In regard to your request for a special discount for the US Forces, we would like to advise you that such special discount is only made to certain specific industrial export consumers, whose contracted power demand is less than 200KW, and does not affect all the energy consumed, but affects only the portion which was consumed for the production of manufactured goods exported during the previous month. As for municipal water services operated by governmental agencies, not all the energy consumed is discounted, but only the power consumed for the delivery of water from the reservoir to the residences and security lights.

F2791-068-SA3

한국전력주식회사

116

68-2-22

KECO

As you are also aware, this company has made every possible effort to cooperate with you for the power supply services; for example, this company has cooperated with 1,500KW power demand increase at 6175th Air Base, Kunsan, even though this company has not approved any new connections or power demand increases since 7th of December 1967 because of power shortage. To give reliable power services and to exclude U.S. Forces from power curtailment, this company has installed exclusive feeders at several U.S. Compounds at our own expense. Also, this company is trying to provide new connections to several U.S. Army locations, such as Camp Humphreys, Changsan VHF, Camp J. Williams and SASF #10 & K-46, even though no new connections have been made for Korean consumers.

Please fully understand our situation in this matter. This undue delay on your part in paying at the new price for the power consumed since 1 November 1967 results in financial and operational problems for our company and has caused to delay some improvements scheduled to be financed from this additional income on our part.

Additionally, we would like to point out that a further delay in payment may result in a serious situation in the electric power supply service, and it may also cause bad effects on our power services to U.S. Forces stationed in Korea.

We regard you, the United Nations Command and U.S. Forces in Korea, as part of consumers, such as ROK Army, Navy and Air Forces and other governmental agencies, who are in the same service and rate category.

Therefore, we again appeal to you to accept and approve the rate-increase effective on 1 November 1967 and to pay the back payments requested by us.

Thanking you for your full understanding and cooperation in this matter.

Sincerely yours,

HAE-HIUK JUNG
President
Korea Electric Company

F2791-068-SA3   한국전력주식회사

117   68-2-23

KOREA ELECTRIC COMPANY

SEOUL, NAMDAEMOON-RO, CHUNG-KU

SEOUL, KOREA

13 June 1968

CABLE ADDRESS:
KELECCO SEOUL

William J. Porter
The American Ambassador to Korea

Dear Ambassador:

It is my pleasure to remind you that the electric rate was increased by 15 percent on 1 November 1967, and I would like to furnish you a copy of a letter, which was sent to General C. H. Bonesteel, Commander in Chief, UNFK/UNC/Eighth US Army, from Nae-Hiuk Jung, president of the Korea Electric Company pertaining to the electric rate increase.

As you are well aware of it, the invoices for the power consumed by U.S. Forces in Korea are still prepared and paid based on the old rate since 1 November 1967, because the increase in the cost of electricity is in dispute over paragraph 2, Article VI of the Status of Forces Agreement.

In this connection, it appears and we are believed that the intention of article on utilities in SOFA is to provide the energy consumed by U.S. Forces be charged no less favorable than those consumer, who are under the same condition of service and function, such as the ROK Forces.

It is kindly requested to pay your attention to the fact that the energy consumed by the ROK Army, Navy and Air Forces and other governmental and foreign agencies, who are in the same service and rate category, are charged and paid based on the new rate, which became effective on 1 November 1967.

Please fully understand our situation in this matter, and we would like to make request for your kind assistance and cooperation for the sttlement and solution of this problem at an early date.

Your kind cooperation and assistance in this matter are greatly appreciated.

Sincerely yours,

/s/ Chung-Ho Lee
CHUNG-HO LEE
Chief
Business Operation Dept.

118

68-2-24

2 4 JUN 1968

Dear General Jung:

This is in reply to your 11 June 1968 letter concerning nonpayment by the United States for the increased power rate differentials which went into effect on 1 November 1967. I recognize the adverse impact this situation creates in the fiscal management of the Korea Electric Company and am most sorry. However, resolution of this matter is beyond my immediate control.

The problem is a legal matter affected by Status of Forces Agreement of 9 July 1966 to which the United States Government and the Government of the Republic of Korea are signatories. Thus, the derivation of an agreement to provide the basis of payment cannot be arranged between you and me. Rather, it must be made within the administrative structure established by SOFA under the provisions of the aforementioned government to government agreement.

The issue at question is concerned with SOFA Article VI, paragraph 2, which states: "The use of such utilities and services by the United States shall be in accordance with priorities, conditions, and rates or tariffs no less favorable than those accorded any other user." As I am sure you must be fully aware, the KECO rate schedules effected 1 November 1967 contravene the agreement between our two governments since more favorable rates are given several classes of customers than are given to the United States. Specifically, discount rates are provided to export industry customers with 200 KW of contracted demand or under, to industry customers whose power charges account for more than 20% of their total production cost, and to municipal water services.

Let it be clearly understood that I do not question the right of your government to subsidize its industry and public utilities. Let it be equally understood, however, that under United States law, it is manifestly illegal for me to authorize payment of the increased rates so long as these rate schedules are at variance with the provisions of the Status of Forces Agreement.

119

I reiterate the suggestion, offered by the United States Chairman of the SOFA Utilities Subcommittee, that the United States would concur in the 1 November 1967 electric power rate increase if the preferential rate schedules which grant discount subsidies to preferred customers are eliminated. Adoption of this procedure would not, of course, preclude the granting of subsidies by some other means. That done, payment for increased power rate differentials could be effected immediately retroactive to 1 November 1967 since I have directed that funds be reserved for that purpose. Unfortunately, however, the extensive delay of almost eight months in your Government's not resolving this issue, has placed me in the unpleasant situation of having to withhold payment and to have received threats of reprisal action. It was most surprising to me that your letter to me dated 11 June seems to hint at possible reprisal action in the event that a further delay in payment occurs. At this time, when the North Korean's are becoming increasingly threatening and bellicose, any interruption of KECO services would have adverse effects on our military capabilities in the ROK, which would be most unfortunate. I would appreciate your early reassurances on this matter.

I trust that through appropriate action under SOFA arrangements, the problem of payments to KECO can be rapidly resolved. I want to assure you that I wish to pay up the back payments just as soon as I can legally do so.

Sincerely,

C. H. BONESTEEL, III
General, United States Army
Commander

General JUNG Nae-Hiuk
President
Korea Electric Company
52 Ka Namdaemoon-Ro, Chung-Ku
Seoul, Korea

Copy:
Honorable CHOI Young Hi
Minister of National Defense
Republic of Korea
Seoul, Korea

2

120

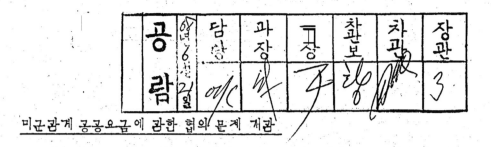

미군관계 공공요금에 관한 협의 문제 개관

1. 관계 군대지위협정 조항
   제 6 조 합의의사록

   " 1. It is understood that any changes determined
   by the authorities of the Republic of Korea in priorities,
   conditions, and rates or tariffs, applicable to the
   United States armed forces shall be the subject of
   consultation in the Joint Committee prior to their
   effective date."

   제 6 조 2항

   " 2. The use of such utilities and services by the
   United States shall be in accordance with priorities,
   conditions, and rates or tariffs no less favourable than
   those accorded any other user."

2. 경 위
   가. 합동위원회는 1967. 9. 28. 제15차 회의에서 6조 합의의사록
       소정 협의 절차를 정하는 과제를 상무분과위원회에 부여 (당시
       철도 및 전기요금 인상이 예견되고 있었음.)
   나. 1967. 10. 19. 합동위원회 제16차 회의에서 한국 대표는 10. 16. 부터
       인상 철도요금이 시행되고 11. 1. 부터 전기 요금을 인상시행 한다는
       경정이 있었음을 지적하고 상무 분과위원회가 협의 절차에 합의하지

121 룡굴□께淡재띄 6/22 내   68-2-28

못하였고 등 합의까지는 상당 시간이 소요될 것이므로 당서 인상요금
에 관하여는 협정 시행이 불가능함에 유의하여 다음과 같이 제안
미국 대표의 동의를 얻음.

(1) 상무 분과위원회는 본 건 협의절차 심의를 촉진한다.

(2) 철도 및 전기 요금에 관하여는 현행 약정 (existing arrangements
)을 최대한 이용하여 한.미 양측 관계당국
간에 실제 협의와 교섭을 행한다.

다.. 상무분과위원회는 수차의 회합끝에 동 분과위원회가 본 건 처리에
부적당하다는 결론에 도달 합동위원회 제20차 회의 (68. 1. 18.)
에 경제기획원을 주축으로 하는 공공용여 분과위원회의 신설과
협의 절차 심의 과제의 동 위원회 이관을 건의 채택함.

박. 신설된 공공용여 분과위원회는 합동위원회 제22차 회의 (68. 3.22.)
에 동 협의절차를 건의하여 채택하였는바, 동 절차 골자는 다음과같음.

(1) 공공요금 인상에 관하여는 정책 입안 단계에서 부터 양측
분과위원장이 비공식 비밀전제로 정보를 교환 협의한다.

(2) 인상이 공식 결정되면 한국측 분과위원장이 전 요율표를
첨부하여 조속히 이를 미측 위원장에게 통고하고 미측은 6조 2항
저촉 여부를 확인하고 저촉 없음을 확인하였다고 통고하면
협의가 완료된 것으로 간주하고 이를 합동위원회에 보고, 채택
하여 절차 완료.

(3) 양측에 이견이 있는 경우에는 동 사실 (split recommendation)
을 합동위원회에 보고

(4) 동 절차가 신요율 시행일 후 7까지 완료되지 않는 경우에는
협의완료시까지 구요율을 지불하되 절차 완료 후 시행일자 부터
신 요율을 소급 적용한다.

122

68-2-29

마. 전기 절차 채택후 협의완료 건수는 다음과 같음.

  (1) 부산지구 수도료 인상 (67. 12. 1. 시행) ─ 22차 회의 (68.3.14.)

  (2) 대구지구 수도료 인상 (68. 1. 1. 시행) ─ 22차 회의 (68. 3.14.)

  (3) 철도요금 인상 (67. 10. 16. 시행) ─ 22차 회의 (68. 3.14.)

  (4) 체신요금 인상 (68. 1.1. 시행) ─ 23차 회의 (68. 4.4.)

바. 계류중의 문제

  전기요금 (67. 11. 1. 인상) 및 인천수도요금, 전기요금에 관하여는 수출 제조업자에 대한 할인, 상수도용 특수전기 요율, 가로등 용 특수전기 요율등은 미군 요율보다 저율인바 협정 6조 2항 규정에 의하여 미군측은 최저율 적용을 주장, 특히 수출업자 요율이 논의의 대상이 되고 있으며 한국측의 수출 보조금 적 성질주장에 대하여 보조금 지불은 우리측의 자유나 보조금이라면 별도 지불될 성질의 것이고 요율표에 그것이 표시되어 있는 이상 미군에게도 최저요율이 적용되어야 한다고 주장하고 있음. 인천 상수도에 관하여도 극빈자 특수요율이 논난되고 있음.

3. 참고사항

  가. 철도요금에 관하여 수출 물자에 대한 특수 화물 운송요율이 있는바 미측은 그 사실을 알고도 미측은 priorities 및 conditions 상 많은 혜택을 누리고 있으므로 상쇄한다는 취지로 문의한바 있음. 따라서 6조 2항의 no less favourable 이 priorities conditions and rates 에 총체적으로 적용되어야 할 것인지 priorities conditions 및 rates 가 개별적으로 no less favourable 하여야 한다고 해석할 것인지의 문제가 있음.

123

68-2-30

나. 공공용역 분과위원회에서 **split recommendations** 을 제출하고
합동위원회에서도 합의에 도달하지 못하는 경우 협의 절차는 일단
완료한 것으로 간주하고 신요율을 적용하되 **no less favourable**
조항에 관한 문제 협정위반 문제로 별도 취급할 것인가, 협의절차의
미완상태로 볼 것인가의 문제가 제기됨.

4. 결 론

가. 협정 6조 2항 문맥으로 우리측 주장은 무리인 것으로 사료됨.

나. 현 공공요율 책정 과정, 특히 지방 단체가 정하는 요율 책정에 있어서
협정 조항의 존재가 무시되고 있어 허다한 정의가 예견되는바 이러한
정의를 방지하기 위하여 다음 조치가 필요할 것으로 사료됨.

(1) 국내 요율 체재를 변경하여 공공요율은 일률적으로 표준 요율
을 징수하되 할인을 요하는 특수 수요자에게는 별도 보조금을
지급하는 정책을 수립.

(2) 전 조항 조치가 불가능한 경우 미군에게 최저 요율을 적용.

"비고" 협정 개정교섭 — 6조 2항을 "한국군과 동일한 대우"로 개정하는
교섭을 상정할 수 있으나 미측이 동의할 가능성은 없음.

124   '68-2-31

電氣料金表

1. 月間電氣料金表

(1) 一般電力甲 (住宅用과 4KW以下의 其他需用)
　　　　전압 100 V 200 V

(가) 最低料金은 129.40 원으로 합니다

(나) 電力量料金

　　처음 3 KWH 까지　　　　　　　　　　　129.40원

　　다음 27 KWH 에 對하여 KWH 當　　　　12.25원

　　다음 180 KWH 에 對하여 KWH 當　　　　9.30원

　　210 KWH 超過分에 對하여 KWH當　　　　7.20원

　　但 最大電力 3KW超過分에 對하여는 KW當 90

　　KWH 를 9.30 원 適用塊量에 追加합니다

(2) 一般電力乙 (4KW以上의 모든 需用)

　　　전압. [20KV] 10KV EKV 3KV 200

1. 常時電力

(가) 需用料金

　　契約電力의

　　처음 50 KW 에 對하여 KW 當　　　　　　144 00 원

　　　　　　　　　　　-9500-

125

다음 450 KW 에 對하여 KW 當 115.00 원

500 KW 超過分에 對하여는 KW 當 86.00 원

(나) 電力量料金

契約電力에 對한

처음 90時間使用 該當電力量에 對하여

KWH 當 7.50 원

다음 90 "   "   5.15 원

다음 180 "   "   3.70 원

360 時間超過使用 該當電力量에 "   2.50 원

2. 倂用深夜電力

(가) 需用料金

深夜契約電力을 常時電力에 加算하여 常時電

力需用料金을 適用하되 深夜契約電力分에 對

하여는 80% 割引한 것으로 합니다

(나) 電力量料金

常時電力에 依한 使用電力量에 合하여 常時

契約電力을 基準하여 計算합니다

3. 單独深夜電力

(대) 需用料金

常時電力需用料金의 80% 割引한 것으로 합니다

(매) 電力量料金

모든 使用電力量에 對하여 KWH當 3.34원

(3) 特高压電力

1. 常時電力

特高圧 A (20 KV 以上 1,000 KW 以上)

(가) 需用料金

契約電力의

처음 500 KW 에 對하여 KW當 120.00원

500 KW 超過分에 " " 80.00원

(나) 電力量料金

契約電力에 對한

~11~

처음 90 時間使用該當電力量에 對하여 KWH當 7.50원

다음 90 " " " 4.88원

다음 180 " " " 3.40원

360 時間超過 " " 2.15원

特高壓 B (150 KV 以上 1,000 KW 以上)

(가) 需用料金

契約電力에 對하여 KW當 80.00원

(나) 電力量料金

契約電力에 對함

처음 90 時間使用該當電力量에 對하여 KWH當 7.50원

다음 90 " " " 4.83원

다음 180 " " " 3.33원

360 時間超過 " " 2.14원

2. 併用深夜電力

(가) 需用料金

深夜契約電力을 需時電力에 加算하여 需時

電力需用料金을 適用하되 深夜契約電力分에

對하여는 80% 割引한 것으로 합니다

(나) 電力量料金

常時電力에 依한 使用量料金과 合하여 常

時電力을 基準하여 使用합니다

3 單獨深夜電力

(가) 需用料金

常時電力 需用料金의 80% 割引한 것으로

합니다

(나) 電力量料金

모든 使用電力量에 對하여 KWH當 ３０５원

(4) 農事用電力

(가) 需用料金

契約電力에 對하여 KW當   43.00원

(나) 電力量料金   KWH當   ２.76원

(5) 街路灯 (100V. 200V)

—13—

129

(다) 最低料金은 72.45 원으로 합니다

(나) 電力料金

　　　負荷設備容量에 對하여　　　W當　　　2.18원

(6) 定額電灯 100 V 200 V

(다) 最低料金은 72.45 원으로 합니다

(나) 電力料金

　　　負荷設備容量의

　　　처음 60 W에 對하여　　　W當　　　4.30원

　　　60 W 超過分에　　　　　　　　　　2.90원

(7) 特殊産業料金

200 KW 以下의 輸出産業과 電力費가 總製造原

價의 20% 以上의 業種에 對하여는 商工部長

官이 定하는 바에 依하여 다음과 같이 料金

을 割引합니다

(다) 200 KW 以下의 輸出産業은 (30%)

(나) 電力費가 總製造原價의

① 20% 以上 30% 未満은 15%

② 30% 以上 40% 未満은 20%

③ 40% 以上 50% 未満은 25%

④ 50% 以上은 30% ✓

(8) 上水道用電力料金

現適用料金의 15% 引上 (1967. 11. 1 料金의 (467%) 割引) 합니다

(9) 電氣供給系統上 孤立된 島嶼地域에 對하여는 商工部長官의 認可를 얻어 別途料金을 設定할 수 있읍니다

Ⅱ 料金의 適用

1967年 11月 1日부터 本料金을 適用합니다

動力   1.447.893 Kw
전등   7.581 696 등(46 □□)
        (348.758 Kw)
計   1.796. 651 Kw

가 200 Kw 以下   5.455 Kw (1.3%)   77 개소
나 상수도   34.015 Kw (1.9%)   281 개소

~15~

仁川上水道料金改正表

	從前			現行			引上率	
	基本量 t	基本料 원	超過料 원	基本量 t	基本料 원	超過料 원	基本料	超過料
家庭用	7	70 (10)	10	7	100 (143)	15	42.9	50.0
私設共用	25	250 (10)	10	25	350 (14)	15	40.0	50.0
浴場用	50	600 (12)	14	300	6000 (20)	21	66.7	50.0
特殊專用	20	300 (15)	18	30	750 (25)	30	66.7	66.7
工場用	50	600 (12)	18	100	2000 (20)	21	66.7	50.0
鐵道船舶用			18			30		66.7
公設共用			10			14		40.0
臨時用			15			30		100.0
私設消火栓			100			150		50.0

공통서식 1—1 (을)
1967. 4. 4. 승인
(18절지) (특급인쇄용지 42g/m²)
(조달청) (2,000,000매 인쇄)

132

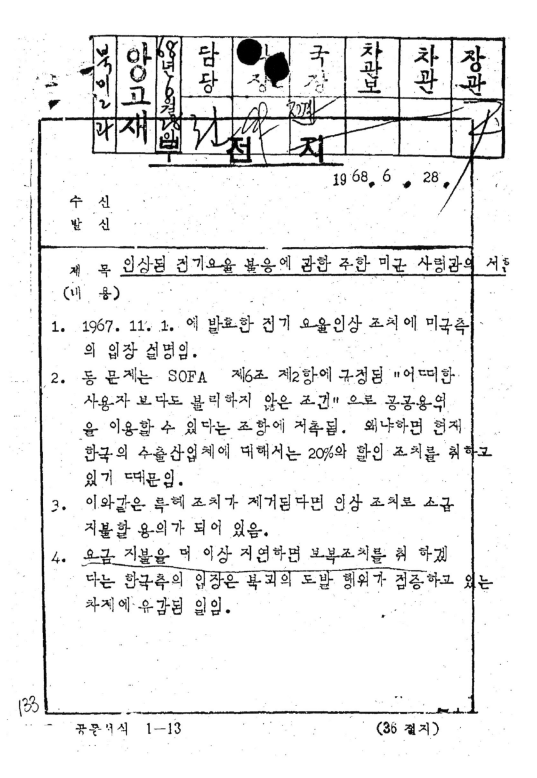

	북미과	앙고재	68년 6월 결재필	담당	과장	국장	차관보	차관	장관

接 지

19 68. 6 . 28.

수 신

발 신

제 목 인상된 전기요율 불응에 관한 주한 미군 사령관의 서한

(내 용)

1. 1967. 11. 1. 에 발효한 전기 요율 인상 조치에 미국측
   의 입장 설명임.

2. 동 문제는 SOFA 제6조 제2항에 규정된 "어떠한
   사용자 보다도 불리하지 않은 조건" 으로 공공용역
   을 이용할 수 있다는 조항에 저촉됨. 왜냐하면 현지
   한국의 수출산업체에 대해서는 20%의 할인 조치를 취하고
   있기 때문임.

3. 이와같은 특혜조치가 제거된다면 인상 조치로 소급
   지불할 용의가 되어 있음.

4. 요금 지불을 더 이상 지연하면 보복조치를 취 하겠
   다는 한국측의 입장은 북괴의 도발 행위가 접증하고 있는
   차제에 유감된 일임.

133

공문서식 1—13   (36 절지)

기 안 용 지

분류기호 문서번호	미이 722.2	(전화번호)	전결규정	조 항
			국장	전결사항

처리기한		기 안 자	결 재 자
시행일자		북미이과 권순대	*7*
보존년한		68. 6. 28	

보 조 기 관	북 미 2 과 장		

협 조		
경 유		
수 신	경제기획원 장관 물가정책과장	정
참 조		서
제 목	전기요금 인상에 관한 미군 사령관 서한 전달	

미8군 사령관은 한국전력주식회사 사장에게 보내는 그의 회신에서

인상된 전기요율은 SOFA 제6조에 저촉되므로 그 요율대로 따르기가

곤란하다는 요지를 언급하였으므로 동 회한의 사본을 별첨 송부하오니

참고하시기 바랍니다.

첨부 : 동 서한 사본 1 부.   끝

914

외   무   부

미이 722.2   1968. 6. 29.

수신 : 경제기획원 장관

참조 : 물가 정책과장

제목 : 전기 요금 인상에 관한 미군 사령관 서한 전달

     미8군 사령관은 한국전력 주식회사 사장에게 보내는
그의 회신에서 인상된 전기요율은 SOFA 제6조 제2항에
저촉되므로 그 요율대로 따르기가 곤란하다는 요지를 언급
하였으므로 동 회한의 사본을 별첨 송부하오니 참고하시기
바랍니다.

첨부 : 동 서한 사본 1부.   끝.

          외   무   부   장   관

UNITED STATES FORCES, KOREA
OFFICE OF THE COMMANDER
APO SAN FRANCISCO 96301

2 4 JUN 1968

Dear General Jung:

This is in reply to your 11 June 1968 letter concerning nonpayment by the United States for the increased power rate differentials which went into effect on 1 November 1967. I recognize the adverse impact this situation creates in the fiscal management of the Korea Electric Company and am most sorry. However, resolution of this matter is beyond my immediate control.

The problem is a legal matter affected by Status of Forces Agreement of 9 July 1966 to which the United States Government and the Government of the Republic of Korea are signatories. Thus, the derivation of an agreement to provide the basis of payment cannot be arranged between you and me. Rather, it must be made within the administrative structure established by SOFA under the provisions of the aforementioned government to government'agreement.

The issue at question is concerned with SOFA Article VI, paragraph 2, which states: "The use of such utilities and services by the United States shall be in accordance with priorities, conditions, and rates or tariffs no less favorable than those accorded any other user." As I am sure you must be fully aware, the KECO rate schedules effected 1 November 1967 contravene the agreement between our two governments since more favorable rates are given several classes of customers than are given to the United States. Specifically, discount rates are provided to export industry customers with 200 KW of contracted demand or under, to industry customers whose power charges account for more than 20% of their total production cost, and to municipal water services.

Let it be clearly understood that I do not question the right of your government to subsidize its industry and public utilities. Let it be equally understood, however, that under United States law, it is manifestly illegal for me to authorize payment of the increased rates so long as these rate schedules are at variance with the provisions of the Status of Forces Agreement.

136

68-2-82
723. 16(2) -3

I reiterate the suggestion, offered by the United States Chairman of the SOFA Utilities Subcommittee, that the United States would concur in the 1 November 1967 electric power rate increase if the preferential rate schedules which grant discount subsidies to preferred customers are eliminated. Adoption of this procedure would not, of course, preclude the granting of subsidies by some other means. That done, payment for increased power rate differentials could be effected immediately retroactive to 1 November 1967 since I have directed that funds be reserved for that purpose. Unfortunately, however, the extensive delay of almost eight months in your Government's not resolving this issue, has placed me in the unpleasant situation of having to withhold payment and to have received threats of reprisal action. It was most surprising to me that your letter to me dated 11 June seems to hint at possible reprisal action in the event that a further delay in payment occurs. At this time, when the North Korean's are becoming increasingly threatening and bellicose, any interruption of KECO services would have adverse effects on our military capabilities in the ROK, which would be most unfortunate. I would appreciate your early reassurances on this matter.

I trust that through appropriate action under SOFA arrangements, the problem of payments to KECO can be rapidly resolved. I want to assure you that I wish to pay up the back payments just as soon as I can legally do so.

Sincerely,

C. H. BONESTEEL, III
General, United States Army
Commander

General JUNG Nae-Hiuk
President
Korea Electric Company
52 Ka Namdaemoon-Ro, Chung-Ku
Seoul, Korea

Copy:
Honorable CHOI Young Hi
Minister of National Defense
Republic of Korea
Seoul, Korea

2

한 국 전 력 주 식 회 사

(22- 5101 - 279)

한전업(영)910- 4372   1968.   7.   4.

수신   외무부 장관

제목   미군에 대한 인상요금적용

　　1. 한전업(영)910-4265 (1968. 6. 28)과 관련된 사항입미다

　　2. 당사전기요금 인상에 따라 미군에 대한 신전기요금적용에
대하여 주한미대하에게 협조를 요청한바 있읍니다(한전업(영)910-
3949 (68. 6. 18) 참조)

　　3. 이에 대하여 미대사관으로부터 이문제는 한미행협합동위
원회에서 해결될것미라고 별첨과 같이 회시하여 왔가에 사분을 송부
하오니 참조하시기 바라며 이문제가 조속 해결되도록 협조하여 주시
기 바랍니다.

유첨   미대사관 회신서한 사본 1부.   끝

사 장   정   태

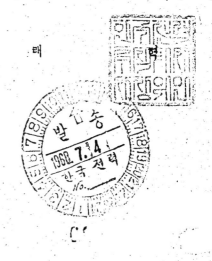

<u>COPY</u>

EMBASSY
OF THE
UNITED STATES OF AMERICA

SEOUL, June 27, 1968

Mr. Chung-Ho Lee
Chief
Business Operation Department
Korea Electric Company
#5 2-Ka Namdaemoon-Ro, Chung-Ku
Seoul, Korea

Dear Mr. Lee:

The Ambassador has asked me to reply to your letter
of June 13, 1968, regarding the electric power rates
paid by United States Forces, Korea.

I understand this problem is being examined by the
ROK-US Joint Committee established by the Status of
Forces Agreement and that this is the proper forum
for consideration of the problem. I hope that the
Committee will reach a mutually acceptable solution.

Sincerely yours,

/s/ R. A. Ericson
Richard A. Ericson, Jr.
Counselor of Embassy for
Political Affairs

139

68-2-36

FACT SHEET

SUBJECT: Conf   between SOFA and Power Rates

TO: Chief of Staff   FROM: ULC/JA

1. PROBLEM: To appraise the Chief of Staff of a conflict between an article in SOFA and the Rate Schedule of the Korea Electric Company.

2. FACTS:

a. Paragraph 2, Article VI of SOFA on utilities reads as follows: "The use of such utilities and services by the United States shall be in accordance with priorities, conditions, and rates or tariffs no less favorable than those accorded any other user."

b. On 1 November 1967 the Korea Electric Company (KECO) increased the cost of purchased electricity by 15 percent.

c. The review of the new rate schedule disclosed that the rates for the US Forces are not the most favorable ones and that certain industrial consumers receive discounts from 15 to 30 percent and Municipal Water Works receive discounts of 46.7 percent.

d. The US Forces are in Category B for electric service which covers consumers with a demand of four or more kilowatt.

e. The most favorable rate KECO has is for residental service and other service with a demand of four or less kilowatt. No US Army facilities are in this category.

f. The investigation of the rate increase disclosed that the ROK Armed Forces are being charged the same new rates as are applicable to the US Forces.

기안자	계 장	과 장	차 장	부 장	이 사
/111 /일/시명	일 시 분	일 시 분	일 시 분	일 시 분	일 시 분

140

SUBJECT: Conflict between SOFA and Power Rates

g. Invoices submitted by KECO for electric power consumed by USFK are still based on and paid for at the old rate. However, KECO made numerous appeals in the past several months to effect payment at the new rate and arrange for payment of accumulated arrears.

h. This subject was discussed between the ROK and US Subcommittees of SOFA for Utilities, but no agreements could be reached.

i. The matter has reached an impasse. Funds are set aside for payment of the increase in the cost for the eight month period in FY 1968 estimated to amount close to $400,000 or to $585,000 per year. However, payment cannot be accomplished until this problem is solved to the satisfaction of both sides.

j. It is doubtful that the article on utilities in SOFA intended to offer the US Forces lower rates than the ROK Forces. However, since such a possibility exists, it appears necessary that State Department personnel involved in the writing of this article be queried on the interpretation and intent of this paragraph.

2

3. 요금대비

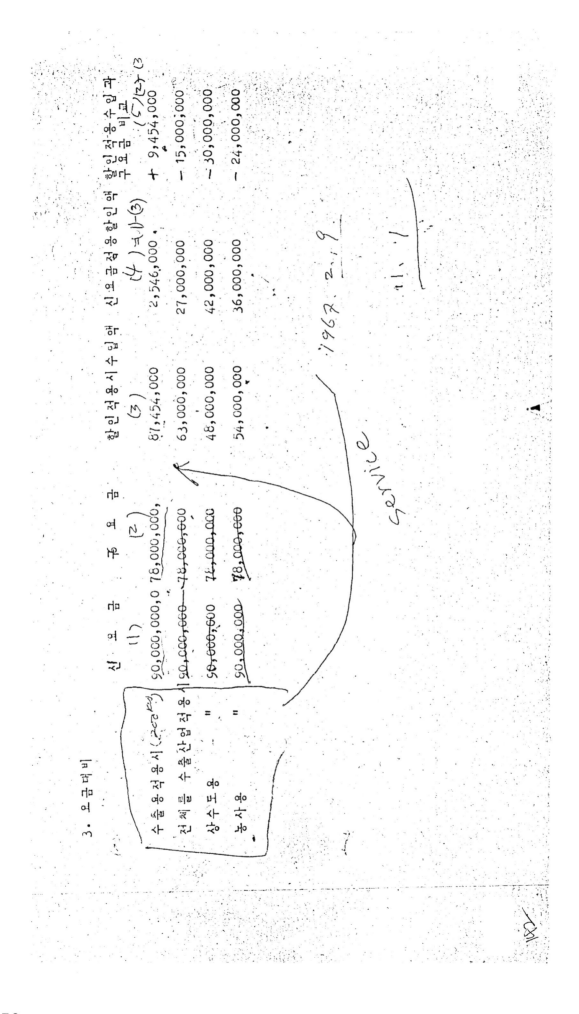

구 분	신 여 금 (1)	종 여 금 (2)	할인적용서비스수입해 (3)	신요금적용할인해 (가)=(1)-(3)	할인적용수입과 비요급여부 (나)-(3)
수출용적용시 (2.78 kg)	90,000,000	90,000,000, 0 78,000,000,	81,454,000	2,546,000	+ 9,454,000
전체를 수출산업적용 시	90,000,000	~78,000,000	63,000,000	27,000,000	~ 15,000,000
상수도용	90,000,600	78,000,000	48,000,000	42,000,000	~ 30,000,000
농사용	90,000,000	78,000,000	54,000,000	36,000,000	~ 24,000,000

service

1962. 2. 9

RATE SCHEDULES
For
ELECTRIC SERVICE

EFFECTIVE DATE : NOVEMBER 1, 1967

KOREA ELECTRIC COMPANY

143

TARIFF 1

GENERAL SERVICE A

APPLICABLE:

    To residential service without limit and general service of 4 kw demand or under.

TYPE OF SUPPLY:

    Single or three phase supply at any one of the Company's available standard voltages, 100 v or 200v.

MONTHLY BILL:

    Basic Rate :
        Energy charge:
        ₩ 129.40 for the first 3 kwh.
        ₩ 12.25 per kwh for the next 27 kwh.
        ₩   9.30 per kwh for the next 180 kwh.☆
        ₩   7.20 per kwh for each additional kwh.
    ☆ Add 90 kwh at ₩9.30 block for each kw in excess of 3 kw of demand.
        The demand shall be determined in same way as "Determination of Contract Demand" of "General Service B".

    Minimum Charge: ₩129.40

TARIFF 2

GENERAL SERVICE B

APPLICABLE:

    To general service of 4 kw of contracted demand and over.

TYPE OF SUPPLY:

    Single or three phase supply at any one of the Company's available standard voltages, 20kv, 10kv, 6kv, 5.2kv, 3kv, 200v, 100v or others.

- 1 -

144

MONTHLY BILL:

Basic Rate :

a. Demand Charge:
   ₩ 144.00 per kw for the first 50 kw of contracted demand.
   ₩ 115.00 per kw for the next 450 kw of contracted demand.
   ₩ 86.00 per kw for each additional kw of contracted demand.

b. Energy Charge:
   ₩ 7.50 per kwh for the first 90 kwh per kw of
   contracted demand.
   ₩ 5.15 per kwh for the next 90 kwh per kw of
   contracted demand.
   ₩ 3.70 per kwh for the next 180 kwh per kw of
   contracted demand.
   ₩ 2.50 per kwh for each additional kwh.

c. Minimum contracted kw of demand: 4 kw

DETERMINATION OF CONTRACTED DEMAND:

The KW of contracted demand shall be determined
multiplying total input of the connected load by following factors;

     100% for the first 75 kw of connected load.
      85% for the next 75 kw of connected load.
      75% for the next 75 kw of connected load.
      65% for the next 75 kw of connected load.
      60% for all over 300 kw of connected load.

     a. In computing the contracted kw of demand any
fraction of 1 kw will be taken as a full kw.

     b. In the case that any of the units of connected
load exceeds 75 kw, the connected load of such unit or
units beginning with the largest shall take place of
75 kw steps in above table.

     c. In the case the Company considers the contracted

- 2 -

kw of demand that is computed with above table is too
small than actual maximum kw of demand, the Company
may install a demand meter at its expense for determining the contracted kw of demand.
In the case a customer considers the contracted kw of
demand that is computed with above table is too large
than actual maximum kw of demand, the customer may
install a demand meter at his expense for determining
the contracted kw of demand.

d. In the case service is supplied through a transformer exclusively used by one customer, contracted
kw of demand shall not be more than load limitation of
the transformer.

e. To a customer with a demand meter, the maximum
kw of demand for twelve months ending current billing
month shall be used as contracted kw of demand.

POWER FACTOR:

Customer shall maintain 85% lag or better, in this
purpose, if it is necessary, customer shall install
corrective equipment at his expense.
When less than 85%, demand kw shall be adjusted as
follows and the Company shall bill with it for General
Service B, High Tension Service and Irrigation Service.

Contracted Demand ÷ actual power Factor x 0.85

LOAD BALANCE:

A customer taking service at three phase shall at
all times balance his load between phases in such a
manner that the difference in the load between any
two phases will not exceed ten percent of the most
heavily loaded phase. When more than ten percent, the
Conpamy shall bill with three times of kw and kwh
supplied by the most heavily loaded phase.

- 3 -

146

COMBINED OFF PEAK SERVICE PROVISION

APPLICABLE:

To a General Service B customer whose demand
during off peak time (10:00 P.M to 6:00 A.M) exceeds
regular contracted kw of demand.

CONTRACTED KW OF DEMAND:

Contracted kw of demand for off peak shall be the
excess demand of regular contracted kw of demand on
off peak time, but no more than two times of regular
contracted kw of demand will be permitted.

MINIMUM CONTRACTED KW OF DEMAND: 50KW

MONTHLY BILL:

For contracted kw of demand for off peak, demand
charge of basic rate shall be discounted by 80%.
Energy charge of basic rate will be applied with
regular contracted kw of demand to total kwh consumed
by both regular and off peak service.

METER:

KW and KWH shall be measured by recording meter
or other meter authorized by the Company. Meter installation shall be made at customer's expense.

INDEPENDENT OFF PEAK SERVICE PROVISION

APPLICABLE:

To a customer of General Service B category who
desires service only on off peak time(10:00 P.M to
6:00 A.M) and 24 hours on Sunday. Installation of
private line from Company's substation and seperate
connected load from regular contracted load, if there
is, are required at customer's expense.

MONTHLY BILL:

Demand Charge: Basic rates shall be discounted by
80%.

- 4 -

Energy Charge: ₩ 3.34 per kwh for each kwh.
Minimum contracted kw of demand: 50 kw.

TARIFF 3
HIGH TENSION SERVICE

HIGH TENSION SERVICE A

APPLICABLE:

To service 1,000 kw of contracted demand and over, and 20 kv and over.

TYPE OF SUPPLY:

Three phase supply at any one of the Company's available standard voltages, 20kv and over.

MONTHLY BILL:

Basic Rate:
a. Demand charge;
   ₩ 120.00 per kw for the first 500 kw of contracted demand,
   ₩ 80.00 per kw for each additional kw of contracted demand.
b. Energy charge:
   ₩ 7.50 per kwh for the first 90 kwh per kw of contracted demand.
   ₩ 4.88 per kwh for the next 90 kwh per kw of contracted demand.
   ₩ 3.40 per kwh for the next 180 kwh per kw of contracted demand.
   ₩ 2.15 per kwh for each additional kwh.
c. Minimum contracted kw of demand: 1,000 kw.

DETERMINATION OF CONTRACTED DEMAND:

Same as "General Service B".

- 5 -

148

POWER FACTOR

    Same as "General Service B".

LOAD BALANCE

    Same as "General Service B".

HIGH TENSION SERVICE B

APPLICABLE:

    To service of 150 kv and over.

TYPE OF SUPPLY:

    Three phase supply at any one of the Company's available standard voltages 150 kv and over.

MONTHLY BILL:

    Basic Rate:
    a. Demand Charge:
       ₩ 80.00 per kw of contracted demand.
    b. Energy Charge:
       ₩ 7.50 per kwh for the first 90 kwh per kw of contracted demand.
       ₩ 4.83 per kwh for the next 90 kwh per kw of contracted demand.
       ₩ 3.33 per kwh for the next 180 kwh per kw of contracted demand.
       ₩ 2.14 per kwh for each additional kwh.

DETERMINATION OF CONTRACTED DEMAND:

    Same as "General Service B".

POWER FACTOR

    Same as "General Service B".

LOAD BALANCE

    Same as "General Service B".

- 6 -

149

COMBIND OFF PEAK SERVICE PROVISION

APPLICABLE:

To a high tension service customer whose demand during off peak time (10:00 P.M to 6:00 A.M) exceeds regular contracted kw of demand.

CONTRACTED KW OF DEMAND :

Contracted kw of demand for off peak shall be the excess demand of regular contracted kw of demand on off peak time, but no more than two times of regular contracted kw of demand will be permitted.

MINIMUM CONTRACTED KW OF DEMAND: 50KW

MONTHLY BILL:

For contracted kw of demand for off peak, demaand charge of basic rate shall be discounted by 80%. Energy charge of basic rate will be applied with regular contracted kw of demand to total kwh consumed by both regular and off peak service.

METER:

KW and KWH shall be measured by recording meter or other meter authorized by the Company. Meter installation shall be made at customer's expense.

INDEPENDENT OFF PEAK SERVICE PROVISION

APPLICABLE:

To a customer of High Tension Service category who desires service only on off peak time (10:00 P.M to 6:00 A.M) and 24 hours on Sunday. Installation of private line from Company's substation and seperate connected load from regular contracted load, if there is, are required at customer's expense.

- 7 -

MONTHLY BILL:

    Demand Charge: Basic rate shall be discounted
            by 80%.
    Energy Charge: ₩ 3.05 per kwh for each kwh.
    Minimum contracted kw of demand: 1,000 kw.

TARIFF 4

IRRIGATION SERVICE

APPLICABLE:

    To service required for the operation of pumps
which are used to irrigate land for the cultivation
and growing of grain for food purpose.
Lighting necessary and incidential to the operation
of pumps is permitted.

TYPE OF SUPPLY:

    Same as "General Service B".

MONTHLY BILL:

    Basic Rate:
        Demand Charge: ₩ 43.00 per kw for contracted
                demand.
        Energy Charge: ₩ 2.76 per kwh for each kwh.

DETERMINATION OF CONTRACTED DEMAND:

    Same as "General Service B".

POWER FACTOR

    Same as "General Service B".

LOAD BALANCE

    Same as "General Service B".

TARIFF 5

STREET LIGHTING SERVICE

APPLICABLE :

To service for operation of lighting of streets, parks and similar places for the benefit and convenience of public.

TYPE OF SUPPLY:

Single phase at either 100 v or 200 v.

MONTHLY BILL :

Basic Rate: ₩ 2.18 per watt for connected load.
Minimum Charge: ₩ 72.45.

TARIFF 6

FLAT RATE LIGHTING SERVICE

APPLICABLE:

To lighting service (including radio substituted one set as one lamp), principally limited to 100 watts of connected load with three lamps or under. One radio set shall be counted as 20 watts.

TYPE OF SUPPLY:

Single phase supply at either 100 v or 200v

MONTHLY BILL:

Basic Rate:

    ₩ 4.30 per watt for first 60 watts of connected load.
    ₩ 2.90 per watt for additional watts of connected load.
Minimum Charge: ₩ 72.45

- 9 -

SPECIAL PROVISIONS

1. SPECIAL INDUSTRY:

To export industry custmers with 200 kw of contracted demand or under, and to industry customers whose power charges occupy more than 20% of the total production cost who are designated by the Minister of Commerce and Industry.

DISCOUNT:

Monthly bill shall be discounted as follows:

a. 30% Discount: for export industry customer with 200 kw of contracted demand or under.

b. 15% Discount: for the industry customer whose electric charges occupy 20% and over, of the total production cost.

20% Discount: for the industry customer whose electric charges occupy 30% and over, of the total production cost.

25% Discount: for the industry customer whose electric charges occupy 40% and over, of the total production cost.

30% Discount: for the industry customer whose electric charges occupy 50% and over, of the total production cost.

2. MUNICIPAL WATER SERVICE

Rate for Municipal Water Service shall be discounted by 46.7%.

3. ISLAND AREA:

Special rates may be established for island area which is isolated from mainland power system, subject to approval by the Minister of Commerce and Industry.

- 10 -

SPECIAL PROVISION FOR SUBSIDY

1. Special subsidy may be provided for the following categories of customers as may be separately determined by the Ministry of Commerce and Industry:

    a. Special Industry

    b. Municipal Water Services

    c. Island Area

2. The subsidy may be given ~~by subtracting~~ based on ~~certain proportion of the amount of the~~ monthly ~~bill for the electric service.~~

(NOTE: Draft handed to the US side, on 30 July 1968, to replace page 10 of the RATE SCHEDULE, This was envisaged as a possible compromise after considerable preliminary discussion and the US side was to accept or propose modification after study.)

154

局長께서 紹介院에 直接 商議하여 후意에서 解除하는
親睦으로서 照會하는 方式 採択를 要請하고 그 規程가 計에
될때까지 回答 保留토록 要望함.

경 제 기 획 원

물 정 · 331.24 - 287 (72.9714) 1968. 7. 8
수 신 · 외무부장관
제 목 · 한미합동위원회 공공용역분과위언회에 관한 건

    1. 한미행정협정 합의의사록 6조 1항에 의
거 당원의 경제기획국장과 미 8군의 Col. Waltz 를
위원장으로 하는 Utility Subcommittee 의 설치와
위원회의 협의 절차를 1968.3.14 제 22차 한미합동
위원회에서 공식합의 한바 있읍니다.
    2. 이러한 협의 절차에 따라 현재까지
        1) 상수도요금
            부산 (효력일자 1967. 12. 1)
            대구 (효력일자 1968. 1. 1)
        2) 철도요금 (효력일자 1967. 10. 16)
        3) 통신요금 (효력일자 1968. 1. 1)
의 인상안에 대하여는 협의를 완료하였으나 인천의
상수도요금 (개정일자 1968.2.1) 과 전력요금 (개
정일자, 1967.11.1) 에 관한 협의절차는 완료되지
못하였읍니다.

24093

북 미 2과

물 정 . 331.24   1968. 7. 8

  3. 미군측의 요구에 의하면 전력요금에 대하여는 수출산업, 상수도등에 부여하고 있는 46.7%의 할인에 비하여 미군에 적용하는 요율이 불리하다는 것이며, 인천시 상수도의 경우에는 미군에 적용되는 소위 제4종 수용자 요금을 한국군, 관공서, 은행, 학교등 모든 공공이용자들에도 적용하고 있는데도 불구하고 가정용, 사설공용요금과 비교하여 불리하다고 하여 양자 모두 행정협정 6조 2항에 위배된다는 점을 들어 협의절차를 거부하고 있을 뿐만 아니라 그 결과로 인상된 요금수납이 지연되고 있는 실정에 있읍니다.

  4. 따라서 미군측이 협정의 문자에 철저히 고착하여 문제의 합리적 해결을 거부하는 한 현재의 고착상태는 물론 앞으로 제기될 똑같은 문제에 대하여도 공공요금분과위원회로서는 해결할 수 없는 것으로 사료되니 협정문언을 수정하던지 현재의 협정하에서 행정협정의 최고 합의기관인 합동위원회를 통하여 문제의 해결을 위한 긴급하고도 합리적인 조치를 강/구하여 주시기 바랍니다.

156

물 정 . 331.24 —   1968. 7. 8

이 조치가 취하여 질때까지 공공요금분과위원회는
더 이상 협의를 진행시킬수 없는 것으로 판단됨
을 첨신합니다.

첨 부 : 1. 미국측분과위원장의 전력요금변경에
            대한 이익 공한사본
         2. 전력요금에 대한 분과위언회 회의록
            사본
         3. 상공부로 부터 전기요금문제해결촉구
            공문사본
            가) 미측에 대한 한전의 문제해결촉구
                서한 사본
            나) 가) 에 대한 회신사본
         4. 미국측에 대한 인천상수도요금변경
            통보사본
         5. 인천상수도요금변경에 대한 미측의 이
            의 공한 사본 각 1통   끝.

         경 제 기 획 원

8 March 1968

USFK DJ-O

SUBJECT: Consultation on Change in Electric Rates

To: Republic of Korea Chairman, Utilities Subcommittee

        1. Reference: Paragraph 2 and Agreed Minute 1 of Article VI of the Status of Forces Agreement.

        2. The consultation process initiated by the Republic of Korea concerning an increase in electric rates has been reviewed and while the requirement for the increased rates is understood, the United States component of the Utilities Subcommittee takes this opportunity to express its views.

        3. The meaning and intent of paragraph 2, Article VI, SOFA, is very clear, in stating that the United States shall be furnished utilities and services in accordance with priorities, conditions, and rates or tariffs no less favorable than those accorded any other user. The United States has been advised through the rate schedule published by Korea Electric Company that certain export industries and Municipal Water Works receive electricity rates that are more favorable than those being charged the United States Armed forces. The rates being charged the United States are clearly not in accordance with Article VI of SOFA.

        4. The United States does not question the right of the Republic of Korea to raise electricity rates, however, the provisions of SOFA must be complied with, by both parties. The United States is prepared to pay electricity rates set in accordance with paragraph 2, Article VI of SOFA and until such rates are furnished, this consultation on electricity rates cannot be concluded.

                        COL FLOYD R. WALTZ, JR., USA
                        United States Chairman
                        Utilities Subcommittee

누락되었음 -

19 March 1968

SUBJECT: Minutes of Meeting - 11 March 1968.

1. Subcommittee Members:

Republic of Korea	United States
LEE HEE Il, Chairman	COL Floyd R. Waltz, Jr., Chairman
SUH Suck Joon, Secretary	COL John T. Horrocks, Jr.,
LEE Man Hee, Member	Alternate Chairman
HAN Byung Il, Member	LTC Walter A. Brown, Jr., Secretary
KIM Soo Hak, Member	Mr. Francis K. Cook, Member
Nam, Mun Hee, Member	Mr. Samuel Pollack, Member
KIM, Sang Woo, Member	LTC James A. Jolley, Member
LEE, Yong Shick, Member	Mr. Oliver J. Kennedy, Member
OH, Myong Too, Member	LTC John J. Hamparian, Member
	MAL Ray E. Willis, Member

2. Purpose of the meeting was to discuss ways and means to conclude consultation on the electricity rate increase of 1 Nov 1967. The meeting was held at the ROK Economic Planning Board conference room and was chaired by Mr. Suh acting for Mr. LEE, Hee Il, ROK Chairman, who was absent. COL Waltz responded for the US side.

3. Mr. Suh stated the ROK position concerning the electricity rate increase and the special industry rates. Mr. Suh stated that the same basic electricity rate is charged all users, with certain users being given discounts because of this status. These preferential users are identified as municipal water works and export industries. The export industries are subsidized thru electricity rates on an infant industry concept. Mr. Suh stated that if the US Armed forces "exported" or produced water, then the discounted rates would apply to the U.S.

4. COL Waltz stated that the US position was the same as that formally transmitted to the ROK Chairman on 8 March 1968. Briefly, the U.S. is prepared to pay electricity rates set in accordance with paragraph 2, Article VI of SOFA. The rate schedule of KECO, as now published, is not in accordance with Article VI of SOFA.

159

63-2-13

19 March 1968

SUBJECT: Minutes of Meeting - 11 March 1968.

5. There was general discussion concerning these two positions but no agreement. It was mutually decided that a split decision memorandum would be written and sent to the Joint Committee for resolution. Prior to adjournment of the meeting, Mr. OH Myong Too asked COL Waltz if the ROK subsidized the export industries in some manner other than by reduced electricity rates, what would be the US position. COL Waltz replied that how the ROK subsidized industries was not the concern of the US, unless the manner of subsidy was in conflict with SOFA.

BUH SUCK JOON.,
Secretary,
ROK Utilities Subcommittee

WALTER A. BROWN, JR.
Lt Colonel   USAF
Secretary, US Utilities Subcommittee

APPROVED:

FLOYD R. WALTZ, JR.
Colonel, United States Army
Chairman, US Utilities Subcommittee

LEE HEE IL.,
Chairman,
ROK Utilities Subcommittee

160

63-2-14

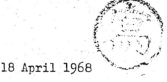

18 April 1968

Mr. SHIN Chung Sup
Republic of Korea Secretary
ROK-US Joint Committee

Dear Mr. Shin:

In the course of our discussion, on Saturday, 13 April, concerning the
problem of US-ROK consultations on recent increases in the electric
power rates of the Korean Electric Power Company, you expressed a
desire for anstatement in writing of the United States position on this
issue. I am inclosing a copy of a letter of 8 March 1968, from the
Chairman of the US component of the Utilities Subcommittee to his ROK
counterpart stating the US position on this subject, which was dispatched
in accordance with the Joint Committee-approved procedures (Format B,
Inclosurel11, minutes of the twenty-second Joint Committee meeting)/

The US Government position is based on the language of Ariticle VI of
the SOFA, and its Agreed Minutes, especially the following:

     a. Agreed Minute 1 to Article VI, which makes it clear that the
authorities of the Government of the Republic of Korea determine utility
rates or tariffs. (There is not believed to be any disagreement between
the United States and the Republic of Korea in the Joint Committee on
this point.)

     b. In accordance with Agreed Minute 1 of Article VI, there will be
US-ROK consultation in the Joint Committee, in accordance with the
Joint Committee-approved procedures, prior to the effective date of
any changes in priorities, conditions, and rates or tariffs, applicable
to the United States armed forces. (There is not believed to be any US-
ROK differences on this point.)

161

18 April 1968

Mr. Shin

c. Paragraph 2 of Article VI provides that US use of utilities and services "shall be in accordance with priorities, conditions, and rates or tariffs no less favorable than those accorded any other user."

There does not appear to be any basis for significant differences of opinion on the meaning of the SOFA language on the foregoing points; however, a problem has arisen as a result of the Government of the Republic of Korea giving a preferential electric rate to certain cate-gories of Korean customers. Under paragraph 2 of Article VI, such preferential rates would also be clearly applicable to the US armed forces in Korea. In resolution of this problem, it appears that there are two readily apparent solutions, as follows:

a. Permit the US armed forces to have electric power charges "no less favorabe than those accorded any other user,""in this case, the same rates as given the preferred industrial users; or

b. Revise the electric power s hedule, to eliminate the preferer-tial rates granted to certain export industries and Municipal Water Works, and thereby make the US armed forces subject to the standard rates. Of course the Government of the Republic of Korea has the sovereign right to subsidize any preferred industries which it chooses to favor; however, if this subsidy should be granted through preferential utility rates, or if the subsidy is based on utility rates, then the US armed forces are eligible, under the provisions of the SOFA, to similar rates.

It appears that the key to the Joint Committee resolution of this problem, under the SOFA provisions, lies in the decision of the Gover-nment of the Republic of Korea to decide either to maintain existing rate schedules and grant the United States Forces, Korea rates no less favorable than those accorded any other user, or modify its procedured which utilize preferential utility rates to subsidize certain cate-gories of users.

Sincerely,

1 Inclosure
Copy of 8 March letter

ROBERT A. KINNEY
United States Secretary
US-ROK Joint Committee

162

상 공 부

전 정. 1321 -   (74 - 3362) 1968. 4. 27
수 신. 경제기획원장관
제 목. 미군전기요금

    1. 한국전력주식회사장으로 부터 미군수
용가의 전기요금에 관하여 별첨과 같이 건의가 있
는바

    2. 한미행정협정 제6조의 규정에 모순되
는 문제점이 해결될시까지 전기요금 차액 (1967. 11.
1 전기요금 15% 인상분)을 지급할수 없다는 미
8군의 공한이 있으며

    3. 한전은 미군의 전기요금 미수로 인하여
전원개발사업자금 확보에 막대한 지장을 초래하고
있는 실정입니다.

    4. 이상과 같이 한전의 건의가 있아오니
미군의 전기요금 미수액이 조속히 수금되도록 적극
협조하여 주시기 바랍니다.
첨 부 : 1. 한전업 (영) 910 - 2485. 사본 1부

        2. 한전요청서한 사본   1부

        3. 미.8군 회신서한 사본   1부 끝.

            상 공 부 장 관

63

한국전력주식회사

한전업 (영) 910 - 2485   1968. 4. 19
수 신·상공부장관
참 조·전기국장
제 목·미군 수용의 전력요금 지불 요청의 건

        1. 1967.11.1 을 기하여 전기요금이 인상된
바 있으며 인상된 전기요금의 미군 적용에 관한 사항
입니다·

        2. 당사는 과거 요금 인상시는 미8군과의
전력수급계약에 따라 미육군성 전력구매관 또는 그대
리인 미태평양지구 사령부 전력구매관의 승인을 득한
후 소급시행하는 전제 조건으로 미8군 (구매처) 과 가
계약을 체결하고 승인 즉시 미수금 (차액) 을 회수하여
왔으며 금번 1967.11.1요금인상시에도 상기한 방법
으로 1967.11.14 mod # 90으로 가계약을 체결하였
읍니다·

        3. 금번 상기한 mod # 90 이 1968.4.5 일자로
미태평양지구 사령부로 부터 승인을 득하였기 별첨과
같이 전력요금 (차액) 지불을 요청한바 있으나 이에
대하여 미8군으로 부터 첨부와 같이 (한미행정협정
시행절차에 따라 한미행정협정 제6조의 규정에 모순
되는 문제점이 해결될시까지 차액을 지급할수 없다고)
회시하여왔기 의뢰하오니 별첨 서한을 참조하시여

164

4. 미군으로 부터의 미수금으로 인하여 당사는 재정상에 막대한 지장을 초래하고 있음을 양찰하시어 한미행정협정(SOFA)본 위원회 또는 공익사업분과위원회 (utilities Subcommittee) 에 조속 건의하여 상기한 차액을 조속 회수가능토록 조치하여 주시기 바랍니다.

첨 부 : 1. 당사요청서한 사본   1부
          2. 미 8 군 회신서한 사본   1부

끝.

사 장 정 래 혁

155

April 29, 1968

Headquartes
US Forces Korea/United Nations Command

Attn: Col. Waltz, Chairman of the Utilities Subcommittee, SOFA

Dear Sir:

Reference is made to our letter of 15 April 1968 to the Eighth
US Army Engineer, in which we requested acceptance of the latest price
increase which became effective on 1 November 1967 and appropriate
back payments, and the reply dated 17 April 1968, which pointed out
that the difference of opinion between the American and Korean side of
the SOFA Utilities Subcommittee has not been settled.

In regard to your request for a special discount for the US Forces
we would like to advise you again that such special discounts are only
made to certain specific industrial export consumers, whose contracted
power demand is less than 200 KW and municipal water services operated
by governmental agencies. The special discount given to export firms
is meant to be an inducement for such firms to carry on their exporting
business and to lower their operational expenditures.

This undue delay in paying for the power consumed since 1 November
1967 at the new price results in financial and operational problems
for our company and delays certain improvements which have been scheduled
to be funded from this additional income.

It is further pointed out that this delay in payment may result in
a serious situation in the electric power supply service. Therefore, we
again appeal to you to accept and approve the increase which was effected
on 1 November 1967 and to effect the required back payments, especially
since all consumers which are in your category of service, such as the
ROK Army, Air Force and Navy and all Governmental agencies are in the
same rate category as the United Nations Command and the US Forces Korea.

Very truly yours,

CHUNG-HO LEE
Chief
Commercial Operation Dept.

166

63-2-18

17 April 1968

Korea Electric Company

Gentlemen:

Reference is made to your letter of 15 April 1968 in which you request payment for electricity based on the 15 percent increase which became effective on 1 November 1967.

Until the establishment of SOFA a year ago the USARPAC Power Procurement Officer was the approving authority for increase in the cost of electric power and other utilities.

In accordance with US Army procurement Regulations (ASPR), Government to Government agreements, such as SOFA have precedence over the US Army regulations which delegate the approval authority to the power Procurement Officer.

In view of the fact that the US Component of the SOFA Utilities Subcommittee is of the opinion that the increase in the cost of electricity is in conflict with Article VI of the agreement the requested payment can not be effected until the issue is resolved through SOFA procedures.

Very truly yours,

L. A. GROSSMAN
CPT. AGC
Asst AG

167

68-2-15

한 국 전 력 주 식 회 사

(22 — 5101 —279)

한전업(영)910— *서명*   1968. 7. 10

수신 외 무 부 장 관

제목 미군수용에 대한 신전기요금 적용

    1. 한전업(영)910-4392 (68. 7. 4)와 관련된 사항입니다

    2. 미군수용에 대한 신전기요금적용 문제에 대하여 참고코자
요청하신 당사에서 할인 적용하고있는 200^{KW}이하의 수출산업체 및 상
수도에 대한 계약전력 대 당사총계약전력과의 대비를 아래와 같이 통
보하오니 참조하시기 바라오며

    3. 상기한 문제가 조속 타개되도록 귀부의 적극협조를 요청하오
니 선처하여 주시기 바랍니다

        가. 당사의 총계약전력 (1968. 5월말 현재)

            동력   1,447,893^{KW}

            전등   7,581,696등 (1등을 46^{W}환산348,758^{KW})

            계   1,796,651^{KW}

        나. 할인업체의 계약용량 및 비율

        (1) 200^{KW}이하 수출산업체

            5,455^{KW} (0.3%) 수급호수 77호

        (2) 상수도

            34,015^{KW} (1.9%) 수급호수 291호.   끝

1051

    사 장   정   래

168

전　　　　도　　　　청

화물 1512 — 1747   1968.7.13

수신　외무부장관 (참조· 구미국장)

제목　국련군 철도 군사수송 계약서중 개정.

　　　　1969 년도 유엔군 철도 군사 수송계약을 1968.6.28 별첨과 같이 체결

하였음을 통보 합니다.

첨부· 1969년도 유엔군 철도 군사수송계약서 사본 1부· 끝

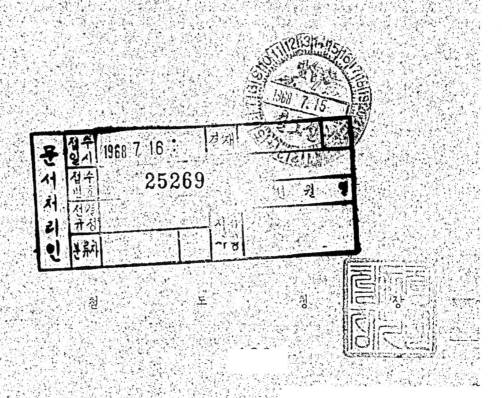

전　　　　도　　　　청

부미2과

169

유엔군 철도군사 수송 계약서중 개정  1968.7.13

지시제   호

유엔군 철도군사 수송계약서 (66.7.23 지시제263호)중 다음과 같이 개정하여
68.7.1 부터 적용한다.

1. 본 계약서중 "에이"는 "미국정부" 또 "비"는 "계약관" 으로한다.

2. 제2절 1.화물수송 비.임시열차의 (1)로 다음에 다음을 가한다.

   (2)임시열차는 국방 또는 공적(公的)의 비상사태와 특수한 화물수송의
경우를 제외하고는 기관차 견인정수의 70% 이상의 차량을 연결 할때에만
운행한다.

3. 1. 화물수송 에프.기관차 임환료 "279원"을 "523원" 으로한다.

4. 제2절 2 여객수송 씨.부가요금중 보통급행 부가요금 "8789원" 을
"12900원" 으로 특별급행 부가요금 "18096원" 을 "25800원" 으로 준급행
요금 "4500원" 을 "6450원" 으로한다.

5. 제2절 2.여객수송 지. 개인여행의 (3)을 다음과 같이한다.

   (3) 특급열차의 승차권과 보급,준급및 모든열차의 2등승차권은 좌석을
보유한다. 상기승차권을 동용개시전 임의 열차 출발전이 반환하였을때에는
수수료 2할을 공제한 잔액, 동용개시 당일의 열차 출발전에 반관하였을때에
는 수수료 5할을 공제한 잔액을 반환한다.

6. 제3절 미국정부 사유조차중 1.으.에이 의 "174량"을 "25량" 으로한다.

7. 제5절의 계약기간을 1968.7.1 부터 1969.6.30 까지로한다.

   제6절 연장

   1. 미국정부의 요구이따라 계약관은 본계약상의 일반적인 수송연장에
대한 고섭을 행함이 동의한다. 즉, 1971년 6.30 이후까지 수송연장이 되지
않을 경우를 제외하고 1969.6.30 이전 적어도 60일 간의 연장에 대한 고섭
을 하기위하여 서면으로 계약관에게 동지한다.

— 1 —

2. 계약관은 그러한 연장의 수락을 할수없다는 서면통지서를 미국정부에게 답으로서 회계년도(6.30)말에 본계약의 연장을 거부할수 있으며 계약관은 현행 계약기간의 종료일전 적어도 120일전에 그러한 통지를 함에동의한다.

3. 계약관은 또한 차기 계약체결에 있어 미국정부와의 동일한 협조와 최종 계약관리를 위하여 본규정에의한 1개월간의 본계약 연장의 선택을 미국정부에게 주는데 동의한다.

9. 지·피─6 책임의 9조 다음에 다음을 추가한다.

10. 계약관의 요구에 의하여 미국정부가 화물수송을위한 도송인을 첨승한다는 합의를 미국정부와 한국정부간에 이루어졌을때에는 본책임에관한 조항을 즉시 수정한다.

10. "지·피─8 세금 "을" 지·피─9세금"으로하고 이하 지·피 번호를 순차적으로 옮긴다.

11. "지·피─22수입장고" 다음에 다음을 추가한다.

"지·피─23 홍콩·싱가폴(에취·큐·에이)구매

에이. 계약관은 미국정부의 사전 서면승인없이는 본계약 수행을위하여 홍콩,싱가폴에서 물자공급의 하청계약이나 직원채용을 할수없다.

비. 계약관은 본조항에 의하여 이하의 모든 하청계약이 포함됨을 동의한다.

첨   도   청   장

부 전 지

수　신	외무부장관	1968. 7. 18.
발　신		

제　목　改美向き.

(내　용)

하명 AI2-1747 (68.7.15)의
제保조類인 내무 鉄道부
車輛運輸約書 를 追送하
니다

　　　　　賀物課長

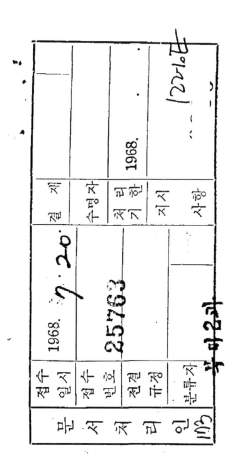

문 서 처 리 인 (2)	접수 일시	1968. 7. 20.	결 제	
	접수 번호	25763	수명자	
	처결 규정		처리 기한	1968.
	분류자		지시	
			사항	

STANDARD FORM 26, JULY 1966
GENERAL SERVICES ADMINISTRATION
FED. PROC. REG. (41CFR) 1-16.101

AWARD/CONTRACT

PAGE 1 OF 1

1. CONTRACT (Proc. Inst. Ident.) NO.	2. EFFECTIVE DATE	3. REQUISITION/PURCHASE REQUEST/PROJECT NO.	4. CERTIFIED FOR NATIONAL DEFENSE UNDER BSDA REG. 2 AND/OR DMS REG. 1.
DAJB03-68-D-0216	1 Jul 68	DF,EAGC-FA,8 Feb 68 (LTR-47)	RATING: N/A

5. ISSUED BY	CODE	DAJB03	6. ADMINISTERED BY (If other than block 5)	CODE	7. DELIVERY

5. ISSUED BY CODE DAJB03
Headquarters
US Army Korea Procurement Agency
ATTN: Services Section
APO 96301 Buyer: Mr. Yi C.W./Tel: YS-5028 or 4-2163

6. ADMINISTERED BY (If other than block 5) CODE
N/A

7. DELIVERY
☐ FOB DESTINATION
☒ OTHER (See below)

8. CONTRACTOR NAME AND ADDRESS	CODE		FACILITY CODE		9. DISCOUNT FOR PROMPT PAYMENT

8. CONTRACTOR NAME AND ADDRESS
(Street, city, county, State, and ZIP code)

Korean National Railroad
Republic of Korea
Seoul, Korea

9. DISCOUNT FOR PROMPT PAYMENT
None

10. SUBMIT INVOICES (4 copies unless otherwise specified) TO ADDRESS SHOWN IN BLOCK
5

11. SHIP TO/MARK FOR	CODE	12. PAYMENT WILL BE MADE BY	CODE

11. SHIP TO/MARK FOR CODE
Commanding Officer
25th Transportation Center (MC)
APO 96301

12. PAYMENT WILL BE MADE BY CODE
Finance & Accounting Officer
Eighth United States Army
APO 96301

13. THIS PROCUREMENT WAS ☐ ADVERTISED, ☒ NEGOTIATED, PURSUANT TO:
☒ 10 U.S.C. 2304 (a)(6)
☐ 41 U.S.C. 252 (c)( )

14. ACCOUNTING AND APPROPRIATION DATA All orders placed in accordance with PART IV of the Contract
Schedule shall contain a certificate of availability of funds quoting the procurement allotment to be used in making Payment.

15. ITEM NO.	16. SUPPLIES/SERVICES	17. QUANTITY	18. UNIT	19. UNIT PRICE	20. AMOUNT
	THE CONTRACTOR shall provide complete rail service on all railroad lines within the Republic of Korea in strict accordance and compliance with the contents of this contract.			See PART II of CONTRACT SCHEDULE.	
					Estimated

21. FIRM FIXED REQUIREMENT TYPE CONTRACT: TOTAL AMOUNT OF CONTRACT $ 2,000,000.00

CONTRACTING OFFICER WILL COMPLETE BLOCK 22 OR 26 AS APPLICABLE

22. ☐ CONTRACTOR'S NEGOTIATED AGREEMENT (Contractor is required to sign this document and return 10 copies to issuing office.) Contractor agrees to furnish and deliver all items or perform all the services set forth or otherwise identified above and on any continuation sheets for the consideration stated herein. The rights and obligations of the parties to this contract shall be subject to and governed by the following documents: (a) this award/contract, (b) the solicitation, if any, and (c) such provisions, representations, certifications, and specifications, as are attached or incorporated by reference herein. (Attachments are listed herein.)

26. ☐ AWARD (Contractor is not required to sign this document.) Your offer on Solicitation Number _____, including the additions or changes made by you which additions or changes are set forth in full above, is hereby accepted as to the items listed above and on any continuation sheets. This award consummates the contract which consists of the following documents: (a) the Government's solicitation and your offer, and (b) this award/contract. No further contractual document is necessary.

23. NAME OF CONTRACTOR	27. UNITED STATES OF AMERICA
BY s/Kim Kwang Hyun (Signature of person authorized to sign)	BY s/Alexander J. Fekete, Jr. (Signature of Contracting Officer)

24. NAME AND TITLE OF SIGNER (Type or print)	25. DATE SIGNED	28. NAME OF CONTRACTING OFFICER (Type or print)	DATE SIGNED
t/KIM KWANG HYUN Dir of Transportation Bureau, KNR	28 JUN 1968	t/ALEXANDER J. FEKETE, JR. Captain, TC	28 JUN 1968

CONTRACT SCHEDULE

AGREEMENT

This contract is entered into as of 1 July 1968, by and between the United States of America, hereinafter called US Government, representative by the Contracting Officer executing this contract, and Korean National Railroad, hereinafter called Contractor, done at Seoul, Korea and existing under the laws of Republic of Korea.

PART I - SCOPE OF CONTRACT:

1. Contractor shall provide complete rail services on all railroad lines within the Republic of Korea in strict accordance and compliance with the contents of this contract. The services specified in this contract shall be limited to official rail transportation services for US Government. These services include passenger and freight transportation by regularly scheduled trains or special movements.

2. a. In the event it is determined by the Commander-in-Chief, United Nations Command, Korea that an emergency exists, US Government shall enjoy the priority use of rolling stock and motive power of Contractor.

    b. US Government shall retain title to buildings and such other facilities as were constructed by US Government, and may use, move, remove or otherwise dispose of them. US Government may continue to use buildings and facilities as secured by US Government for performance of this contract.

3. Unless otherwise provided in this contract, services shall be conducted in accordance with the provisions of Railway Passenger and Freight Service Regulations, Supplementary Rules thereof, and other rules governing Railway traffic as established by the laws of the Republic of Korea.

4. Contractor agrees to maintain all cars and other facilities used in connection with the performance of this contract in a state of acceptable cleanliness and sanitation.

    a. Box cars, Gondolas, and Flat Cars:

        (1) Floors to be broom cleaned, except cars used for movement of POL drum.

        (2) All paper, blocking, nailing strips, wire strapping or any other obstruction to be removed prior to placement for loading.

    b. Passenger Cars and Sleeping Cars - prior to every run:

        (1) Floors to be broom swept and mopped.

        (2) Inside of cars and seats to be free of dust by brushing and wiping.

(3) Washrooms and toilet facilities to be clean and sanitary with wash bowls and toilets clean, in working order and properly supplied with water.

(4) Windows washed inside and outside of car.

(5) Cars to be disinfected.

(6) Clean head linen.

5. Contractor agrees that all rail cars leased by US Government from Contractor will be legibly stenciled on both sides "US ARMY LEASED" with letters a minimum of six (6) inches high.

The transportation officer procuring transportation for property and personnel under this contract shall have the right to reject any car that does not meet the above mentioned standards.

PART II - RATES, FARES AND CHARGES:

The applicable rates, fares and charges for services shall be as indicated below:

1. FREIGHT SERVICE:

   a. Carload Freight.

      (1) Rental Car. Contractor shall be paid fifty eight Won fifteen Chon (58.15) per car per kilometer for carload freight, provided that the minimum rate per car shall be two thousand eighty (2,080) Won.

      (2) US Government Owned Car. Contractor shall be paid forty nine Won forty Chon (49.40) per car per kilometer for carload freight.

      (3) Carload freight is defined as freight of all commodities in any quantity loaded in any type of freight car, except that such loading Party B shall have the right to reject cars that Contractor determines are not properly loaded and secured.

      (4) Charges for carload freight shall be computed on the basis of the longest rail distance, as published in official tariff distance tables of Contractor, between the tariff station nearest the point of delivery. Computation shall be made via junctions resulting in the longest distance between point of origin and destination. In the absence of specific routing by US Government nothing herein shall be construed as limiting the right of Contractor to select the route of movement considered most feasible for operational reasons.

176

2

b. **Special Train Service.** Charges shall be assessed at the rate specified in Para 1 a of PART II above, or Para j below as applicable with a minimum charge of one hundred twenty five thousand seven hundred thirty (125,730) Won per each special train operated at the request of US Government.

(1) Special Train Service is defined as a freight train operated exclusively for US Government on Schedules equal to the fastest freight trains now scheduled or that may hereafter be scheduled by Contractor.

(2) Special train operations, except emergency in national defence or public exigency and special cargo as determined by the Contracting Officer, shall be restricted to those cases in which at least 70% of the locomotive traction capacity will be utilized.

c. **Demurrage.** Charges shall be assessed at the rate of one thousand six (1,006) Won per car per each six (6) hours, or fraction thereof, for all detention beyond the initial free time allowed for loading, unloading, reconsignment or diversion, subject to the following conditions:

(1) For freight cars placed and notification given, the "Initial Free Time" for loading and unloading shall be as follows:

Cars Placed	Expiration of Free Time
Between 0001 hours & 0600 hours	by 1200 hours the same day
Between 0601 hours & 0900 hours	by 1400 hours the same day
Between 0901 hours & 1200 hours	by 1700 hours the same day
Between 1201 hours & 2400 hours	by 1200 hours the following day

(2) For cars placed on tracks used exclusively by Contractor.

(3) For cars placed on all other tracks the time of actual spotting shall be the time notice of arrival is received by US Government.

(4) No extension of the initial free time shall be allowed on account of Sundays or holidays.

(5) No extension of the initial free time shall be allowed, except that under abnormal weather conditions and/or as a result of such conditions i.e., typhoons, hurricanes and sub-freezing temperatures, which prevents normal loading or unloading, an oral request, confirmed in writing, may be made to Contractor for an extension of the initial free time. In such cases Contractor agrees to grant such extension of the initial free time as conditions may warrant.

(6) When empty cars are ordered or loaded cars received which can not be accepted because of some disability on the part of US Government, such cars shall be considered as "constructive" placement, and the initial free time shall commence immediately following notice by Contractor of the time of such "Constructive" placement.

3

(7) Contractor shall notify the local Transportation Officer of US Government by the presentation of a Nr. 3 copy of KNR Bill of Demurrage of any demurrage incurred within ninety (90) days after the fact.

(8) When a specific number of cars are requested by US Government from Contractor for movement on a Special Train, and any part of these cars can not be spotted due to non-availability of suitable cars for loading of desired freight, those cars which have been spotted and loaded shall not be construed as constructive placement and therefore will be exempted from demurrage charge while waiting for a Special Train.

d. Diversion or Reconsignment. Contractor shall be paid two thousand sixteen (2,016) Won for each car for which US Government requests diversion or reconsignment after Contractor has spotted the car(s) for unloading. Contractor shall not be paid if the request is received prior to spotting. All requests for diversion or reconsignment shall be made in writing. Request for Diversion or Reconsignment may be made orally; however, written request will be delivered to the appropriate KNR Station Master for attachment to GBL prior to actual diversion or reconsignment.

e. Cars Ordered, Spotted and not Used: Charges shall be assessed at the rate of one thousand four (1,004) Won per car for empty cars ordered, spotted and not used, provided the car spotted by Contractor was in acceptable condition for the loading of the commodity for which car was ordered by US Government.

f. Switching. For each loaded car switched on all sidings now being used by US Government, excluding station facilities of Contractor, Contractor shall be paid five hundred twenty three (523) Won.

g. Stopoff in Transit. Contractor shall be paid nine hundred thirty nine (939) Won per car for each stop enroute as required by US Government. In the event the car is required to be placed on sidings now being used by US Government, except station facilities of Contractor, Contractor shall be paid switching charges in addition to stopoff in transit charge.

h. Equipment Rental. Contractor agrees to reserve such rolling stock for the exclusive use of US Government as may be requested in writing, from time to time, by the Contracting Officer. The both parties shall mutually agree on the number of cars, types of cars, or specific cars, and necessary equipment for which US Government desires exclusive use.

(1) Contractor shall be paid seven hundred ninety eight (798) Won per day for each available and serviceable car reserved for the exclusive use of US Government. Whenever such cars are not available and/or serviceable, Contractor shall not be paid for the period commencing the day a car is deemed unavailable or not serviceable and ending the day the car is returned to service.

(2) Cars in the exclusive use of US Government for which a per diem rental is being paid are exempt from demurrage.

4

i. Bad Order Cars.

(1) Contractor agrees to furnish cars for loading which are suitable for the commodity to be loaded, and which are mechanically safe for movement. US Government agrees to load and unload cars in a manner acceptable to Contractor. However, if freight is transferred to another car because of mechanical defects of the car, or shifting of the load as a result of rough handling by Contractor, such reloading shall be accomplished by or at the expense of Contractor.

(2) Whenever Contractor shall move a bad order car from its home station to another station for purpose of effecting repairs thereon, the cost of moving the car to the point of repair and from point of repair to home station shall be borne by Contractor.

j. Deadhead Movement of Rented Freight Cars.
Contractor shall be paid fourteen Won thirty Chon (14.30) per car per kilometer for deadhead movement of freight cars for which per diem rental is paid by US Government: Such charges shall be computed in accordance with paragraph 1a(4) of PART II.

k. Surcharge for Oversized Freight.
A surcharge of forty two Won sixty Chon (42.60) per car per kilometer shall be assessed for cars loaded with with individual pieces of freight exceeding 10 meters in length, or 30 metric tons and/or 50 cubic meters. The surcharge shall be applicable to idler cars used in conjunction with movement of such freight.

l. Shipment of US Government Locally Purchased Supplies.
When transporting supplies locally purchased by the US Government, on a commercial Bill of Lading, Contractor agrees to convert commercial Bill of Lading to a Government Bill of Lading at destination and rate of payment shall be at the contract rate: Contractor from whom there supplies are purchased shall submit an application for freight movement to the KNR station master at point of origin, after he has obtained authority for movement from the Contracting Officer. KNR will then issue a KNR Bill of Lading on the shipment. Contractor will annotate all copies of Contractor Bill of Lading by stamping "TO BE CONVERTED TO GBL". KNR Bill of Lading is composed of four (4) copies. Distribution of the KNR Bill of Lading is as follows:

Copy A (Kap)	Consignor
Copy B (Eul)	Accompanies Shipment
Copy C (Byung)	Finance Bureau, KNR
Copy D (Jung)	Destination Stationmaster through KNR Registered Mail System

Copy D (Jung) will be presented to the consignee by the destination stationmaster at the time the shipment arrives at destination. The consignee will issue US Government Bill of Lading and make appropriate distribution. Copy D of the KNR Bill of Lading will be retained by the Consignee for his file.

5

179

2. **PASSENGER SERVICE:** Contractor agrees to provide for the lighting and heating of all passenger equipment in a manner acceptable to and as required by the US Government.

    a. **Definitions of the Passenger Type Cars.**

        (1) Business car is defined as a passenger car consisting of lounge, observation, sleeper, dining room, kitchen, shower, and toilet.

        (2) Sleeper car is defined as a passenger car contained bed accommodations.

        (3) Hospital car is defined as a passenger car which contains bed accommodation, laboratory, operating room, lounge, and/or dining room.

        (4) Kitchen car is defined as a car other than freight car or caboose, in which kitchen facilities are located.

        (5) Passenger coach is defined as a car equipped with seats and toilet facilities used in commercial service by Contractor.

        (6) Mail car is defined as a baggage type of car usually used for loading of mail and/or mail bags.

        (7) Baggage car is defined as a baggage type of car usually used for loading of common baggage.

        (8) Combination car is defined as a car consisting of compartments in combination for baggage and/or mail, and passengers.

        (9) Troop main is defined as passenger cars normally used for group passenger movement.

    b. **Basic Rate.** Contractor shall be paid one hundred thirty four Won seventy Chon (134.70) per car per kilometer for all types of cars in the exclusive use of US Government when moved in regularly scheduled passenger or mixed trains, or in special trains moving on ordinary, common express or special express time schedule.

        (1) Contractor agrees to accomplish cleaning services including cleaning services in-transit on US/UN exclusive use coaches in accordance with the US Government's standard operating procedure (SOP) for car janitor. This Standing Operating Procedure for car janitor shall be furnished to Contractor. Contractor shall be paid four hundred fifty (450) Won per car per day for cleaning services including in-transit cleaning services rendered on US/UN exclusive use coaches.

        (2) The cars listed and defined in para 2a of PART II above, shall be considered as types of equipment subject to the basic rate prescribed in para 2b of PART II above.

6

c. Special Train Service. Except as provided below, charge for Special Train Passenger Services will be assessed at the basic rate specified in paragraph 2b of PART II above with a minimum charge of sixty three thousand five hundred seventy five (63,575) Won. Special Passenger Train Service is defined as a train consisting of an engine and one or more passenger cars operated by Contractor, at the request of and for the exclusive use of US Government not on a published time table schedule of Contractor.

d. Self-Propelled Motor Coach is defined as a self-powered coach operated by Contractor at the request of and for the exclusive use of US Government not on a published time table schedule of Contractor. Contractor shall be paid one hundred thirty four Won seventy (134.70) Chon per coach per kilometer plus a surcharge of eight thousand seven hundred eighty nine (8,789) Won for the movement of self-propelled Motor Coaches while in the exclusive use of US Government, except that the minimum charge shall be sixteen thousand seven hundred sixty seven (16,767) Won. The minimum charge of sixty three thousand five hundred seventy five (63,575) Won applicable to Special Train Service will not apply to Self-Propelled Motor Coaches.

e. Surcharges.

(1) Common Express

In addition to the basic rate prescribed in paragraph 2b and 2c of PART II above Contractor shall be paid twelve thousand nine hundred (12,900) Won for each passenger type car of a regularly scheduled or special train moving on "Common Express" time schedule. Such time schedules shall not be less than those of trains designated as common express on officially published time tables of Contractor.

(2) Special Express

In addition to the basic rate prescribed in paragraph 2b and 2c of PART II above, Contractor shall be paid twenty five thousand eight hundred (25,800) Won for each passenger type car of a regularly scheduled or special train moving on "Special Express" time schedule. Such time schedule shall not be less than those of train designated as special express on officially published time table of Contractor.

(3) Semi-Common Express

In addition to the basic rate prescribed in 2b and 2c of PART II above, Contractor shall be paid six thousand four hundred fifty (6,450) Won for each passenger type car of a regularly scheduled or special train moving on "Semi-Common Express" time schedule. Such time schedules shall not be less than those of trains designated as semi-common express on officially published time tables of contractor.

7

181

0945

(4) Troop Trains

The surcharges prescribed in Part e(1), (2) and (3) above, shall not apply to cars operated in Special Trains designated by US Government as "Troop Train" when such trains are operated exclusively for the movement of troops. Provided further, that such Troop Trains will be moved on time schedules not less than those of common express trains, as defined in sub-paragraph (1) above.

(5) Cancellation of Surcharge

The surcharge prescribed in subparagraphs (1), (2) and (3) above shall not apply when trains operated on common or special express time schedule arrive at destination one (1) hour or more later than their originally scheduled arriving time.

f. Escort Personnel. Contractor shall not be paid for the Transportation of personnel riding on any car or cars when such personnel are performing assigned duties in connection with the operation or movement of such car, cars or train, or returning to home station after performance of such duties.

g. Individual Travel.

(1) Individual travel performed in cars or on trains not operated for the exclusive use of US Government shall be paid for at the rates prescribed in the officially published railroad passenger tariff effective on the date travel ticket is purchased for the class of accommodations requested by US Government, and furnished by Contractor. Purchase of train tickets by use or for travel on Contractor operated trains in US Government Transportation Requests will be allowed three (3) days in advance of the date of travel.

(2) Unused tickets for regular trains may be returned to station of issue for cancellation of the TR (Transportation Request) at any time prior to departure of the train, without charge.

(3) Tickets for Special Express, 2l Class of Common Excess & Semi-Express Trains and 2d Class Coaches on all trains involve reserve seats. Therefore if tickets purchased by TR's are returned to Contractor on the day prior to scheduled departure of train, 80% of the ticket charge will be refunded by the Contractor to the U.S. Government. If ticket is returned to Contractor on the day of scheduled departure but prior to actual departure of trains a charge of 50% will be assessed for the cancellation. Return of tickets under this provision must be accomplished by the appropriate Transportation Officer or his representative who will annotate the TR accordingly.

(4) For all tickets returned for cancellation after train departure time, full payment will be made to Contractor for lost revenue.

8

h. **Equipment Rental.** Contractor agrees to reserve such rolling stock for the exclusive use of US Government as may be requested in writing, from time to time, by the Contracting Officer. The parties shall mutually agree on the number of cars, types of cars, or specific cars, and necessary equipment for which US Government desires exclusive use.

(1) Contractor shall be paid at the following rates for applicable type of equipment reserved for the exclusive use of US Government. Whenever such cars are not available and/or serviceable, Contractor shall not be paid for the period commencing the day a car is deemed unavailable or not serviceable and ending the day the car is returned to service.

(a) One thousand one hundred ninety six (1,196) Won per day for each Business Car, Sleeper, Hospital Car, Dining Car, Kitchen Car or Passenger Type Coach.

(b) Nine hundred fifty six (956) Won per day for each Baggage, Mail Car, or Combination thereof.

(c) One thousand seventy six (1,076) Won per day for each combination car.

i. **Deadhead Movements.** Stabling points for holding reserved passenger equipment will be established as mutually agreed between the parties concerned. When cars are ordered for loading they will be furnished from the stabling point nearest the point of loading.

(1) Contractor shall be paid twenty Won five Chon (20.05) per car per kilometer for deadhead movement of passenger cars rented by US Government other than business cars, except that no such charges will be assessed for the movement of rented cars between storage yards and origin or destination station when it is the general practice to similarly deadhead the regularly scheduled trains of Contractor between such points for the purpose of inspection, cleaning or storage.

(2) When cars are ordered for loading by US Government and are not loaded after having been moved to the loading point, the aforementioned deadhead charge shall be assessed for the distance from stabling point to loading point and return; provided that no charge shall be assessed for such deadhead movement when the loading point is within the normal switching limits of the stabling point.

(3) Passenger type equipment shall be considered as being in deadhead movement when occupied only be personnel regularly employed on or assigned for duty on such cars; except that this provision shall not apply to cars during the time they are in regular operation in scheduled trains of Contractor.

j. **Transportation of Sentry Dogs.** Contractor agrees to transport Sentry Dogs in Baggage Cars not operated for the exclusive use of US Government.

9

183

Each Sentry Dog shall be caged in a 102cm x 94cm x 71cm cage furnished by US Government and accompanied by US Government escort personnel at all times while in transit. No food or water is required to be furnished by Contractor. US Government personnel accompanying dog are responsible for loading, unloading, trans-loading and caring for the Sentry Dogs. Government Bill of Lading will be used for ordering services and payments for services rendered therefor.

(1) Contractor shall be paid at the following rates per dog.

(a) For less than 100 Km three hundred sixty nine (369) Won.

(b) For more than 100.1 Km and less than 200 Km six hundred twenty one (621) Won.

(c) For more than 200.1 Km and less than 500 Km eight hundred thirty four (834) Won.

(d) For more than 500.1 Km one thousand seventy one (1,071) Won.

(2) Travel fares for persons accompanying Sentry Dogs for the purpose of escort shall be in accordance with paragraph "g" above.

3. DOCUMENTATION: All documents used for the procurement of services by US Government, and documents certifying accounts due Contractor for payment therefore shall be printed in English and Korean. Except as provided below all required forms for documentation will be furnished by and at the expense of US Government.

a. Freight Service.

(1) "U.S. Government Bill of Lading" EA Form 332 (EK) for the procurement of following types of services:

(a) Carload Freight

(b) Special Train Service

(c) Switching

(d) Stopoff in Transit

(e) Deadhead Movement of Rental Freight Cars

(f) Surcharge for Oversized Freight

10

(2) "Bills for Accessorial Service" EA Form 332 (EK) for the procurement of following types of services. This form shall be supported by "Bill of Demurrage" (Form KNR) furnished by Contractor for Demurrage, or for charges accruing for cars ordered, spotted and not used.

(a) Demurrage

(b) Cars Ordered, Spotted and not used.

(3) Diversion and/or Reconsignment EA Form 332-8 (EK) for the procurement of services of Diversion and/or Reconsignment.

(4) "Certificate In Lieu of Lost U.S. Government Bill of Lading" EA 376-1 (EK) 20 November 1958, will be used in the event original "Bill of Lading" is lost or destroyed after issuance to Contractor.

(5) Authorized "Car Rental Report" for the rental of reserved freight equipment.

(6) "Public Voucher (Std Form 1034) for the submission of the individual documents prescribed in subparagraph (1), (2), (3), (4) and (5) above, to US Government for payment.

b. **Passenger Service.**

(1) "Transportation Request for Passenger Equipment" (EA Form 332-2 (EK) and "Passenger Travel" (EA Form 332-1 (EK) will be used for the procurement of all services under SECTION II,2 except for Equipment Rental.

(2) Authorized "Car Rental Report" for rental of reserved passenger equipment.

(3) "Transportation Request for Passenger Equipment" EA Form 322-2 (EK) will be used for deadhead movements of reserved passenger equipment.

(4) A Passenger Car Cleaning Report", in the authorized format, and prepared by US Government, will be used for documentation of payment for car cleaning services, including cleaning services in transit, of US/UN coaches.

(5) "Public Voucher" (STD Form 1034) for the submission of the individual documents prescribed in sub-paragraphs (1), (2), (3) and (4) above, to US Government for payment.

PART III - U.S. GOVERNMENT OWNED CARS:

1. Contractor agrees to take custody of, operate, maintain, repair and perform all maintenance as required by procedures and regulations of Contractor when, as and if required by US Government for the exclusive use of US Government as follows:

11

18

a. 254 Each FSN 2220-262-0752 US Government owned tank cars, railway car, tank petroleum, 10,000 gallon, 56½ gauge: 49 Each FSN 2220-354-2726, US Government owned tank cars, railway car, tank petroleum 10,800 gallon, 56½ gauge.

b. 72 US Government owned railway cars, refrigerator, 56½ gauge, 40 ton capacity, 8 wheel FSN 2220-262-0754 and 28 US Government owned railway cars, refrigerator, 56½ gauge, 50 ton capacity, 8 wheel FSN 2220-875-1536, total 100 US Government owned refrigerator cars.

c. The term maintenance means all maintenance including but not limited to normal maintenance, running repairs, and heavy maintenance as required by regulations and procedures implemented by Contractor, as per attached reference, titled "Korean National Railroad, Regulations for Inspection and Repair of Railway Passenger and Freight Equipment", dated 1 January 1962.

2. Performance of maintenance on US Government owned cars shall be performed by Contractor in the same manner as for its own cars. US Government without cost to Contractor shall furnish only the following items, parts and/or components required in connection with performance of all maintenance on US Government owned cars:

Description	Unit	Unit Price
Wheel, chilled solid, (Including an Axle and two (2) wheels)	Set	$ 320.00
Wheel, Tired (one (1) wheel)	Ea	$ 153.00
Axle	Ea	$ 78.00
Coupler	Ea	$ 90.00
Draft Gear	Ea	$ 90.00
Triple Valve	Ea	$ 70.00
Bolster Spring	Ea	$ 93.00
Side Frame	Ea	$ 110.00
Brake Beam	Ea	$ 23.00
Bolster	Ea	$ 120.00
Paint: Black	Kg	$ 1.40
Red Lead	Kg	$ 1.40
White	Kg	$ 1.40
Silver	Kg	$ 2.00
Thinner	Kg	$ 1.40

12

All parts, items, components other than those specified herein required for the performance of maintenance on US Government owned cars, e.g., labor, items, parts, components, facilities, tools, and equipment, etc., will be furnished by Contractor at its own expense. In the event the items, parts and components specified herein are not on hand for issue by US Government, Contractor shall furnish such items, parts, and components and Contractor shall be reimbursed by US Government for the cost, of such items, parts, or components shall be replaced in kind by US Government.

The necessity for replacing items, components, and parts specified above shall be determined by the point inspection of both parties. Contractor agrees to notify US Government of the time, date and location of the inspection of US Government owned cars 72 hours prior to disassembly of the car. In the event US Government does not make inspector available, Contractor may proceed to inspect and perform maintenance as required by Contractor's regulations.

Contractor agrees to furnish paint for periodic repainting of US Government owned cars when, as and if requested by US Government. The quality of the paints furnished will be in accordance with the Korean Railroad Standards as established by Contractor. Payment for paints furnished shall be made to Contractor at the end of each month subsequent to passing the inspection of repainted cars by US Government's inspector. The following rates of consumption are applicable to the equipment cited:

Type of Car	Color of Paint	Quantity Per Car	Unit
POL Tank Car	Black	24	Kg
	Red Lead	10	Kg
	White	1	Kg
	Thinner	3	Kg
Refrigerator Car	Silver	30	Kg
	Red Lead	10	Kg
	Black	14	Kg
	Thinner	2	Kg

Government furnished material shall be receipted for by Contractor and stored in a dry, secure location apart from Contractor's material to avoid commingling of same. Contractor shall not utilize US Government property for any other purpose than that specified in this agreement.

All scrap material generated from replacing parts, items and components of US Government owned cars with Contractor furnished property will be stored within Contractor's premises for disposal by the Property Administrator of US Government and shall be loaded aboard US Government furnished transportation by Contractor as necessary.

13

3. No alterations, modifications, or major rehabilitation of said cars will be made without prior written approval of both parties; and as may be mutually agreed upon by both parties when such changes are made, US Government will bear the expense thereof, except as provided in paragraph 8 below.

4. The operational procedures and implementation thereof as applicable to US Government owned cars shall be performed by Contractor in the same manner as for its own cars. All necessary inspection to ascertain that cars are in operable condition will be performed by Contractor in accordance with the attached reference, titled "Korean National Railroad Regulations for Inspection and Repair of Railway Passenger and Freight Equipment" dated 1 January 1962. US Government reserves the right to make any additional inspections other than those normally performed by Contractor.

The attached forms are to be maintained on all US Army rolling stock and made available to the US Army Contracting Officer's Representative upon request:

    (1) KNR (Form No. 1) Bad Order Car Report

    (2) KNR (Form No. 2) Rolling Stock Inspection & Repair & Register

    (3) KNR (Form No. 3) Train Inspection Log

5. No demurrage or equipment rental charges will be paid on US Government cars.

6. US Government reserves the right to remove from service at any time any or all of the number of US Government's cars provided Contractor is given adequate time to move the cars to a point designated by US Government. Payment for the movement of any such cars will be at the applicable rate.

7. Specific details concerning car types, car numbers, and number of cars involved, and/or the location where such cars may be accepted by or delivered to either party shall be determined by mutual consent of both parties.

8. When it is determined by Contractor that good and sufficient cause exists to consider any of the US Government owned cars subject to this contractual instrument unserviceable or inoperable such cars may be removed from service at any time and US Government upon proper advance notice will remove such cars from the rail lines of Contractor, provided that if cars are operable, Contractor will move such cars to a point designated by US Government, at applicable rate for such movement.

9. Contractor shall not be liable for any damage to the above mentioned US Government owned cars while such cars are in its custody, except when such damage is caused by the wrongful act or negligence of the employees, or agents of Contractor.

14

a. US Government will be responsible for fastening of all dome covers and ice bunker covers and for placing of seals on all dome covers, car doors, and ice bunker covers.

b. Contractor has the right at any time prior to acceptance of a US Government owned car for movement, to reject such car when dome covers and/or ice bunker covers and car doors of such car are not properly fastened or seals are not properly placed on such dome covers, ice bunker covers and/or car doors.

10. The flushing, cleaning, and testing of US Government's tank cars will be accomplished by Contractor only on written request of the Contracting Officer, except that Contractor will be responsible for flushing, cleaning, and testing of US Government's tank cars free of charge when contamination of the tank occurs as the result of negligence or misconduct of the agents, employees or servants of Contractor.

11. Title to all US Government owned cars shall remain with US Government. Contractor will not use any US Government owned car in any undertaking not in connection with this contract.

12. US Government shall pay to Contractor as compensation for the maintenance and operation of US Government owned cars the rates and charges specified in this contract for operation of KNR equipment.

13. Contractor shall submit periodic reports of the Status and Conditions of US Government owned cars to the Contracting Officer's Representative:

a. Every 30 days for cars in backshop facilities of Contractor.

b. Not less than annually for all US Government owned cars.

14. US rail car inspector appointed by US Government reserves the right to deadline any US Government owned rail car, if the inspector determines that further operation of the car might result in further serious damage to the car, loading, death or injury to personnel. Any rail cars so deadlined will not be operated further until a mutual agreement is reached between the rail car inspector and a responsible Contractor representative as to the action necessary to correct the defect.

PART IV — ORDERING:

This contract is for GENERAL UTILIZATION by the US Armed Forces and US/UN Forces, Korea. All calls on contract or orders for delivery or services hereunder shall be issued either by the Contracting Officer on Delivery Orders or by the Transportation Officer or his authorized agent on Bills of Lading, Car Rental Reports, Freight & Demurrage Bills, Transportation Requests for Passenger Travel & Equipment, or Bills for Accessorial Services and WILL CONTAIN THE CERTIFICATE OF AVAILABILITY OF FUNDS, QUOTING THE PROCUREMENT ALLOTMENT TO BE USED IN MAKING PAYMENT.

15

189

PART V – <u>PERIOD OF CONTRACT:</u>   0953

   1. The contract shall begin on 1 July 1968 or effective date of contract. if subsequent thereto and shall end 30 June 1969 both dates inclusive, provided however, that any work started before and not completed by the expiration of this contract period shall be governed by the terms of the contract.

   2. <u>AVAILABILITY OF FUNDS:</u> (SEPT. 1962)

      Funds are not presently available for this procurement. US Government's obligation hereunder is contingent upon the availability of appropriated funds from which payment for the contract pruposes can be made. No legal liability on the part of US Government for payment of any money shall arise unless and until funds are made available to the Contracting Officer for this procurement and notice of such availability, to be confirmed in writing by the Contracting Officer, is given to Contractor.

PART VI – <u>OPTION TO EXTEND:</u>

   1. At the option of US Government, Contractor agrees to negotiate for the continuance of services of the general type hereunder; provided that, the US Government notifies Contractor in writing of the intention to negotiate for such continuation at least sixty (60) days prior to the 30th day of June 1969 except that in no event shall services be continued beyond 30 June 1971.

   2. Contractor may refuse annual continuance of the services of the general type hereunder at the end of any fiscal year (30 June) by giving the Contracting Officer a written notice to the effect that such continuance will not be accepted, and Contractor agrees to give such notice at least one hundred and twenty (120) days prior to the end of the current contract period.

   3. Contractor further agrees to given US Government an option to extend this contract under the terms thereof for one month for final contract administration and simultaneous cooperation with any contractor who may be awarded a contract for an subsequent period.

PART VII – <u>CONTRACTUAL CONTENTS:</u> This contract consists of:

   1. SIGNATURE PAGE (Standard Form 26).
   2. CONTRACT SCHEDULE – PART I thru VII – Page 1 thru 16.
   3. APPENDIX "A" – dated 2 June 1966 – Pages 1 thru 3.
   4. APPENDIX "B" – "Regulation for Inspection and Repair of Railway
                  Passenger and Freight Equipment" dated 1 January 1962 –
                  Page 1 thru 5.
   5. GENERAL PROVISIONS for Rail Services – Clause 1 thru 23 – Page 1 thru 9.

16

1. Contractor shall have the right to inspect the loading of all cars. In the event a car is rejected by Contractor, US Government will be informed of the reason for rejection.

2. All freight loaded by US Government shall be considered shipper's weight, load, and count.

3. a. The signature or official stamp (dochang) of Contractor's employee or agent on all copies of Bill of Lading will constitute prima facia evidence of receipt for the freight or cargo delivered to Contractor, concealed damage excepted.

b. The signature of US Government's employee or agent on the No. 1, 5 and 7 copies of Bill of Lading will constitute prima facia evidence of receipt for the freight or cargo delivered to US Government, concealed damage excepted.

4. Unless noted on a Bill of Lading, items loaded on a freight car will be presumed to be in apparent good order, concealed damage excepted.

5. Contractor's responsibility for custody of freight and cargo terminates when a car is spotted or constructively placed at destination. Spotting is defined as placement at the location designated by US Government for unloading. Constructive placement is defined as placement at a location other than normal unloading track(s) of US Government, because of congestion or other reasons arising from the convenience of US Government, reasonable notice thereof having been given to US Government. In the event a car can not be spotted, it will be handled in accordance with instructions from US Government. In case a car can not be placed at a location designated by US Government it will be placed at a location within destination station yard limits.

6. Under the following circumstances any loss or damage incident to shipment will be determined as the responsibility of US Government, and no claim will be initiated against Contractor.

a. When a carload arrives with the seals intact, and there are no other circumstances to which shortage may be attributed, such as evidence of forced entry through floor, or roof, or end of the car.

b. When packages or boxes, known to have been packed by the shipping agency, or known to be as originally packed, arrive with no external evidence of tampering or repacking in transit, and there are no other circumstances to which the shortage may be attributed.

c. When damage results from improper loading, blocking, and bracking of freight in or on cars.

191

7. US Government's Transportation Officer or his representative at destination will take the following action when there is an indication that a shipment has been pilfered, damaged, or other loss incurred:

a. Contractor's destination stationmaster or his representative will be notified of any discrepancy incident to shipment as soon as practicable after discovery. Such notice will be given prior to breaking of seals and/or unloading of car, if indications of discrepancies are evident at that time; or when KNR seals have been applied. If discrepancy is noticed during unloading operations, or thereafter, Contractor's destination Stationmaster, or his representative, will be notified as soon as possible, after discovery and in no event more than 14 days after delivery of car. A reasonable period of time will be allowed to Contractor's representative for the investigation but this period will not be extended to the point of allowing the rail car to go into demurrage time. If additional time is required by Contractor an extension of the free time will be obtained in writing from the contractor's local station master or his representative.

b. Contractor's destination stationmaster or his representative will be requested to be present for a joint inventory-inspection of shipment. When discrepancy is noted prior to unloading, car unloading will be postponed for a reasonable time to allow Contractor's representative to be present. If discrepancy is discovered during or after unloading operations, Contractor's destination stationmaster or his representative will be requested to make a joint-inventory-inspection as soon as possible after discovery.

c. After joint inventory-inspection, Contractor's destination stationmaster or his representative will prepare a Carrier's Inspection Report (KNR Form) and will provide 2 copies thereof to US Government as soon as possible. It is understood that the Carrier's Inspection Report is merely a statement of fact and does not constitute an admission of liability on behalf of Contractor.

d. The US Government will accomplish Bills of Lading promptly, noting on the reverse side on ORIGINAL, COPY 5 and COPY 7 any discrepancy in so far as it can be determined at that time.

8. Once a month, or more often if either party requests it, a meeting shall be held to discuss and attempt to settle disputed claims.

9. Contractor will pay all claims promptly after settlement, in Won, by certified check payable to the Treasurer of the United States, delivered to the Contracting Officer.

10. Bills of Lading and Bills for Accessorial Charges will be accomplished promptly and normally within three working days after unloading of the car and receipt of original Bill of Lading or other Accessorial Billing, as applicable, whichever occurs later.

192

2

11. The US Government will be notified promptly by Contractor as soon as practicable after discovery of any incident which may be the basis for US Government responsibility under paragraph 7, GP-6 of General Provisions, and in no event more than 90 days after the incident has occurred.

12. When freight shifts because of improper blocking and/or bracing and it becomes necessary to reload, such expenses attendant to this operation will be borne by US Government.

13. Notwithstanding the provisions of PART II para. 1c(1) of this agreement, the US Government will initiate procedures and assure compliance to effectively reduce detention of cars during the period of initial free time for loading and unloading of rail cars.

3

193

APPENDIX "B"

KOREAN NATIONAL RAILROAD

Regulation for Inspection and Repair
of Railway Passenger and Freight Equipment   1 January 1962

1. Inspection and repair of passenger and freight equipment will
be effected in accordance with provisions contained in this regulation,
unless otherwise provided.

2. For the purpose of this regulation the following definitions
apply:

a. Rolling Stock - Railway passenger and freight cars.

b. Back Shop - Mechanical shop facilities where manufacture,
modification, or general inspection of rolling stock is made. The
back shop has responsibility for production and/or repair of rolling
stock component parts, and performance of heavy repair.

c. Rolling Stock Office - General designation of main, branch
and sub-branch offices of Rolling Stock Office. These offices are
responsible for conducting train inspection, lubrication inspection,
partial inspection and ordinary inspection of rolling stock; and performance of minor repairs.

d. Terminal Inspections - General designation of stations and
marshalling yards where train inspection and minor repairs are performed.

3. Inspection and repair of rolling stock is classified in two (2)
categories as follows:

a. Train inspection.

b. Periodic inspection

4. Train inspection is defined as external inspection of condition and
functions of major component parts of rolling stock and repair action thereof, as necessary, performed on cars arrived, to be departed or being delayed
in terminals.

5. Periodic inspection is defined as periodic performance of inspection
on entire rolling stock during the specified time. The specific inspection
schedule will be based on time periods specified herein and utilization of
each car.

194

0958

6. The periodic inspection is further classified in the following categories:

     a. Lubrication Inspection.

     b. Partial Inspection.

     c. Ordinary Inspection.

     d. General Inspection.

7. At the time lubrication inspection is made, lubrication with journal oil will be done and inspection and repair of wheel journal lubrication device will be made simultaneously.

8. Lubrication inspection will be effected at the specified time as indicated below:

     a. Freight car (excluding caboose) 30 days.

     b. This period may be postponed or curtailed for a 5 day period.

9. Partial inspection will be conducted inspecting and repairing as required on this following components:

     a. Journal brass (including wedge) and contact are between journal bearing.

     b. Couplers.

     c. Air Brake and hand brake systems.

     d. Sources of electricity.

     e. Electric power distributing devices.

     f. Light fixtures and electricity connecting assembly.

10. Partial inspection will be made at the time specified below:

     a. Passenger cars and caboose - every 30 days.

     b. Freight cars (excluding caboose) - every 120 days.

The inspection times indicated above may be postponed or curtailed within 10 day period for passenger cars and 30 day period for freight cars. In case partial inspection of freight cars is postponed, lubrication inspection will be made in lieu thereof.

2

195

11. At the time of ordinary inspection, the following component parts will be disassembled for inspection and repair required thereby:

     a. Valves of air brakes, connecting devices and brake cylinders.

     b. Draft gear.

     c. Generator and converters.

     d. Batteries.

     e. Loud speaker system and recorder.

12. The ordinary inspection is required to be made every 8 months. The inspection time may be, if extremely necessary and condition of the car permits, postponed or curtailed within one month period, provided that partial inspection for passenger cars and lubrication inspection for freight cars is made in lieu thereof, when the specified inspection time is postponed.

13. General inspection will be effected covering entire car completely disassembling to insure complete operational condition of the car. However, riveted and welded parts are exempted from disassembling.

14. General inspection will be made at the times stipulated below:

     a. Passenger cars - every 16 months.

     b. Freight cars - every 24 months.

     The inspection time mentioned above may be postponed or curtailed within 2 month period, if it is extremely necessary and condition of the car permits, provided that partial inspection is made in lieu thereof in case postponed.

15. A road test that has been completed on newly manufactured rolling stock, is considered same as general inspection has been performed. When general inspection is to be made on a car, the inspection and repairs required in the ordinary, partial and lubrication inspections will simultaneously be performed at this time. At the time ordinary inspection is made, inspection and repair required in lubrication inspection will also be performed at the same time.

16. For rolling stock which is not continuously operated, the periodic inspections may be postponed as indicated below:

     a. General Inspection.

       (1) Passenger car - 36 months.
       (2) Freight Car - 60 months.

3

b. Ordinary and Partial Inspection.

As much time as length of period that the car was not operated. If the car is suspended from operations for a long period, it may be applied to the provision of the preceding paragraph.

17. For rolling stock placed on repair track of a Rolling Stock Officer, due to damage or inoperable defects, the ordinary inspection will be made; and if the damage was made to electrical devices, the partial inspection will be made. However, if the car is loaded with cargo and repair of damage is needed, the requirement of this Article may be waived.

18. When a car is placed in back shop for heavy repairs or major modification periodic inspection will be made at the same time as indicated below:

a. Major modification or rehabilitation of heavy damage is to be made to all type of rolling stock-General Inspection.

b. When the rolling stock is specifically in need of general inspection - General Inspection.

c. If a freight car is scheduled to be deadlined for general inspection within a 6 months hence - General Inspection.

d. Others - Ordinary Inspection.

19. Inspection and repairs will be conducted according to applicable type of inspection in such manner as described below:

a. The train inspection will insure safe operation of cars without impediment due to wear or loosening of components during operation on train until arrival at final destination by repairing and maintaining the cars always in operable condition. However, when unavoidable situations arise, the car may continue its operation to the next station where train inspection can be made and when safe operation assured.

b. In case of periodic inspection, safe operation of the car until the next scheduled inspection date must be insured.

20. The following stock which falls under the following categories will be placed on road test empty prior to return to services. However, if required, it may be placed on road test loaded:

a. Passenger and freight cars newly manufactured or on which major modification is made.

4

b. Passenger cars which have just completed general inspection.

c. Passenger or freight cars requiring a road test for a particular reason.

21. All rolling stock will be marked with the following information in accordance with procedure provided in applicable rules:

a. When a periodic inspection is made, the date and location where the inspection is made.

b. When any defect which may cause obstruction to normal operation is detected, its causes and extent of restriction and location where such determination is made.

22. Location where train inspection is normally to be made and trains to be inspected will be designated by the Director, Mechanical and Electrical Bureau.

23. In regard to performance of the periodic inspection, the Director, Mechanical and Electrical Bureau will provide procedures for the following matters:

a. Maintenance performance target in amount of cars for Back Shops and Rolling Stock Offices.

b. Special authorization for performance of general inspection by the Rolling Stock Office.

c. Special Authorization for performance of partial and/or ordinary inspection (minor repair) by Back Shop.

d. Application of paragraph 16a to rolling stock.

5

198

GENERAL PROVISIONS
FOR
RAIL SERVICES

1. __DEFINITIONS:__

As used throughout this contract, the following terms shall have the meanings set forth below:

a. The term "head of the agency" or "Secretary" means the Secretary, the Under Secretary, any Assistant Secretary, or any other head or assistant head of the executive or military department or other Federal agency, and the term "his duly authorized representative" means any person or persons or board (other than the Contracting Officer) authorized to act for the head of the agency or the Secretary.

b. The term "Contracting Officer" means the person executing this contract on behalf of the US Government, and any other officer or civilian employee who is a properly designated Contracting Officer; and the term includes, except as otherwise provided in this contract, the authorized representative of a Contracting Officer acting within the limits of his authority.

c. When used in this contract the term "US Government" refers to the Government of the United States of America, including its various departments, branches and agencies, and includes the United Nations Command in Korea. The term "Contractor" refers to the Korean National Railroad, an agency of the Republic of Korea represented by the Director of Transportation Bureau.

2. __PAYMENT:__

Contractor shall be paid promptly for services satisfactorily completed and accepted by the Transportation Officer on the submission of properly certified invoices, properly supported by the documents enumerated herein, by the appropriate Disbursing Officer indicated on the cover page hereof. Payment shall be made in the amount shown in Contractor's invoices, provided that the US Government can deduct the amount of any overpayment to Contractor from amounts subsequently found to be due to Contractor. Payment shall be made in dollars, effective 1 July 1968, at the official Eighth United States Army Dollar-Won conversion rate which is in effect on the date of the GBL/BAS. It is agreed that this rate is published by the Eighth United States Army Finance and Accounting Office on Thursday of each week and that copies of this rate will be made available to the Korean National Railroad.

3. __EXTRAS__ (JUL. 1949)

Except as otherwise provided in this contract, no payment for extras shall be made unless such extras and the price therefore have been authorized in writing by the Contracting Officer.

199

4. NOTICE OF ACCIDENTS:

0963

a. Whenever it is known and clearly evident to Contractor's personnel, all cases of personal injury requiring medical attention or death of any US/UN Personnel in the performance of this contract will be verbally reported by Contractor to the Contracting Officer's Representative administering this contract within 24 hours, if practicable. A full and completely written report of information available to Contractor will be submitted to the Contracting Officer of this contract at the U.S. Army Korea Procurement Agency, Seoul, Korea within twenty days following the verbal report.

b. In all cases where any US Government's equipment is damaged to an extent requiring removal from service to effect repair or is destroyed while in the possession of or under the control of Contractor a preliminary report of such damage, or destruction shall be submitted to the Contracting Officer's Representative administering this contract within 72 hours. A full and completely written report of such damage or destruction will be submitted the Contracting Officer at the U.S. Army Korea Procurement Agency within 20 days.

c. In all cases where any of Contractor's equipment and facilities in the possession of or under the control of U.S. Government personnel are damage or destroyed in the performance of this contract, or in the use of the facilities by US Government's personnel, a preliminary and verbal report of such damage, or destruction shall be submitted to the Director of Transportation of the Korean National Railroad within 72 hours. A full and completely written report of such damage or destruction will be submitted to the aforementioned Director within 20 days.

5. NOTICE TO US GOVERNMENT OF LABOR DISPUTES:

Whenever Contractor has knowledge that any actual or potential labor dispute is delaying or threatens to delay the timely performance of this contract, Contractor shall immediately give notice thereof, including all relevant information with respect thereto, to the Contracting Officer.

6. LIABILITY

a. Contractor shall be liable to US Government for all loss or damage to freight delivered to its custody under the terms of this contract while the same is in Contractor's custody, except when such loss or damage results from an Act of God, the Public enemy, the inherent nature or quality of the goods, or due to the act or fault of US Government.

b. Contractor shall be liable to US Government for bodily injury to, or death of persons caused by the negligence or fault of Contractor, or its employees in performance of services under this contract.

2

c. Contractor shall not be liable to US Government as stated above, if such loss, damage, injury or death was due to an act or omission of US Government, or its employees; or of the person or persons injured; or resulted from compliance by Contractor, or employees of Contractor with specific directions of authorized representatives of US Government that are reasonably within the scope of this contract.

d. Claims against Contractor under the provisions of this contract will be brought to the attention of Contractor through the Contracting Officer at the time loss, damage, or injury is discovered, or within a reasonable time thereafter. No claim will be filed unless Contractor has been notified of the loss, damage or injury by the Contracting Officer in writing, within six (6) months of the date when shipment was delivered or incident occurred.

e. The monetary value of claims will be expressed in dollars and payment, when made, will be in Won at the official conversion rate of exchange prevailing at the time payment is made.

f. Claims arising under the terms of this contract will be determined and processed in accordance with the procedures established in Appendix A, attached hereto and made a part hereof, or as otherwise mutually agreed between both parties.

g. US Government is responsible for repair of damage to and for loss of Contractor's equipment when such equipment is in the custody and control of US Government and such loss or damage is caused by a wrongful or negligent act or omission of US Government's officers, agents, or employees in connection with performance of service under this contract. It is understood by both parties that the interior of guard cars when occupied by US/UN security guards provided for the use of US/UN Security guards will be considered in custody and control of US Government. US Government will be responsible for damage to Contractor's freight equipment resulting from US Government's actions in welding car doors or hatches or in opening such welded car doors or hatches.

h. US Government shall be liable to Contractor for bodily injury to, death of persons, or damage to property caused by the US Government owned Sentry Dogs in transit.

i. Contractor shall be liable to US Government for damage to property of US Government, e.g., US Government owned rolling stock, fence gate, loading ramps, rail car stopper, etc., when such damage is caused by negligence or wrongful acts by the employees of the Contractor.

j. Notwithstanding the provisions as outlined above, the liability clause shall be immediately changed by a modification of contract when and if an agreement is made between the US Government and ROK Government that the US Government will provide security guard services upon request by the Contractor for protection of cargoes.

3

7. THIRD PARTY CLAIMS:

Contractor will be held harmless by US Government from Claims of third parties for loss, damage, bodily injury or death suffered by third parties arising out of negligent act or omissions of US Government or its employees occurring within Contractor's station facilities in performance of duties directly related to services rendered by Contractor under this contract.

8. ASSIGNMENT OF CLAIMS:

No claims under this contract shall be assigned.

9. TAXES: (JUL. 1960)

a. The contract price, including the prices in any subcontracts hereunder, does not include any tax or duty which the Government of the United States and the Government of Republic of Korea have agreed shall not be applicable to expenditures made by the United States in Republic of Korea, or any tax or duty not applicable to this contract or any subcontracts hereunder, pursuant to the laws of Republic of Korea. If any such tax or duty has been included in the contract price through error or otherwise, the contract price shall be correspondingly reduced.

b. If, after the contract date, the Government of the United States and the Government of Republic of Korea shall agree that any tax or duty included in the contract price shall not be applicable to expenditures by the United States in Republic of Korea, the contract price shall be reduced accordingly.

10. UNITED STATES OFFICIAL NOT TO BENEFIT: (JUL. 1949)

No member of or delegate to Congress of the United States, or resident commissioner of the United States, shall be admitted to any share or part of this contract, or to any benefit that may arise therefrom; but this provision shall not be construed to extend to this contract if made with a corporation for its general benefit.

11. COVENANT AGAINST CONTINGENT FEES: (JAN. 1958)

Contractor warrants that no person or selling agency has been employed or retained to solicit or secure this contract upon an agreement or understanding for a commission, percentage, brokerage, or contingent fee, excepting bona fide employees or bona fide employees or bona fide established commercial or selling agencies maintained by Contractor for the purpose of securing business. For breach or violation of this warranty US Government shall have the right to annul this contract without liability or at its discretion to deduct from the contract price or consideration or otherwise recover, the full amount of such commission, percentage, brokerage, or contingentfee.

12. GRATUITIES: (MAR. 1952)

a. The US Government may, by written notice to Contractor, terminate the right of Contractor to proceed under this contract if it is found after notice and hearing by the Secretary or his duly authorized representatives, that gratuities (in the form of entertainment, gifts, or otherwise) were offered or

4

given by Contractor, or any agents or representative of Contractor to any Officer or employee of US Government with a view toward securing a contract or securing favorable treatment with respect to the awarding or amending, or the making of any determinations with respect to the performing, of such contract; provided that the existence of the facts upon which the Secretary or his duly authorized representative make such findings shall be in issue and may be reviewed in any competent court.

b. In the event this contract is terminated as provided in paragraph "a" hereof, US Government shall be entitled:

(1) To pursue the same remedies against Contractor as it could pursue in the event of a breach of the contract by Contractor, and

(2) As a penalty in addition to any other damages to which it may be entitled by law, to exemplary damages in an amount (as determined by the Secretary or his duly authorized representative) which shall be not less than three nor more than ten times the costs incurred by Contractor in providing any such gratuities to any such officer or employee.

c. The rights and remedies of US Government provided in this clause shall not be exclusive and are in addition to any other rights and remedies provided by law or under this contract.

13. EXAMINATION OF RECORDS: (FEB. 1962)

a. Contractor agrees that the Comptroller General of the United States or any of his duly authorized representatives shall, until the expiration of three years after final payment under this contract, have access to and the right to examine any directly pertinent books, documents, papers and records of Contractor involving transaction related to this contract.

b. Contractor further agrees to include in all its subcontracts hereunder a provision to the effect that the subcontractor agrees that the Comptroller General of the United States or any of his duly authorized representatives shall, until the expiration of three years after final payment under the subcontract, have access to and the right to examine any directly pertinent books, documents, papers, and records of such subcontractor, involving transactions related to the subcontract. The term "subcontract" as used in this clause excludes (i) purchase orders not exceeding $2,500 and (ii) subcontracts or purchase orders for public utility services at rates established for uniform applicability to the general public.

14. REVIEW OF TRANSPORTATION RECORDS:

a. US Government agrees that the Director of Finance, Korean National Railroad of the Republic of Korea or any of his duly authorized representatives, shall until the expiration of three years after the final payment under this contract, have access to and the right to examine any retained copies of Bills of Lading, Bills for Accessorial Services, Demurrage Bills, Transportation Requests, and Vouchers of US Government involving transactions relating to this contract.

5

203

b. For the purpose of this contract the reference to "directly pertinent books, documents, papers and records" in paragraphs a and b of Clause 13 and a of this provision shall include retained copies of Bills of Lading, Bills for Accessorial Charges, Demurrage Bills, Transportation Requests, and Copies of Vouchers.

15. STATUTORY CLAUSES:

It is understood by both parties that Clause 10 - United States Officials Not to Benefit, Clause 11 - Covenant Against Contingent Fees, Clause 12 - Gratuities and Clause 13 - Examination of Records are clauses which are required to be included in this contract by the laws of the United States and, although binding on the parties hereto, are not intended to imply that Contractor has ever conducted its business with the United States or is likely to conduct such business in a manner contrary to such provisions.

16. DISPUTES:

Any dispute under this contract between local representatives of US Government and Contractor, which is not disposes of by agreement, shall be referred to the Korean National Railroad, Republic of Korea, and the Head of Army Procuring Activity for the Western Pacific Area for consideration. In the event the Korean National Railroad, Republic of Korea, and the Head of the Army Procuring Activity for the Western Pacific Area are unable to reach a mutual understanding on the dispute, the problem will be the subject of discussions between appropriate officials of the two Government.

17. TRANSLATIONS:

a. Contractor will, on request of the Contracting Officer, furnish a translation of any law, rules and regulations of the Republic of Korea, pertinent to transportation services rendered by Contractor under the terms of this contract.

b. In the event of any disagreement between the English text of this contract and any translation thereof, or any ambiguity in any such translation, the English text shall govern.

18. CHANGE OF RATES:

The rates and charges established in the general schedule hereto are based on the commercial tariff rates of Contractor. In the event that such commercial tariff rates are changed by the law of the Republic of Korea, the parties hereto agree to negotiate expeditiously and in good faith to adjust the rates quoted herein and to execute a supplemental agreement that will be fair and equitable to both parties to this contract. In no event will negotiations extend beyond 30 days after effective date of change of rates. Contractor agrees to notify the Contracting Officer by formal written notice of the occurrence of a future rate revision as decreed by Republic of Korea law on the effect if date of the revision. If Contractor fails to make this notification, this failure shall not preclude the parties

6

to this contract from negotiating for an adjustment of contract rates.
The negotiated adjusted rate will be effective on the date of the rate
revision as decreed by Republic of Korea Law.

19. __COMPETITIVE RATES AND CHARGES:__ XXXXXXXXXX

Contractor agrees that rates and charges applicable to US Government indicated
in the General Schedule hereto shall be no less favorable than the rates
and charges as may from time to time be applicable to ministries and agencies
of the Republic of Korea.

20. __COMMUNIST AREAS__ (OCT. 1966)

a. Unless he first obtains the written approval of the Contracting
Officer, the Contractor shall not acquire for use in the performance of this
contract:

  (i) any supplies or services originating from sources within
      the following communist areas: Albania; Bulgaria; China,
      excluding Taiwan (Formosa), but including Manchuria, Inner
      Mongolia, the provinces of Tsinghai and Sikang, Sinkiang,
      Tibet, the former Kwantung Leased Territory, the present
      Port Authur Naval Base Area, and Lianoning Province;
      Communist-controlled area of Vietnam and Communist-controlled
      area of Laos; Cuba; Czechoslovakia; East Germany (Soviet
      Zone of Germany and the Soviet Sector of Berlin); Estonia;
      Hungary; Latvia; Lithuania; North Korea; Outer Mongolia;
      Poland and Danzig; Rumania; Union of Soviet Socialist Republics;

  (ii) any supplies, however processed, which are or were located
       in or transported from or through China (as described in (i)
       above), North Korea, North Vietnam, or Cuba;

  (iii) any of the following supplies, if of foreign origin and
        however processed, unless acquired directly from the
        countries indicated for particular supplies:

        Bamboo, split . . . . None
        Braids, straw . . . . Italy, Japan
        Bristles, hog, including such bristles   None
          in knots or other processed conditions.

        Brushes, paint (including parts thereof, con--   None
          taining hog bristles, if any such bristle
          is more than 1 1/2 inches in total length or
          more than 1 1/4 inches in length cut of the
          ferrule.

        Eggs, poultry:
          Whole in the shell, other than chicken . . . . .   None
          Whole, dried . . . .   None

7

```
Albumen, dried . . . . . . . . . . . . . . . . . . . . . .    None
Yolks, dried . . . . . . . . . . . . . . . . . . . . . .     None
```

Floor coverings, grass and straw, including   Japan
seagrass mats and quares.

Fur skins:

```
Goat and kid . . . . . . . . . . . . . . .    Argentina, Ethiopia
                                              (including Eritrea),
                                              Iran, Iraq.

Koliasky. . . . . . . . . . . . . . . . .     Republic of Korea
Weasel . . . . . . . . . . . . . . . . . . . . . . . . . Canada
```

Garments, Chinese type . . . . None

Jade, stones, cut but not set and suitable   None
for use in jewelry.

Menthol, natural and synthetic (Other than   Brazil
racemic)

Silk, piece goods, tussah and muga . . . . None

Silk, tussah and muga . . . . None

Tea, Chinese type . . . . Formosa

Tung oil . . . . Argentina, Brazil, Paraguay.

Walnuts . . . . France, Iran, Italy, Turkey

(iv) any of the following supplies, however processed, which
are or were located in or transported from or through Hong
Kong, Macao, or any communist area listed in (i) above:
Agar-agar; Bamboo (Bags, baskets and other manufactures,
excluding furniture) (Poles and sticks); Brocades and
brocade articles; Camphor, natural and synthetic; Camphor
oil, natural and synthetic; carpets; Castor bean; Castor oil;
Chinaware, other than Dresdenware and Meissenware; Citronella
oil; Cotton manufactures; Cotton waste; Earthenware; Edible
marine products; Embroideries and embroidered articles;
Feather manufactures; Glass sheet (window); Graphite; Hair
nets, regardless of the material from which made; Hand-
kerchiefs; Hardwood manufactures, including furniture other
than bentwood furniture; Hats, paper; Honey; Ivory manufactures;
Lace and lace articles; Linen manufactures, excluding wearing
apparel other than wearing apparel made in whole or in part
of brocade, embroidery or lace; Ores and metals (Antimony,
Bismuth, Quicksilver, Molybdenum, Tin, Tungsten); Peanuts and
peanut products; Poultry, including pigeons, frozen or otherwise prepared or preserved; Ramie; Rugs; Seagrass and straw
manufactures, excluding floor covering; Sesame, oil and seed;
Shoes, leather-soled with non-leather upper, except ladies'
high-heel shoes; Silk (Raw and manufactures other than Western
style suits and Indian saris) (Waste); Skins, deer and goat;
Stones, semiprecious, and manufacture thereof, including jewelry;
Tapestries, including needlework tapestries; Tapioca, including
tapioca flour.

                              8

```
```

21. CONTROL OF SECURITY PASSES:

a. Where it is necessary for Contractor employees to enter US/UN Forces compounds in the official performance of the contract and where Contractor is issued passes for personnel concerned with the performance of the contract, Contractor will make all reasonable effort to return to the Contracting Officer or his authorized representative as appropriate, any or all of such passes issued under the contract:

(1) Upon completion or termination of the contract.

(2) Upon termination, suspension or removal of an employee who has been issued such a pass.

(3) Upon specific request of the Contracting Officer or his authorized representative when the fact of abuse of the use of any pass has been established by either Contractor, Contracting Officer or his authorized representative.

22. RECEIVING OFFICER:

The Receiving Officer under this contract shall be any Transportation Officer duly authorized to execute and accomplish accountable transportation documents.

23. HONG KONG AND/OR SINGAPORE PURCHASES (HPA):

a. The Contractor agrees he shall not make nor allow any subcontractor to make any purchases of supplies and services or recruitment of personnel in Hong Kong and/or Singapore for use in performance of this contract without the prior written approval of the contracting officer.

b. The Contractor further agrees to insert the provisions of this clause, including this paragraph b, in all subcontracts hereunder.

9

207

공공요율에 관한 진 외무차관과 Porter 주한 미국대사간의

면담요록

일 시 : 1968. 8. 2. 하오 3:30

장 소 : 외무부 차관실

(진 외무차관은 미국과 북월맹간의 제15차 파리협상을 부리핑 하기 위하여
내방한 Porter주한 미국대사와의 회답이 끝난후 우리정부와의 공공요율
인상과 SOFA 집행에 관하여 아래와 같은 요지의 면답을 교환함.)

진 차 관 :   공공요율 인상문제 (특히 전기요율 문제)가 상당한 기간동안
미해결상태하에 있는데 이 문제를 조속 타결하는 것이 양국
정부의 이의이 될줄믿는다.

SOFA 규정에 "no less favorable than any other
user" 라는 구절 때문에 미측이 인상됨 전기요율의 지불을
지연시키고 있는데 우리나라의 경제실정에 의하여 특별 수출
산업과 상수도용 전기요율 또는 농수용 수도요율등에 할인제를
실시하고 있는 것은 정부의 경제정책의 목적상 불가피한 일이며
이는 내용적으로 간접적인 정부보조로 간주되고 있다.
그리고 또 정부는 빈민촌에 공급되는 수도에 대하여도
할인 요율을 적용하고 있다.

여하한 의미에서도 미군 당국이 우리의 특별 경제 정책에
의한 보조요율 적용이나 빈민에 대한 자비적 원조 (Mercy Help)
를 "any other user"   와 결부시키는 것은 미국의

208

723.16(2)-4

본의가 아닌것으로 믿는다.

이와같은 특별 조치는 SOFA 의 범주밖에 속하는 것이 아니겠는가? 정부의 간접 보조를 "any other user" 라는 어구와 비교하여 고려할수는 없으며 이것은 SOFA 의 "Frame" 밖에서 해결하여야 될줄 믿지 않는가?

Porter 대사 : 본인도 이 문제에 대하여 관심있게 진전을 보고받고 있다. 주한 미군은 인상된 요율의 대소는 문제시 하지 않으며 또 한국 정부가 요율을 인상하는 것도 문제시 하지 않는다. 그러나 수출산업을 권장한다하여 요율에 자꾸만 차별을 둔다든지 또는 동사용 수도를 특별할인 하는등 이것저것 한국정부에서 특별 고려를 멋대로 하면 미국의 입장에서볼때 SOFA 의 규정에 적합한 조치라고 보기가 어렵다. 미군 재무관의 입장에서 보면 SOFA 규정에 묶여 있어 융통성 있는 재량권이 없다.

그반면 한국 정부는 자유로운 입장에서 보조금을 일정한 업체나 사용자에게 줄수 있다고 믿는다. 예컨데, 세금에서 보조금을 주도록 절차를 만들수 있지 않겠는가? 그리하여 공공요율은 단일 "Form" 으로 일률적인 적용을 하면 좋지 않겠는가? 다시 말하면 이러한 방법으로 요율을 인상시키면 미군으로 부터 말성없이 더많은 요율을 징수할수 있으며 따라서 정부는 더많은 수익을 올릴수 있지 않는가?

미국 정부는 요율의 액수의 다과는 논하지 않는다.

162

209

진 차관 : 한국정부가 국민에 대한 과세조정을 하는것이 신축성 있게 용이한 일은 아니다. 물론 특수산업등에 대한 보조금을 국민의 세금에서 주도록 하면 SOFA 적용상 간편하고 좋은 방법이겠으나 이와같은 방법을 택하려면 국회가 개입 하여야 하며 기타 여러가지 복잡한 문제가 개재되기 때문에 상당한 시간을 요할뿐만 아니라 수속 절차가 매우 복잡하다. 그렇다고 하여 이 문제를 언제까지나 미결상태로 둘수는 없으니 미측에서도 협조하여 조기 락결되는 방법을 모색 하기 바란다.

Porter 대사 : 다시 검토 시키겠다. 그러나 잠정적인 방법으로 문제의 해결시도는 미측으로선 곤난하다. 그것은 잠정적인 방법이 고정되어 이것이 확정되어 후에 다시 이것을 고치기가 어렵기 때문이다.

진 차관 : ~~하여서~~ 하여서 pending 상태를 너무 오래 繼續 로 두는것은 相互 좋은 일이 못되니 善處 를 要請한다

210

공공요율에 관한 진 외무차관 과 Porter 주한 미국대사간의

대담요록

일 시 : 1968. 8. 2. 하오 3:30

장 소 : 외무부 차관실

(진 외무차관은 미국과 북월맹간의 제15차 파리협상을 부리핑 하기 위하여
내방한 Porter주한 미국대사와의 회담이 끝난후 우리정부와의 공공요율
인상과 SOFA 집행에 관하여 아래와 같은 요지의 대담을 교환함.)

진 차 관 :   공공요율 인상문제 (특히 전기요율 문제)가 상당한 기간동안
미해결상태에 있는데 이 문제를 조속 타결하는 것이 양국
정부의 이익이 될줄믿는다.

SOFA 규정에 "no less favorable than any other
user" 라는 구절때문에 미측이 인상된 전기요율의 지불을
지연시키고 있는데 우리나라의 경제실정에 의하여 특별 수준
산업과 상수도용 전기요율 또는 농수용 수도요율등에 할인제를
실시하고 있는 것은 정부의 경제정책의 목적상 불가피한 일이며
이는 내용적으로 간접적인 정부 보조로 간주되고 있다.
그리고 또 정부는 빈민촌에 공급되는 수도에 대하여도
할인 요율을 적용하고 있다.

이러한 의미에서도 미군 당국이 우리의 특별 경제 정책에
의한 보조요율 적용이나 빈민에 대한 자비적 원조 (Mercy Help)
룰 "any other user" 와 견부시키는 것은 미국의

211

68-2-35

본의가 아닌것으로 믿는다.

이와같은 특별 조치는 SOFA 의 범주밖에 속하는 것이
아니겠는가? 정부의 간접 보조를 "any other user"
라는 어구와 비교하여 고려할수는 없으며 이것은 SOFA 의
"Frame" 밖에서 해결하여야 될줄 믿지 않는가?

Porter 대사 : 본인도 이 문제에 대하여 관심있게 진전을 보고받고 있다.
주한 미군은 인상된 요율의 대소는 문제시 하지 않으며
또 한국 정부가 요율을 인상하는 것도 문제시 하지 않는다.
그러나 수출산업을 권장한다하여 요율에 차등만 차별을
둔다든지 또는 동사용 수도를 특별할인 하는등 이것저것
한국정부에서 특별 고려를 먼데로 하면 미국의 입장에서볼때
SOFA 의 규정에 적합한 조치라고 보기가 어렵다.
미군 재무관의 입장에서 보면 SOFA 규정에 묶어 있어
융통성 있는 재량권이 없다.
그반면 한국 정부는 자유로운 입장에서 보조금을 인정한 업체나
사용자에게 줄수 있다고 믿는다. 예컨대, 세금에서 보조금을
주도록 정책를 만들수 있지 않겠는가? 그렇하여 공공요율은
단일 "Form 으로 일률적인 적용을 하면 좋지 않겠는가?
다시 말하면 이러한 방법으로 요율을 인상시키면 미군으로
부터 말성없이 더많은 요율을 징수할수 있으며 따라서 정부는
더많은 수익을 올릴수 있지 않는가?
미국 정부는 요율의 액수의 다과는 놓하지 않는다.

212

68-2-36

진 차관 :　한국정부가 국민에 대한 국세조정을 하는것이 신축성 있게 용이한 일은 아니다. 물론 특수산업등에 대한 보조금은 국민의 세금에서 주도록 하면 SOFA 적응상 간편하고 좋은 방법이겠으나 이와같은 방법을 뢰하려면 국회가 개입하여야 하며 기타 여러가지 복잡한 문제가 제기되기 때문에 상당한 시간을 요할뿐만 아니라 수속 절차가 매우 복잡하다. 그렇다고 하여 이 문제를 언제까지나 미결상태로 둘수는 없으니 미측에서도 협조하여 조기 타결되는 방법을 모색하기 바란다.

Porter 대사 :　다시 검토 시켜겠다. 그러나 잠정적인 방법으로 문제의 해결시도는 미측으로선 곤난하다. 그것은 잠정적인 방법이 고정되어 이것이 확정되어 후에 다시 이것을 고치기가 어렵기 때문이다.

진 차관 :　~~╌╌╌╌╌╌╌~~
　　　　　　하여간 pending　상태를 너무 오랜 미해결로 두는 것은 상호 좋은 일이 못되니 선고를 요청한다.

23

68-2-31

증산·수출·건설

한국전력주식회사

(22 - 5101 -279)

한전업(영)910-   1968. 10. 21.

수신 외무부장관
참조 구미국장
제목 미군에 대한 인상요금 적용

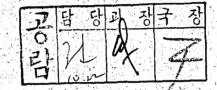

1. 한전업(영)910-4545 (68. 7. 10)과 관련사항입니다.

2. 미군에 대한 신전기요금 적용문제에 대하여는 한국측 한미
행협 공공용역 분과위원회 및 본위원회에서 미측에 제시한 "합인요금
제도"를 요금표에서 삭재하고, 삭재된 요금표를 미측에 제시 미수금
을 회수하는 방안(단, 합인요금 제도는 요금표에서 삭재하되 별도 상
공부령등의 방법으로 심질적으로 동일한 할인제도는 시행됨)이 현재
한·미행협 합동위원회 및 공공용역 합동분과 위원회에서 협의 중에
있는것으로 주지하고 있읍니다.

3. 상기한 한국측 "안"이 미측에 제시한지 근2개월이 지난 현
금까지 아무런 회답이 없으므로 문의하오니 한국측 "안"에 대한 미측
태도 및 가능성 여부등, 추진사항과 예상해결시기에 대하여 상세히 회
시하여 주시면 감사하겠읍니다. 끝

사   장   정   래

납세로 자립경제

236

214

SPECIAL PROVISIONS FOR SUBSIDY

1. Special subsidy ~~to~~ *maybe* provided for the following categories of customers as *maybe* separately determined by the Ministry of Commerce and Industry:

    a. Special Industry

    b. Municipal Water Service

    c. Island Area

2. The subsidy may be given by subtracting certain proportion of the amount of the monthly bill for the electric service.

215

공공 요율 문제에 관한 윤구 미국장및 Freedman 중장과의 대답요록

시 일 : 1968. 11. 1.   16:00 - 17:30시 7까지
장 소 : Freedman   중장 사무실

윤 국장   :   오늘은 거의 일년동안 미결상태하에 있는 공공요율
문제의 해결을 위하여 귀하에게 간곡한 협조를 요청하고저
한다. 작년 11월 1일 공공요율이 인상됨이택 상금도 그
인상됨 요율을 미군측에서 지불받지 못하고 있어 우리정부는
현재 매우 난처한 입장에 있다. 앞으로 국회의 예산 심의
시에 정부가 국회로부터 이 문제에 관하여 추궁을 받을 우려
가 있어 정치문제로 번질 가능성이 많다. 그러므로 본인은
이 문제의 해결에 귀하의 각별한 협조를 요망하는 바다.

아시다 싶이 우리정부가 수출산업을 초합한 특수사용자
에게 공공요율을 할인해주고 있는것은 정부가 정책적으로
유치산업을 권장장려하고 기락정부의 보조를 오하는, 예컨데
도서지방의 거주자나 농수용 급수를 위한 전력사용자에게,
정부로서 원조를 주는 것이다. 그리고 이 예외적으로 보조금
의 혜택을 받고있는 특수사용자의 공공요율 이용율은 전수요
의 불가 0.3 % 밖에 안됨다. 따라서 이는 우리정부정책상

216

68-2-38 231161 2) -6

취해지는 예외 조처이며 결코 미군을 차별하기 위한것은
아니다. 우리정부 기관이나 국군도 미군보다 고율의 요율을
지불하고 있으며 미군에 비하여 세금등을 합하여 약 15 %
나 많은 액수의 요율을 지불하고 있다. 그뿐만아니라 미군은
특수배전을 위하여 우리전력회사가 부가적으로 특별한 시설을
설치하는등 막대한 추가경비를 부담하고 있으므로 우리는
미군을 위하여 특별대우를 하고 있는 셈이다.

그리고 미군이 다른나라와 처결한 SOFA 관계 규정은
모두가 정부기관이나 군대 또는 유사한 상황하의 사용자와
동일한 요율을 적용시키고 있는데 유독 한국에서만 문자그대로
다른 여하한 사용자보다도 불리한 대우를 받지 않겠다고 하는
의도를 모르겠다. 원컨데 미측은 협정의 전체적정신을 고려
하고 문자해석에만 고집하지 말고 의미해석으로 문제를 대국적
견지에서 해결하기 바란다. 문자에만 고집한다면 결코 SOFA
의 운명은 순탄하지 못할것이다. 미측은 이러한 점을 유의하고
이해하여 체납요율의 조속한 지불책이 마련되기 바란다.

Freedman 중장 :   나는 귀하의 입장에 매우 동정적이다. 나도 귀하와
동일한 생각이며 이것은 Bonesteel 사령관도 마찬가지
이다. 본인은 이문제에 관하여 한국측의 요청을 해결하기
위하여 나의 상부 기관인 Porter 대사에게 서신으로
상신한바 있으나 대사관측과 USAID 측에서 이것을 받아
주지 않고있어 해결이 지금까지 지연되고 있다. 본인이

개7

68-2-31

이와같이 이야기하는것은 문제에 대한 책임을 미국대사나

USAID 처장에게 전가시키겠다는 의도는 결코 아니다.

본인은 인상된 요율을 언제라도 지불하기 위한 돈을 가지고

있다. 요는 우리주위에 있는 법률고문관들의 고식적인 이론

때문에 난관에 봉착하고 있는 것이다. 그들의 이론은 요율

에서 보조금이 나가서는 안됩다는 것이다. 본인은 또

경제기획원의 양윤세 국장과도 만나 이 문제를 의논한바

있으며 그와도 의견이 일치됩바 있으나 대사관과 USAID

그리고 법률고문관들을 납득시키는 문제게 남아 있을뿐이다.

와싱톤에 refer 하면 그곳에는 이론만 따지는 법률관

들이 더 많으므로 이 문제의 해결은 일년 이상이 걸릭게 될

것이므로 우리는 이것을 와싱톤에 refer 하지 않고 있다.

본인은 윤국장과 같은 입장에서 이 문제 해결을 위하여 노력

하겠으니 본인에 관한한 아무런 문제가 없을 것이다. 본인은

솔직하게 귀하에게 나의 입장을 밝히는 것이며 앞으로 합심

하여 문제해결을 위하여 성의를 다할것을 다짐한다.

(그후 윤국장및 Freedman 중장은 아래와 같은 세가지 방안을 의논하였

으며 Freedman 중장의 태도는 매우 솔직하고 우호적이며 우리측의 요청을

해결하겠다는 노력이 역력히 엿보였음을 첨기함.)

228

68-2-40

공공 요율 문제 해결을 위한 세가지 방안

1. 현 전기 요율표의 특수 규정의 수정

    지난 7.30 한국측이 제의한 특수사용자에 대한 보조금조로 전기요율을 감액한다는 제 2항을 수정(별첨참조)하는 것을 내용으로하는 서한을 윤국장이 Freedman   중장에게 발송하여 미국대사및 USAID   처장의 동의를 받도록 하는것.

2. 보조금 지불규정을 요율표에서 삭제하고 별도 규정

    우선 한국측에서 특수사용자에 대한 보조금을 공공요율표와 관계없이 별도 규정지불하겠다고 약속하고 그 시행절차는 행정부처간의 조정을 필요로하고 복잡한 수속을 밟아야 함으로 동 규정의 제정 시행은 시일이 소요된다는 양해를 구함. 이 약속과 동시에 미측은 체불됨 요율을 즉시 지불함.

3. 고위층을 통한 미대사와의 해결책 모색

    한 고위층을(국무총리 또는 외무장관)을 통하여 미국대사에게 정책적으로 해결하도록 강력히 압력을 가하는것.

219

68-2-47

SPECIAL PROVISIONS FOR SUBSIDIES

1. Special subsidy may be provided for the
following catagories of customers as may be separately
determined by the Ministry of Commerce and Industry:

    a. Special Industry

    b. Manicipal Water Service

    c. Island Area

2. The subsidies for the special industry will be
in accordance with the percentage of utlities purchersed
and used in pursuant of export.

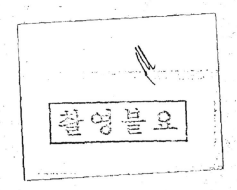

(Draft)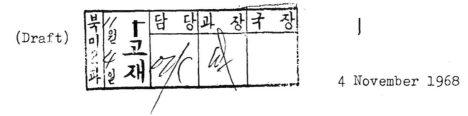

4 November 1968

Dear General Friedman:

I wish to refer to the question of current electicity rates which became effective on 1st November last year, ~~and~~ on which, however, the consultation procedures provided for in the SOFA have not been completed to this day. ~~and to the conversation we had on the matter last Friday, the 1st November.~~

~~You will recall that~~ during the conversation ~~we have~~ discussed as a possible solution reivsion of provisions on sibsidised rates for special industries, as contained in page 10 of the published rate schedule. Inclosed herewith is a draft which will clearly indicate that a special subsidies is involved. I hope that you will be able to notify us as soon as possible official US acceptance of the formula, with modifications if necersary, inasmuch as we share the concern over the delay in solution of the question.

Sincerely yours,

1:encl

Yoon Ha Jong
Republic of Korea Representative
ROK-US SOFA Joint Committee

Lieutenant General Robert J. Friedman
United States Air Force
United States Representative
US-ROK SOFA Joint Committee

SPECIAL PROVISIONS FOR SUBSIDIES

1. Special subsidies may be provided for the following catagories of customers as may be separately determined by the Ministry of Commerce and Industry:

    a. Special Industry

    b. Manicipal Water Service

    c. Island Area

2. The subsidies for the special industry will be *decided* in accordance with the percentage of utlities purchersed and used in pursuant of export.

22|

4 November 1968

Dear General Friedman,

Referring to our conversation on Friday, I am enclosing herewith a draft "Special Provisions for Subsidies" to replace page 10 of the published electric rate schedule, which deemed acceptable to my Government as a result of consultation with the Economic Planning Board.

If it is also acceptable to the United States Forces, Korea, I will officially propose this formula.

Sincerely yours,

Yoon Ha Jong

1:encl

SPECIAL PROVISIONS FOR SUBSIDIES

1. Special subsidies may be provided for the following categories of customers as may be separately determined by the Ministry of Commerce and Industry:

    a. Special Industry

    b. Manicipal Water Service

    c. Island Area

2. The subsidies for the special industry will be decided in accordance with the percentage of utlities purchersed and used in pursuant of export.

US POSITION ON UTILITY RATE PROBLEM

1. There is no question, of course, that the Government of the Republic of Korea has the sovereign right to establish its own utility rates and to subsidize any favored users of utilities in the Republic of Korea as it so desires.

2. Article VI of the SOFA provides that the US armed forces use of utilities and services "shall be in accordance with priorities, conditions, and rates or tarrifs no less favorable than those accorded any other user." It is the US interpretation that the SOFA language entitles the US armed forces to utility rates no less favorable than any other users, public or private.

3. It is recognized that the phrase "any other user" is very broad. It is not the intention of the US to interpret this phrase in an unreasonable or illogical manner. For example: the US does not ask that it be provided rates similar to that of a Korean user of unmetered electricity or of a common-use water faucet. However, if discounts or preferantial rates are offered to favored industrial or commercial users of electric power or water, as part of the utility rate structure, then the US is, under the provisions of the SOFA, also eligible for such favored rates.

68. 11. 26. 韓美 外務長官 會談 에서 美側 이 提示,

(於 USAID)

224   68-2-46

SPECIAL PROVISIONS

1. SPECIAL INDUSTRY:

    To export industry custmers with 200 kw of contracted demand or under, and to industry customers whose power charges occupy more than 20% of the total production cost who are designated by the Minister of Commerce and Industry.

DISCOUNT:

    Monthly bill shall be discounted as follows:

    a. 30% Discount: for export industry customer with 200 kw of contracted demand or under.

    b. 15% Discount: for the industry customer whose electric charges occupy 20% and over, of the total production cost.

    20% Discount: for the industry customer whose electric charges occupy 30% and over, of the total production cost.

    25% Discount: for the industry customer whose electric charges occupy 40% and over, of the total production cost.

    30% Discount: for the industry customer whose electric charges occupy 50% and over, of the total production cost.

2. MUNICIPAL WATER SERVICE

    Rate for Municipal Water Service shall be discounted by 46.7%.

3. ISLAND AREA:

    Special rates may be established for island area which is isolated from mainland power system, subject to approval by the Minister of Commerce and Industry.

- 10 -

68-2-69

INCHON CITY WATER RATES - AS REVISED 1 FEBRUARY 1968

RATE SCHEDULE

Classification	Usage	Rate Schedule	
		Basis Rate	Over Charge
Group I	Domestic use	One hydrant a month 100 won up to 7m^3	15 won/m^3
Group II	Common use of private faucet	One hydrant a month 350 won up to 25m^3	15 won/m^3
Group III	Bathing use	One hydrant a month 6,000 won up to 300m^3	21 won/m^3
Group IV	Special public use	One hydrant a month 750 won up to 30m^3	30 won/m^3
Group V	Industrial use	One hydrant a month 2,000 won up to 100m^3	27 won/m^3
Group VI	Locomotive ship	30 won/m^3	
Group VII	Common use of public faucet	14 won/m^3	
Group V III	Temporary water service	30 won/m^3	
Group IX	Private fire fighting hydrant	150 won a month 200 won for one time's fire fighting drill	
Group X	Special service	To be changed in accordance with Rate Schedule and water , supply condition	

첨부 -3

Water Rates Paid by US Armed Forces in Various ROK Cities

	Present Rates
Seoul	10 won/m^3
ASCOM	18 won/m^3
Inchon	18 won/m^3
Taegu	22 won/m^3
Taejon	15 won/m^3
Pusan	21 won/m^3
Kunsan POL	15 won/m^3
Chunchon	10 won/m^3

The United States-Republic of Korea Joint Committee has been confronted with a divergence of views on the interpretation of Article VI of the Status of Forces Agreement for some time. This problem developed from the practice of the Republic of Korea to grant subsidies or preferential utility rates to certain categories of favored users and from the insistence of the United States armed forces that, under the provisions of the SOFA, is also eligible for similarly lower utility rates.

Intensive discussions between the representatives of our two Governments has revealed that there is a possible basis for solution of the current impasse on the question of utility rates. As the Republic of Korea Representative on the Joint Committee, I would like to propose the following plan to resolve the problem of the utility rates being paid by the United States armed forces for electric power purchased from the Korea Electric Company and for water purchased from the City of Inchon. This plan is also designed to provide a definitive solution to this problem which would minimize the possibility of a recurrence of the present deadlock with regard to consultation on utility rates. The three basic points involved in this proposal are as follows:

a. The Government of the Republic of Korea **pledges** it will eliminate from present utility schedules, subsidies or preferential rates to specified users of utilities within six months from **the date** of US-ROK Joint Committee confirmation of this agreement. **The Govern**ment of the Republic of Korea pledges that if subsidies or **preferential** rates are not eliminated from the utility schedules by the end of six months, it will be prepared to grant US armed forces in Korea similar preferential rates.

b. United States armed forces, in response to the above pledge of the Government of the Republic of Korea to resolve the problem in a definitive way, will agree to pay the Korea Electric Company the 15% increase in electric power rates, retroactive to the date of the increase, 1 November 1967. The US armed forces will also agree to pay its electric power bill on the basis of the 15% increase for six months after this Joint Committee agreement is reached. At the end of the six-month period, the US armed forces will be entitled to the lowest rate charged any favored user, in the event subsidies or preferential rates are still a part of the electric power rate structure.

c. The Inchon water rate question would be resolved by US-ROK agreement for an increase in the water rate paid by the US armed forces from 18 to 21 won per cubic meter, retroactive to the date of the increase in the Inchon water rates on 1 February 1968. This proposal is believed to provide an equitable basis for settlement of this problem, since the 21 won rate is the lowest which is granted to other large users of water in Inchon and is generally comparable to the water rates charged the US armed forces in other cities in the Republic of Korea.

I believe it is mutually agreed that it is strongly in the interest of our two Governments to resolve this problem which has exerted unfavorable

2

influences on the effective operation of utilities in the Republic of Korea and has been a source of considerable misunderstanding between officials in our two Governments. The proposed plan to resolve this problem is believed to be consistent with the intent of the provisions of the SOFA and of the Joint Committee procedures relating to the implementation of Article VI. It is my sincere hope that this plan will provide the basis for early agreement in the Joint Committee to resolve this problem on a basis of equity and mutual interest for both of our Governments.

Sincerely,

기 안 용 지

분류기호 문서번호	미이741-	(전화번호)	전결규정 조 항 국 장 전결사항	
처리기한		기 안 자	결 재 자	
시행일자		북미2과		
보존년한		오 명 두 68. 12. 14.		

보조기관 | 북미2과장

협조

경유
수신
참조 | 경제기획원장관
기획국장 (한.미합동위원회 공공용역 분과위원장)

제 목 | 공공요율 대미군 적용에 관한 이견 조정

1. 작년 10월부터 금년초에 걸쳐 인상된 일련의 공공요금중
    전기요금및 인천시 수도요금은 미군에 대한 최혜대우를
    규정한 한.미군대지위협정 제 6조 2항의 규정과 관련하여
    소정협의 절차를 완료하지 못하여 상금 잠정적으로 구요금을
    납부하고 있읍니다.

2. 전기한 이견을 조정하여 동 문제를 원만타결하기 위하여
    11.1 한.미합동위원회 한국대표는 미국대표와 면담하여 몇
    가지의 가능한 타개책을 논의하였으며, 11.26 에는 미대사관및
    USAID 관계자까지를 포함한 양측실무자 간담회를 개최
    하는외 이 문제에 관하여 교섭을 계속하여 왔읍니다.

공통서식 1-2-1 (갑)
(1967. 4. 4. 승인)

/ 후면계속 /

(18정 시) (2급인쇄용지74g/m²)
(초납징)(300,000매 노쇄)

1

3. 12. 13. 한·미합동위원회 미 양 간사는 일변의 회의끝에 도달한 최종일괄타결안 같은 해결안을 채택하였던바, 이에 대한 귀부의 의견(수락 여부 및 그 이유)를 시급 회시하여 주시기 바랍니다.

4. 동 한국 대표가 미국 대표에게 보내는 공한 형식으로 되어 있어 이를 미국대표가 공식으로 수락하는 방식을 구상한 것인바, 경우에 따라서는 동일문서에 공동서명하는 합의문서의 형식을 취할수도 있을 것인바, 동방안의 골자는 다음과 같읍니다.

   가. 전기요금

   한국측은 합의후 6개월이내에 요율구조에서 특별 우대 요율 또는 보조할인요율을 제기할것을 약속하며, 미측은 이 약속을 근거로 인상요율 시행일자인 67. 11. 1. 부터 소급하여 신요율을 지불하고 향후 6개월간 계속 지불하며, 한국측이 약속을 이행한 경우는 신요율이 확정되며, 6개월후 약속이 이행되지 않은 경우에는 그날부터 최저 요율을 지불한다.

   나. 인천 수도 요금

   인천시의 대량소비자중 최저 요율과 일치시키고, 여타 지역의 대미군 수도요금과의 균형을 유지하기 위하여 입방 미-터 당원의 요율을 적용한다.

   첨부 : 미측 해결안 사본 1통.   끝.

외   무   부

미이 741-   1968. 12. 14.

수신 : 경제기획원 장관

참조 : 기획국장 (한.미합동위원회 공공용역 분과위원장)

제목 : 공공요율 대미군 적용에 관한 이견 조정

1. 작년 10월부터 금년초에 걸쳐 인상된 일련의 공공요금중
    전기요금및 인천시 수도요금은 미군에 대한 최혜대우를
    규정한 한.미군대지위협정 제 6조 2항의 규정과 관련하여
    소정협의 절차를 완료하지 못하여 상금 잠정적으로 구요금을
    납부하고 있읍니다.

2. 전기한 이견을 조정하여 동 문제를 원만타결하기 위하여
    11.1. 한.미합동위원회 한국대표는 미국대표와 면담하여
    몇가지의 가능한 타개책을 논의하였으며, 11.26. 에는 미대사관
    및 USAID 관계자까지를 포함한 양측실무자 간담회를 개최
    하는외 이 문제에 관하여 교섭을 계속하여 왔읍니다.

3. 전기교섭에 입각하여 12.13. 한.미합동위원회 한.미양간사는
    일련의 회의끝에 도달한 최종타결 타결안으로서 대체적으로

233

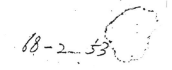

아래와 같은 해결원측에 합의하였는바, (별첨사본 참조)
이에 대한 귀부의 의견(수락 여부와 그 이유를 시급회시하여
주시기 바랍니다.

4. 동 일괄해결안은 한국대표가 미국대표에게 보내는 공한형식
으로 되어있어 이를 미국대표가 공식으로 수락하는 방식을
구상한 것인바, 경우에 따라서는 동일문서에 공동서명하는
합의문서의 형식을 취할수도 있을것인바, 동방안의 글자는
다음과 같습니다.

　가. 전기요금

　　　한국측은 합의후 6개월이내에 요율구조에서 특별우대
요율 또는 보조할인요율을 제거할것을 약속하며, 미측은
이약속을 근거로 인상요율 시행일자인 67.11.1.부터 소급
하여 신요율을 지불하고 향후 6개월간 계속지불하며,
한국측이 약속을 이행한 경우는 신요율이 확정되며, 6개월후
본 약속이 이행되지 않을경우에는 그날부터 그날현재의
최저요율을 지불한다.

　나. 인천 수도 요금

　　　인천시의 대량소비자중 최저 요율과 일치시키고, 여타
지역의 대미군 수도요금과의 균형을 유지하기 위하여 입방
미-터 당 21원의 요율을 적용한다.

첨부 : 미측 해결안 사본 1통. 끝.

　　　　외　무　부　장　관

특수산업용 전기 요금 할인안에 관한 문제점

1. 한.미군 대지위협정 제6조2항은 미군의 공공용역 사용에 있어 최저요율적용을 규정하고 있으며 (주1) 등 조 합의의사록 1항은 요율변경에 있어 미군과의 사전 협의를 규정(주2)하고 있고 이에 따라 합동위원회는 일의 절차를 정한바 있음.

2. 1967년 11월 인상된 전기요율의 대미군적용은 각종 할인요율 중 최저요율을 적용하여야 한다는 미측 주장으로 인하여 1년반이나 보류된후 수출제조 업자할인 조항(계약용량 200킬로와트이하 : 0%할인) 적용전에서 타협되었고, 1968년 2월 인상된 인천수도요금은 상금 인상요율을 징수 하지 못하고 있는 실정임.

3. 본안이 통과되는 경우 미군도 동일할인요율적용을 주장 할 가능성이 있는바 협정문구 해석상으로는 이를 거부할 근거가 박약함.

4. 미군에게도 동일 할인요율적용 용의가 없는 경우는 면세, 보조금 지불등 재정 보조형식을 취함이 가할것임.

5. 그렇지 않으면 본건 미군당국으로부터 동일한 할인요율 적용을 요구 하여 올 경우 정부측으로서도 이에 적의 응할것을 고려하여야 할것임.

235

주 1:　한 미군대지위협정 제6조 2항 ·

　　"합중국에 의한 이러한 공익사업과 용역의 이용은 어느
　　타 이용자에게 부여된것보다 불리하지 아니한 우선권
　　조건 및 사용료나 요금에 따라야 한다."

　　The use of such utilities and services by
the United States shall be in accordance with
priorities, conditions, and rates or tariffs
no less favorable than those accorded any other
user.

주 2:　제6조에 관한 합의 의사록 제1항 ·
　　"합중국 군대에 적용할수 있는 우선권, 조건 및 사용료나
　　요금에 있어서 대한민국 당국이 결정한 변경은 그 효력발생
　　이전에 합동위원회의 협의대상이 될것임을 양해한다.

　　It is understood that any changes determined
by the authorities of the Republic of Korea in
priorities, conditions, and rates or tariffs,
applicable to the United States armed forces shall
be the subject of consultation in the Joint Committee
prior to their effective date.

236

2. 1969년도

231

2. 1969년

1969.

U.N軍 水道料 引上合議에 對한 仁川市側 主張.

仁 川 市

238

UN軍 水道料 引上合議

1. 韓國側의 主張 및 解明

가. 他利用者 보다 不利하지 않다.

UN軍에 適用되는 料率은 絶對 軍隊指揮
協定(韓美行政協定) 事後의 2項 規定에 違背
되지 않다. 理由는 U.N軍用이 數多 되는
給水種別 中4種(種別) 專用은 過去(1962
年以前부터)에도 그러하였으며 國內 用途性格
이 같은 官公署·韓國軍·學校·病院·銀行·會社·
停車場 其他 綜合次(敎會·保育院) 等이 讓多
됨으로 絶對 不利한 料金으로 책정된것은 않음을
主張한다.

나. 給水種別(等級)을 두어 一般 對象用을 처리
하게 率定한 理由.

給水의 明途에 따라 料金의 種類로 區分하며 料率의
等差를 두는것, 비단 仁川市 뿐만 아니라 全國 他都市 와-
世界 各國의 어느 都市의 境遇도 그러고 各級의
差를 두는것이 上水道 事業 本未의 目的인 低所
得層 為하는 것이므로 納稅者인 住民이 使用하는
種別로 低料率보다 저렴하게 策定하는 것이다.

다. 從前의 種別과 變更이 있다.

이번에 策定한 U.N軍 水道料 種別을 特別 特別
等別에 適用시고 것은 變更 또는 變更한 것이 아니고,
特別에 適用시고 것부터 U.N軍과의 給水契約에 따라 種別 그대로
特別 等別에 適用하였으며, 모든 給水種別도 變更이 있다.

라. A.I.D借款 承認을 條件 履行.

仁川市의 水道料 引上은 AID借款行政 條件을 履行한것이다.

마. 他都市 보다 많은 比率로 나눈 理由.

新義州는 1962年에 比한 以末 6年만에 約 69% 라고 하였으나 他都市는 1 以内에 數次에 亘하여 나누었으므로

이 例에 他都市 보다 料率이 비싼 理由는 生産地와 供給地가 距離의 遠距離로 料給 價格이 他都市 보다 비싼 것이다.

바. U.N 軍에는 體制 給水를 하고 있다.

現在는 U.N 軍이 使用의 給水를 爲하여 金井水源地(淨水場)에서 U.N 軍 使給地까지 별도 配管과 같이 送水管을

敷設로 布設하여 一般 需要에게는 制限 給水를 하여도 U.N 軍 使用은 優先的 無制限 給水를 實施하고 있다.

240

수도요금 개정대비

68. 2. 1. 현재

종별	인천시 기본량	인천시 기본료	인천시 초과료	청주 기본량	청주 기본료	청주 초과료	부산시 기본량	부산시 기본료	부산시 초과료	대구시 기본량	대구시 기본료	대구시 초과료
	$7m^3$			$7m^3$			$10m^3$			$10m^3$		
가정용	7	70	10	7	100	15	10	100	21	10	150	21
사업공용	25	250	10	25	350	15			10	7	91	15
목욕용	50	600	14	300	6.000	21	500	12.500	27	200	3.000	21
특수전용	20	300	18	30	750	30	20	500	27	30	720	29
공장용	50	600	18	100	2.000	27	200	5.000	27	60	1.080	27
철도.선박용			18			30			27			27
공설공용			10			14			10	100	1.100	13
급비용			15			30			36			50
시설고처전	1058		100	242		150			300			240

923/6(3)-2

인천시 상수도 사용료 문제

인천시 주장

1. 미군에 대하여는 종전대로 급수종별 제4종(1입방미터당 30원)을 적용하여야 한다.

2. 第4종에 해당되는 급수종별 별게 4종(누별)의 적용을 누비 광공서, 학교, 부대, 병원, 은행, 회사등에 적용되는것으로 타이용자보다 불 비합기 이라고 할수 없다.

3. 제4종(누별) 적용을 시로 적용하는 기준이 아니로 종전에도 적용되어 왔으며 기준이다.(1962년이전부터) 또한 리의 급수 종별에도 변동이 없다.

4. 水도서료에 따른 비용을 인상평가는 심산거와 공급거에 기비가 水도서료에 따른 비용 싱산평가가 비서시가 매매수준이다.(31개월이내)

5. 우 인군에게는 누별급수를 하고있다. (부게한 급수)

미측 주장

1. 누우나에 적용되는 지가준으운(1입방미터당 21원)이 미군에 적용되어야 한다. (가. 미행정의 7.경의 이하여)

이유: 1) 대당수묘되는 접에서 저별비우가 부당하다.
2) 타지방으운과의 균영상이유로도 부우받으음.
(제3종)이 적용되어야 한다.

* 지역별 수도요금 참조

Water Rates Paid by US Armed Forces in Various ROK Cities

	Present Rates
Seoul	10 won/m^3
ASCOM	18 won/m^3
Inchon	18 won/m^3
Taegu	22 won/m^3
Taejon	15 won/m^3
Pusan	21 won/m^3
Kunsan POL	15 won/m^3
Chunchon	10 won/m^3

243

첨부 1 - 2

INCHON CITY WATER RATES - AS REVISED 1 FEBRUARY 1968

RATE SCHEDULE

Classification	Usage	Rate Schedule	
		Basis Rate	Over Charge
Group I	Domestic use	One hydrant a month 100 won up to 7m³	15 won/m³
Group II	Common use of private faucet	One hydrant a month 350 won up to 25m³	15 won/m³
Group III	Bathing use	One hydrant a month 6,000 won up to 300m³	21 won/m³
Group IV	Special public use	One hydrant a month 750 won up to 30m³	30 won/m³
Group V	Industrial use	One hydrant a month 2,000 won up to 100m³	27 won/m³
Group VI	Locomotive ship	30 won/m³	
Group VII	Common use of public faucet	14 won/m³	
Group VIII	Temporary water service	30 won/m³	
Group IX	Private fire fighting hydrant	150 won a month. 200 won for one time's fire fighting drill	
Group X	Special service	To be changed in accordance with Rate Schedule and water supply	

243

1. 행정구역상의 "빈원」은 여기
   라기보다 좀. 거리에서 벗어 있는.
3; 도로에서 지칭한다.
2; category Ⅳ 를 적용하기 바람.   (권원)

(제Ⅲ종을 삭제)   (미)

3. 미군용 학교.공공기관등 과 같이 미정 Ⅳ 종을원
    적용하여야한다. (이견)

4. 지금까지 Ⅳ 종의 요율이 적용되어 있다.

5. 4종이나 5종이나 보의가 되었은 SOFA ~~적용~~
    협정체임 에야 있어 그후 요율체정에
    있어서는 사정이 달라진 것을 의미한다.

6. 권원은 maximum 이다 (미)
    미정부의 확고한 방침이다.

7. 공업용수 적용 측정은 사용량이 공업용수 에
    해당시켜야한다. (미)

8. 시멘트 분야를 도와서 하라는 미군에게는 24시간
    공급을 하고있다. 수원지가 멀기 때문에
    생산원가가 타도시보다 비싸게 먹기 때문에

245

30원을 받지 않고는 안되겠다 (안철)
28.14 (원가계산)→한국측 ● 23.25 (원가계산)→미측

9. 의 원은 싸워할수 없다 (원상준에)
   2원은 한국에서 가장 교율이다、
   이게 예산 입닮을 받으바 있다 (

10. 30원니서니 1원정도의 양보를 할수있다.
    또、Ⅳ등으로 규정하고 미측에 특별한
    원하겠으을
    교래를 할수있다. (이원)
    유물개량은 62년이후 68.2월에 처음샀다.

11. Ⅳ등대응은 노제에 맞지 않는다(경기)

12. SOFA 규정상의 혜택을 포기할수 없다.

246

EXTRACTS OF SOFA'S ON UTILITIES AND SERVICES

Japan (June 23, 1960)

Article VII

The United States armed forces shall have the use
of all public utilities and services belonging to, or
controlled or regulated by the Government of Japan, and
shall enjoy priorities in such use, under conditions no
less favorable than those that may be applicable from
time to time the ministries and agencies of the Government
of Japan.

Republic of China - no provisions (Aug. 31, 1965)

Philippines

Article VII   Use of Public Services

It is mutually agreed that the United States may
employ and use for United States military forces any and
all public utilities, other services and facilities,

airfields, ports, harbors, roads, highways, railroads,
bridges, viaducts, cannals, lakes, rivers and streams in
the Philippines under conditions no less favorable than
those that may be applicable from time to time to the
military forces of the Philippines.

Australia (May 9, 1963)

Article XXIII   paragraph (1)

The United States Forces and all persons associated
with activities agreed upon by the two Governments may
use the public services and facilities owned, controlled
or regulated by the Australian Government or its instrumentalities.
The terms of use, including charges, shall be no less
favorable than those available to other users in like
circumstances unless otherwise agreed.

Dominican Republic (March 19, 1957)

Article XXVI

The Government of the United States of America shall
have the right to employ and use, in order to carry out
the purposes of this Agreement, all public services, including
any water rights owned or controlled by the Dominican Republic,

subject to the tariffs established by the Dominican laws
and regulations. Utilities and other facilities, bays,
roads, highways, bridges and similar channels of transportation
belonging, controlled or regulated by the Government of
the Dominican Republic shall be used under such terms and
conditions as shall be mutually agreed upon by the two
Governments.

Nicaragua (Sept. 5, 1958)

No provisions

West Indies (Feb. 10, 1961)

Article VII

Public Services and Facilities

(1) The United States Forces, United States contractors
and the members of the United States Forces and contractor
personnel may use the public services and facilities
belonging to or controlled or regulated by the Federal
Government or the Government of the Territory. The terms
of use, including charges, shall be no less favorable
than those available to other users unless otherwise agreed ...

Ethiopia (May 22, 1953)

The Imperial Ethiopian Government grants to the Government of the United States the right to employ and use public and commercial utilities, services, transportation and communication facilities in Ethiopia in connection with operations under this Agreement. The Government of the United States shall pay for any employment or usage of such facilities at the most favorable rates obtained by other public users who employ and use such facilities.

Libya (Sept. 9, 1954)

Article V

Public Services and Facilities

Upon the request of the Government of the United States of America and provided that the Government of the United Kingdom of Libya is assured that the public and private interests in Libya will be duly safeguarded, the public services and facilities in Libya shall be made available as far as practicable for the use of the Government of the United States of America and members of the United States forces. The charges therefor shall be the same as those paid by other users, unless otherwise agreed.

Article IX

1. Members of a force or of a civilian component and their dependents may purchase locally goods necessary for their own consumption, and such service as they need, under the same conditions as the nationals of the receiving State.

3. Subject to agreements already in force or which may hereafter be made between the authorized representatives of the sending and receiving States, the authorities of the receiving State shall assume sole responsibility for making suitable arrangements to make available a force or a civilian component the buildings and grounds which it requires, as well as facilities and services connected therewith. These agreements and arrangements shall be, as far as possible, in accordance with the regulations governing the accommodation and billeting of similar personnel of the receiving State. In the absence of a specific contract to the contrary, the laws of the receiving State shall determine the rights and obligations arising out of the occupation or use of the buildings, grounds, facilities or services.

Germany (Aug. 3, 1959)

Article 47

    1. The Federal Republic shall accord to a force or a civilian component treatment in the matter of procurement of goods and services not less favorable than is accorded to the German Armed Forces.

Greece (Sept. 7, 1956)

    NATO Agr.

252

기 안 용 지

분류기호 문서번호	미이 731-	(전화번호)	전결규정 조 항 국 장 전결사항
처리기한		기안자	결 재 자
시행일자		북미2과	
보존년한		오 명 두 69. 2. 14.	

보조기관	북미2과장		
협 조			
경유 수신 참조	주미대사	통 신 제	발 송 No. 1969 2.14 외무부
제 목	주한미군 공공요금에 관한 대미교섭		

1. 1967년 년말에서 1968년 년초에 증하여 각종 공공요금이 인상되었는바, 주한 미군에 대한 인상 요금 적용에 있어 대부분 원만 해결되었으나, 전기요금및 인천시 상수도 요금에 관하여는 한미간의 이견으로 상금 락결을 보지 못하여 미군은 계속 인상전 구요금을 지불하고 있어 그 해결이 시급합니다.

2. 당지 주한 미군사 및 미국 대사관은 장기간의 접충 끝에 금년 년초 본국정부에 기본 방침에 관한 청훈 전문을 작전한바, 최근 추가 자료 제시를 지시하여 왔으며, 금명간 지시 자료를 전문으로 보고할 단계에 있다 합니다.

3. 귀하는 미국무성(Legal Adviser, Korea Desk,

Bureau of Economic Affairs)및 국방성(International Security Affairs) 당국과 접촉하여 우리측에
유리한 결정이 내려지도록 교섭하시고 그 결과를 보고하시는
동시에 가급적이면 본건에 관한 정확한 통신 내용을 입수
송부하시기 바랍니다.

　　　　4. 본건에 관한 관련 사실은 다음과 같읍니다.

　　　　　　가. 한.미 군대 지위 협정 제 6조 2항은 미군의 공공
용역 사용은 우선 순위, 조건및 요율에 있어 다른 어느 사용자
보다 불리하지 않을것임을 규정하고 있고, 동조 합의 의사록
1항은 대한 민국 정부가 우선 순위, 조건및 요율 변경을 결정
하는 경우 합동위원회의 사전 협의 대상이 된다고 규정하고
있읍니다.

　　　　　　나. 동 협정 한미 합동위원회는 68. 3. 14. 제 22차회의 에서
건기 협의 절차를 채택하였는바, (기송 회의록 참조) 그 개요는
비공식 사전 협의, 공식 결정후 문서 협의를 정하되 미측은
6조 2항 규정 이행을 확인 할것이며, 협의 완료시가지는 구
요금을 지불하고 협의 완료후 신요금을 시행일자 부터 소급 청산
한다는 취지이며, 본 절차 채택시 한국 대표는 6조 합의록은
"합의" 아닌 "협의"를 규정하고 있으며, 어떠한 경우 에도 동협의
절차가 사실상의 거부권 행사로 변질될수 없다는 유보를
붙였는바, 미국 대표는 이에 동의 하였읍니다.

　　　　　　다. 건기 요금에 관하여는 (별첨 요율표 P. 10 참조)

(1) 계약 용량 200 Kw 이하의 수출업자에게는 30 % 할인

(2) 건기 요금이 총 생산비의 20 % , 30 % , 40% ,및 50 % 에
달하는 생산업자에 대하여는 각각 15% , 20 % , 25% ,및 30%

의 합인

(3) 상수도용 동력에는 46.7% 의 할인

이 각각 규정되어있는바, 미측은 전기 할인 특히 수출산업에 대한

할인에 관하여는 이를 폐지하든지 미군에게도 최대 할인율을 적용

하여야 한다고 주장하고 있읍니다.

   다. 인천 상수도료에 관하여는 미군에 대하여 특수 공공

기관 요율 (1 입방미터당 30원)을 미군에게 적용하고자 하는바,

목욕탕 용수(입방미터당 21원)와 비교하여 대량 수요라는점에서

차별대우가 부당하며, 타 지방요율과의 균형상으로 보아도 목욕탕

요율 적용이 타당하다는것이 미측 주장입니다. (별첨 인천 수도

요율표및 지역별 수도요금표 참조)

   5. 전기 2개 문제중 인천시 수도 요율 문제는 관련 금액의

규모가 비교적 적어서 상금 심각한 절충이 없었으며, 우리측 논거가

박약하다고 사료되므로, 그것이 지방자치단체가 독립 경영한다는

사정으로 인한 시정 절차의 행정기술상의 문제가 있기는 하나

미측요구에 응하는 방향으로 해결될 여지 한다는 것이 본부의

이며, 다만 해결시기는 전기 요금문제와 일괄 타결함이 하려는것이

본부의 방침입니다.

   6. 한.미합동위원회의 공공요율분과위원회에서 한국측이

공식으로 주장한내용은 다음과 같읍니다.

   가. 특수 산업에 대한 할인은 별도 요율이 아니고, 내용적

으로는 보조금 지불의 성격이며, 6조 1항과는 관계가 없다.

   나. 4종의 특별할인은 목적별 용도별이므로 미군에 대한

차별대우가 아니며, 미군도 소정 목적으로 전기를 사용하는 경우에는

할인율을 적용할것이다.

1072

이에 대하여 미측은 국고 재원으로서 정식으로 보조금을 지불할

경우 아무런 이의가 없다고 하여 그 선에서 해결을 추진하였으나,

보조금 교부가 현실적으로 어렵다는점, 미측의 입장이 수출산업

할인에 관하여서만 문제시하는지 전 할인요율을 문제시 하는지의

태도 불분명, 보조금 형태에 있어 형태 불문이라는 미군 측 입장과

보조금이라 할지라도 전기 요금을 근거로하는 형태는 그 효과가 동일

하다는 USAID 측 견해와의 혼선등으로 해결을 보지 못 하였읍니다.

(별첨 해결안 참조)

7. 이러한 사정으로 본건의 해결이 지연되므로 우리측은 문제를

확대하여 다음과 같은 점을 지적하여 미측의 호의적 고려을 촉구하고

있읍니다.

가. 현 협정 6조 2항은 무리이며, 장기적으로는 개정을

요하며, 적어도 그 해석에 관한 명시적 양해 사항의 채택이 필요하다.

(1) 별첨 협정에서 보는바와 같이 미국이 체결한 군대 지위협정은

거개가 무규정, 내국민 대우, 유사여건하의 여타 사용자와의 동등

이상대우, 주둔국 정부기관 특히 군대와의 동등대우를 규정하고

있는데 반하여 유독 한국만이 최혜대우를 규정하고 있는바, 한국이

차별대우를 받아야할 이유가 없으며, 대한 차별대우가 미국의 의사

라고는 믿지 않는다. 전기 다른국가와의동이 초항정신에미측어볼때

(2) 극빈자, 재해지역을 위한 구호적 특수 요율등 사회정책상의

특수요율, 경제정책상의 특수 요율등 예외적인 재정 보조적 특수

요율을 정하여야할 필요성은 배제할수 없을것이며, 그러한 경우

파견국도 보조대상이 되어야 한다고는 사료되지 않는다.

(3) no less favorable than any other user 라는

어구는 문자 그대로 집행할수 없으며, other users of similar

category under similar circumstances 라는 부차적인

척도에 대한 묵시적 양해가 없는 경우 도저히 상식으로 납득할수

없는 구단적인 경우가 발생함은 예컨대 유아의 경우 철도는 무료

항공기는 1할인바 미군이 타 하여 무료 또는 1할 운임을 주장할수

없음은 명백하다. 또 대부분의 공공요금은 실질비용과 가격

정책상 사용조건, 용도, 사용량에 따라 상이하는 정액, 체감요율

제도를 병행하고 있어 경제 원칙상 타당한 차별과 최혜대우 원칙

간의 한계선을 확정하기는 이론적, 기술적으로 극히 곤란하여

분쟁의 요인이 될수 있다.

(4) 결국 reasonable interpretation 이라는 부차적

척도의 병용이 불가피한바 이러한 이유로 미측의 해석에도 일관성이

결여되고 있으며, 동 규정의 실질 내용의 불안정 합리적 시행을

곤란하게 하고 불필요한 마찰의 요인이 될것이다 ~~우리 입장으로는~~

~~내정관섭의 구실이 될 가능성 마저 있다.~~

이러한 우리 주장에 대하여 미측 실무자는 clarifying

understandings 의 필요성을 인정하고 있으며 any other

user 대신으로 comparable user 라는 개념이 타당

함을 인정하기에 이르렀으며 이에 대한 본국 정부 양해를 구하는것이

전기 청훈의 하나의 목적인것으로 사료됩니다. (다만 이 경우에도

무엇이 comparable 하냐는 내용은 매우 상세히

규정되어야 할것으로 사료됩니다.)

　　나. 협정 6조 2항의 priorities, conditions and

rates or tariffs 가 개별적으로 no less favorable

하여야 하느냐, 그것이 전체적으로 no less favorable

하면 가하느냐의 문제.

공공 용역의 실질 원가는 그 공급 조건과 밀접한 관계가 있는바,

공공용역 시설의 확장과 개선에 막대한 경제 원조를 제공하는

미국의 입장으로서는 수입부족으로 인한 기본투자의 황폐화가

그 본의가 아닐것으로 최소한 원가는 부담하는 것이 그의 의사일

것이고, 요컨대 미군 사용분에 대한 전체 경비의 fair share

이상을 지불하지 않는 것이 미측 목적일것인바 따라서 전체로서

no less favorable   하면 족하다는 것이 우리측 해석임.

전기공사항에서 취급

미측은 개별적으로 no less favorable   하여야 할것으로

해석한다는 발언이 많았으나 선례로서 철도 요금의 경우 화물운임에

있어 특혜 요율이 설정되어 있었으나(수출물자, 연료, 광석) 이에는

이의를 제기치 않았으며, 그 이유는 미군이 우선권, 사용조건등에

여러가지 혜택을 입고 있으므로 상쇄하여 전체적으로 no less

favorable   하다고 인정하여 적절한 예를 들어 반박하면 답변에

궁하게 되고 있음.

　　　다. 이상 전기 요금은 미군에 대한 고의적인 부당한 차별이

아님.

6조 2항 교섭기록에 의하면 우리측은 최후까지 미.일협정유형

(정부각부, 또는 정부기관, 군대와 동일 대우)을 주장한데 대하여

미측이 현 자구를 주장한것은 과거 경험에 의하면 어데까지가 정부

기관인가의 정의에 있어 분쟁이 있었으므로 이를 방지하여야하며,

미측의 목표는 요컨대 요율 조작에 의하여 부당하게 차별대우를

받는것을 방지하는데 있다는 취지의 설명을 하였는바 다음과 같은

사실로 현 전기요금이 고의적이며 부당한 대 미군 차별이 아님은

명백하다.

(1) 한국의 특수한 제도로서 전기 요금에 15% 의 전기 까스세를

부과하고 있는바, 미군의 실제 부담은 동 세금 면제로 정부기관,

국군에 비하여 15% 적다.

(2) 미군부대에 대하여는 상시 송전을 위하여 단독 송전 시설,

신규 송전 시설등으로 최우선 배전을 하고 있으며, 이를 위한

막대한 경비를 부담하고 있다.

(3) 미측이 문제시하고 있는 특수 산업용 배전은 한전의 총 배전량

의 0.3%에 미달하며, 이는 예외적 요율이다

      박. 미측 입장의 일관성 결여

(1) 철도 요금의 경우에는 특수 요율을 문제시하지 않으면서

전기, 수도 요금에서만 문제를 제기함은 이해키 곤란하며, 미측은

그 이유를 명시하여야 할것이다.

(2) 전기 요금에 있어서도 상수도용 및 도서지역 특수 요금은

문제시 하지 아니하고 유독 수출산업에 관하여서만 역점을 두고

있는데 대하여도 그 이유가 명시되어야 할것이다.

이러한 일관성의 결여는 감면 금액의 중요성에 따라 문제를 택일

하고 있다는 해명이 가능하나 반면에는 미측 이의 제시의 자의성을

말하는 것으로서 우리측의 방침 결정에 곤란을 주는 것으로 볼수 있다.

      마. 미측의 절차상의 무리

(1) 미측이 6조합의 의사록 1항의 협의 절차와 6조 2항 규정을

결합하여 1년 이상이나 신요율 지불을 거부하고 있는 것은 "협의"

를 사실상의 거부권으로 변질시키고 있는것으로서 유감이라 하여야

할것이다.

(2) 현 요금 인상전에도 미측이 문제시하고 있는 특혜 요율은 존재

하였는바 미측이 6조 2항 위반으로서 신요율 지불을 거부한다면

당연히 협정 발효(67. 2.9)직후부터 이를 제기하고 동의자 부터

소급하여 할인 요율 적용을 주장하여야 타당할것인바 그렇지

않고 구요율을 계속 지불하고 있음은 논리적 모순이다

첨부 : 1. - 인상 전기 요율표   p - 10 사본

2 - 인천시 수도 요율표

3 - 미군이 지불하는 지역별 수도 요금표

4 - 미측이 제시한 최종 타협안 (비공식, 매체뿐)

5 - 미국이 체결한 군대 지위협정 중 공공 용역관계

조항표.   끝.

외   무   부

미이 731- 11444.   1969. 2. 14.

수신 : 주미대사

제목 : 주한미군 공공요금에 관한 대미교섭

1. 1967년 년말에서 1968년 년초에 궁하여 각종 공공요금이
인상되었는바, 주한미군에 대한 인상요금 적용에 있어 대부분
원만해결되었으나, 전기 요금및 일천시 상수도 요금에 관하여는
한.미간의 이견으로 상금 타결을 보지 못하여 미군은 계속 인상전
구요금을 지불하고 있어 그 해결이 시급합니다.

2. 당지 주한 미군 당국및 미국대사관은 장기간의 절충끝에
금년 년초 본국정부에 기본방침에 관한 청훈 천문을 마련한바,
화부 당국은 최근 추가 자료를 지시하여 왔으며, 당지 미군당국은
대사관을 통하여 금명간 지시 추가 자료를 전문으로 보고할
단계에 있다 합니다.

3. 귀하는 미국무성(Legal Adviser, Korea Desk,
 Bureau of Economic Affairs   )   및 국방성

 International Security Affairs   )   당국과

261

723.16(3)-3

접촉하여 우리측에 유리한 결정이 내리도록 교섭하시고 그 결과를 보고하시는 동시에 가급적이면 본건에 관한 정확한 통신 내용을 입수 송부하시기 바랍니다.

4. 본건에 관한 관련 사실은 다음과 같읍니다.

가. 한.미 군대지위협정 제6조 2항은 미군의 공공용역 사용은 우선 순위, 조건및 요율에 있어 다른 어느 사용자보다 불리하지 않을것임을 규정하고 있고 동조 합의 의사록 1항은 대한민국 정부가 우선 순위, 조건및 요율 변경을 결정하는 경우 합동위원회의 사건 협의 대상이 된다고 규정하고 있읍니다.

나. 동 협정 한.미합동위원회는 68. 3. 14.제 22차회의 에서 전기 협의절차를 채택하였는바 (기송 회의록 참조) 그 개요는 비공식 사건 협의, 공식 결정후 문서 협의를 경하되 미측은 6조 2항 규정이행을 확인할 것이며, 협의 완료시 까지는 구 요금을 지불하고 협의 완료후 신요금을 시행일자부터 소급정산 한다는 취지이며, 본 절차 채택시 한국 대표는 6조 합의의사록은 "합의"아닌 "협의"를 규정하고 있으며, 어떠한 경우에도 동협의 절차가 사실상의 거부권 행사로 변질될수 없다는 유보를 붙였는 바, 미국대표는 이에 동의 하였읍니다.

다. 전기 요금에 관하여는 (별첨 요율표 p .10 참조)
(1) 계약 용량 200 Kw 이하의 수용업자에게는 30 %할인

262   6P ᵃ 16

(2) 전기 요금이 총생산비의 20 %, 30 %, 40 % 및 50 % 에 달하는 생산업자에 대하여는 각각 15 %, 20 %, 25 %, 및 30 % 의 할인

(3) 상수도용 동력에는 46.7 % 의 할인

이 각각 규정되어 있는바 미측은 전기 할인 유희 수용산업에 대한 할인에 관하여는 이를 폐지하든지 미군에게도 최대할인율을 적용하여야 한다고 주장하고 있습니다.

바. 인천 상수도료에 관하여는 미군에 대하여 특수 공공 기금 요율 (1입방미터당 30원)을 미군에게 적용하고자 하는바, 무유탕 용수 (입방미터당 21원)와 비교하여 대량 수요라는점에서 차별대우가 부당하며, 타 지방요율과의 균형상으로 보아도 무유탕 요율 적용이 마땅하다는 것이 미측 주장입니다. (별첨 인천 수도 요율표및 지역별 수도요금표 참조)

5. 전기 2개 문제중 인천시 수도요율 문제는 관련 금액의 규모가 비교적 적어서 상금 심각한 격론이 없었으며, 오덕측 논거가 박약하다고 사료되므로 그것이 지방자치단체가 독립 경영한다는 사정으로 인한 시정 절차의 행정기술상의 문제가 있기는 하나 미측요구에 응하는 방향으로 해결될수도 있을것이라는 것이

263

본부의 잠정적 견해이며, 다만 해결시기는 전기 요금문제와 일괄 타결함이 좋을것이다는 것이 본부의 방침입니다.

6. 한.미합동위원회의 공공요율분과위원회에서 한국측이 공식 으로 주장한 내용은 다음과 같습니다.

가. 특수 산업에 대한 할인은 요율이 아니고 내용적 으로는 보조금 지불의 성격이며 6조 1항과는 관계가 없다.

나. 4종의 특별할인은 목적별,용도별 이므로 미군에 대한 차별대우가 아니며, 미군도 소정 목적으로 전기를 사용하는 경우 에는 할인율은 적용할것이다.

이에 대하여 미측은 국고 재원으로서 정식으로 보조금을 지불할 경우 아무런 이의가 없다고 하여 그 선에서 해결을 추진하였으나, 보조금 교부가 현실적으로 어렵다는 점, 미측의 입장이 수출산업 할인에 관하여서만 문제시 하는지 전 할인요율을 문제시 하는지의 태도 불분명 소위 보조금 형태에 있어 역할문문 이라는 미군당국의 입장과 보조금이라 할지라도 전기 요금을 근거로하는 형태는 그 효과가 동일하다는 USAID 측 견해와의 혼선등으로 해결을 보지 못하였읍니다. (별첨 해결안 참조)

7. 이러한 사정으로 본건의 해결이 지연되므로 우리측은 문제를

264   6 [3] 8

확대하여 다음과 같은 점을 지적하여 미측의 호의적 고려를 촉구하고 있읍니다.

　가. 현 협정 6조 2항은 무의미하며, 장기적으로는 개정을 요하며, 적어도 그 해석에 관한 명시적 양해사항의 채택이 필요하다.

　　(1) 별첨 협정에서 보는바와 같이 미국이 체결한 군대지위 협정은 거개가 무규정, 내국민 대우, 유사여건하의 여타 사용자와의 동등 이상대우, 주둔국정부기관 특히 군대와의 동등대우를 규정하고 있는데 반하여 유독 한국만이 최혜대우를 규정하고 있는바, 한국이 차별대우를 받아야할 이유가 없으며, 대한 전기 다른 국가와의 동일 조항의 정신에 비추어 본데 대한 차별대우가 미국의 의사라고는 믿지 않는다.

　　(2) 구빈자, 재해지역을 위한 구호적 특수 요율등 사회 정책상의 특수 요율, 경제 정책상의 특수요율등 예외적인 재정 보조적 특수요율을 정하여야 할 필요성은 배제할수 없을것이며, 그러한 경우 파견국도 보조 대상이 되어야 한다고는 사료되지 않는다.

　　(3) no less favorable than any other user 라는 어구는 문자 그대로 집행할수 없으며, other users of

265

similar category under similar circumstances

라는 부차적인 척도에 대한 묵시적 양해가 없는 경우 도저히
상식으로 납득할수 없는 극단적인 경우가 발생함은 예컨대
유아의 경우 철도는 무료 항공기는 1할인바 미군이박 하여 무료
또는 1할 운임을 주장할수 없음은 명백하다. 또 대부분의
공공요금은 실질비용과 가격 정책상 사용조건, 용도, 사용량에
따라 상이하는 경위, 체감요율제도를 병행하고 있어 경제
원칙상 타당한 차별과 특혜대우 원칙간의 한계선을 확정하기는
이론적, 기술적으로 구히 곤란하여 분쟁의 요인이 될수 있다.

(4) 결구 reasonable interpretation   이라는
부차적척도의 병용이 불가피한바 이러한 이유로 미측의 해석에도
일관성이 결어되고 있으며, 동 규정의 실질 내용의 불안정은
합리적 시행을 곤란하게 하고 불필요한 마찰의 요인이 될것이다.
이러한 우리 주장에 대하여 미측 실무자는   clarifying
    understandings 의 필요성을 인정하고 있으며, any
other user   대신으로 comparable user 라는 개념이
타당함을 인정하기에 이르렀으며, 이에 대한 본국정부양해를 구
하는 것이 전기 청훈의 하나의 목적인것으로 사료됩니다. (다만
경우에도 무엇이 comparable 하냐는 내용은 더욱 상세이

규정되어야 할것으로 사료됩니다.

　나.　협정 6조 2항의 priorities, conditions and rates or tariffs 가 개별적으로 no less favorable 하여야 하노냐, 그것이 전체적으로 no less favorable 하면 가하노냐의 문제

공공용역의 실질 원가는 그 공급 조건과 밀접한 관계가 있는바, 공공용역 시설의 확장과 개선에 막대한 경제원조를 제공하는 미국의 입장으로서는 수입부족으로 인한 기본투자의 황폐화가 그 본의가 아닌것으로 최소한 원가는 부담하는 것이 그의 의사일것이고, 으런데 미군 사용분에 대한 전체 경비의 fair share 이상을 지불하지 않는 것이 미측 목적일것인바 따라서 전체로서 no less favorable 하면 족하다는 것이 우리측 해석임. 미측은 전기 각 사항에서 각각 개별적으로 no less favorable 하여야 할것으로 해석한다는 발언이 많았으나 실례로서 철도 요금의 경우 화물운임에 있어 특혜요율이 설정되어 있었으나 (수용물자, 연료, 광석) 이때는 이외를 제기치 않았으며, 그 이유는 미군이 우선권, 사용조건등에 여러가지 혜택을 입고 있으므로 상세하여 전체적으로 no less favorable 하다고 인정하여 막연한 예를 들어 반박하면 답변에 궁하게 되고 있다.

260

다. 인상 전기 요금은 미군에 대한 그 의적인 부당한 차별이 아니다.

6조 2항 교섭기록에 의하면 우리측은 최우가거 미.일협정 유형 (정부각부, 또는 정부기관, 국군과 동일 대우)을 주장함에 대하여 미측이 현 자구를 주장한것은 과거 경험에 의하면 어디까지가 정부기관인가의 정의에 있어 분쟁이 있었으므로 이를 방지하여야 하며 미측의 목표는 오련데 요율 조작에 의하여 부당하게 차별 대우를받는것을 방지하는데 있다는 취지의 설명을 하였는바 다음과 같은 사실로 현 전기 요금이 그의적이며, 부당한 대 미군 차별이 아님은 명백하다.

(1) 한국의 특수한 처지로서 전기 요금에 15%의 전기가스세를 부과하고 있는바, 미군의 실제 부담은 동 세금 면제로 정부기관, 국군에 비하여 15% 적다.

(2) 미군부대에 대하여는 상시 송전을 위하여 단독 송전 시설, 신규 송전 시설등으로 최우선 배선을 하고 있으며, 이를 위한 막대한 경비를 부담하고 있다.

(3) 미측이 문제시하고 있는 특수 산업용 배전은 한전의 총 배전량의 0.3%에 미달하며, 이는 예외적 요율이다.

268

라. 미측 입장의 일관성 결여

(1) 철도 요금의 경우에는 육수 요율을 문제시하지 않으면서 전기, 수도요금에서만 문제를 제기함은 이해키 곤란하며, 미측은 그 이유를 명시하여야 할 것이다.

(2) 전기 요금에 있어서도 삼주도용및 도서지역 육수 요금은 문제시 하지 아니하고 유독 수출산업에 관하여서만 위점을 두고 있는데 대하여도 그 이유가 명시 되어야 할 것이다.

이러한 일관성의 결여는 관련 금액의 중요성에 따라 문제를 국한하고 있다는 태명이 가능하나 반면에는 미측 어의 지시의 자의성을 말하는 것으로서 우리측의 방침 결정에 곤란을 주는것으로 볼수 있다.

마. 미측의 절차상의 무력

(1) 미측어 6조항의 의사록 1항의 협의 절차와 6조 2항 구정을 결합하여 1년 이상이나 심요을 지불을 거부하고 있는것은 "협의" 를 사실상의 거부권으로 변질시키고 있는것으로서 유감이라 하여야 할 것이다.

(2) 현 요금 인상건에도 미측이 문제시하고 있는 육에요율은 존재하였는바 미측이 6조 2항 위반으로서 심요을 지불을 거부한다면

269

6 3 13

당연이 협정 발로(67. 2. 9) 직후부터 이를 제기하고 동일자부터
소급하여 합의 요율 적용을 주장하여야 막당할 지인바 그렇지
않고 구요율을 계속 지불하고 있음은 논리적 모순이다.

첨부 : 1 - 인상 전기 요율표 p - 10 사본
      2 - 인천시 수도 요율표
      3 - 미군이 지불하는 지역별 수도 요금표
      4 - 미측이 제시한 의종 합의안(비공식, 대체불)
      5 - 미국이 체결한 군대지위협정중 공공 용역관지
          조항요. 끝.

                  외 무 부 장 관

전기요금 대 미군 적용에 관한 문제 요약

1. 분쟁점 및 상방 입장

가. 분쟁점

67. 11. 1. 인상전기 요금이 시행되었는바, 신요율표에는
농사용, 상수도 양수용, 도서지역, 및 특수산업용에 대한
특혜요율 또는 할인요율이 정하여 지고 있으며(별첨 요율표
참조) 미측은 특히 특수산업용(수출산업) 할인제를 주목하고
협정 6조 2항의 priorities, conditions and rates or
tariffs no less favorable than any other user
에 위반한다 하여 6조 합의 의사록 1항 소정의 협의절차에서
이의를 제기 상금 구요율에 의한 사용료를 지불하고 있음.
단, 합의된 협의절차에 의하면 협의절차 완료시 신요율
발효시부터 소급하여 신요율을 적용 납부하기로 되어 있고,
주한 미군 사령관은 신요율에 의한 지불 소요자금의 영달을
이미 수령하여 보관중이라고 문서로 언명한바 있음.

나. 미측 주장

(1) 미측은 전기 4종의 특혜요율중 특히 수출산업에 대한
할인(15%, 20%, 30%) 에 대하여 이의를 제기하고, 6조 1항
any other user 에는 아무런 제한어구가 없으므로

미군이 최저요율의 적용을 받아야 하며, 따라서 전기
할인제를 적용한다고 주장, 미군도 외화로 지불하고
있으며, 이점에서 수출산업과 성질이 같다고 지적하였음.

(2) 미측은 요율수준의 고하를 문제시하고 있는 것이 아니고
최혜대우를 받어야 한다는 원측 준수를 요구한다.

(3) 한국정부가 정책상 보조금 지급을 결정하는 권한을 행사
하는 것은 미국이 관여할바 아니나, 보조금이라면 그
취지가 명시되는 방법, 예컨대 국고금 지불, 세금 공제
등의 방식을 취하여야 하며, 요율을 할인하는 경우에는
미측도 동일할인을 받어야 한다.

(4) 현 협정하에서는 신요율표를 인정 지불하는 경우, 법적
책임을 불면한다.

다. 한국측 주장

(1) 특수산업에 대한 할인은 별도 요율이 아니고 내용적으로는
보조금 지불의 성격이며, 따라서 6조 1항과는 관계가
없다.

(2) 수출산업에 대한 할인은 외화획득이 주목적이 아니며,
유치산업보조에 의한 국제경쟁력 강화를 목적으로 하는
것이다.

(3) 4종의 특수요율은 목적별, 용도별이므로 미군에 대하여
차별대우가 아니며, 미군도 소정목적으로 전기를 사용하는
경우에는 동 요율을 적용하는 것이다.

2. 대책

공공요율문제 전반에 근하여 다음 두개의 단기 및 장기대책제을 강구하여야 할것으로 사료됨.

가. 당면대책 - 협의절차의 조속완료에 의한 신요율에 의한 미납요금의 징수·전기요금이 인상시행된지 1년이 경과한 오늘날 까지 미해결(전기요금외에 상수도 요금도 유사한 이유로 협의절차 미완) 상태에 있으므로 더 이상 방치하는 경우 정치문제화하여 양국 우호관계에 영향을 미칠 우려가 있으며 따라서 조속해결이 필요함.

최종타개책으로 현지당국의 법적 책임문제를 고려하여 요율체계의 실질 내용에는 변경없이 보조금이라는 성격을 명시하는 형태로 문서작성하여 미 본국정부의 양해를 얻기로 하고, 그 문서형태를 성안하기 위하여 7월 30일 우리측 초안을 수교한바 상금 반응이 없으나, 현 협정 자구 또는 미측 해석 테두리내에서는 이것이 최선안으로 사료되므로 적극 추진을 노력함이 가하다고 사료됨.

나. 장기대책 - 협정 6조 2항의 개정 또는 해석에 관한 공식 양해 규정

별첨 협정예 집에서도 보는바와 같이 미국이 체결한 군대지위협정은 거개가 무규정, 내국민 대우, 동일여건 여타 사용자와의 동등이상 대우, 주둔국 정부기관, 특히 군대와의 동등대우,

273

를 규정하고 있는데 반하여 유독 한국만이 최혜대우를
규정하고 있어 분쟁이 야기되었는바, 한국만이 차별대우를
받아야 할 특수여건이 없으므로 일반유형 채택을 목적으로 한
협정개정 교섭, 장차의 분쟁 재발 가능성을 제거함이
가장 유리할 것으로 사료됨.

전기 개정교섭이 불가능하거나 부적당하다고 판명되는 경우
에는 후술하는 바와 같이 현 6조 2항 any other user
운운의 자구는 표면상 명백하면서도 현실적으로는 문자 그대로
의 시행이 불가능한 것으로서 결국 "온당한 또는 합리적인
해석" (reasonable interpretation)이라는 부차적
척도의 병용이 불가피하며, 이러한 이유로 타여 미측의 해석
에도 일관성이 결여되고 있는바, 해석에 관한 공식 양해가
채택되지 않을경우 동 협정의 실집내용이 안정성을 결여하여
요율기타 조건변경 때마다 불필요한 분쟁이 발생할 가능성을
내포하고 있으며, 따라서 몇개의 양해사항을 명문화 하는
교섭이 필요하다고 사료됨.

3. 문제에 관련되는 제요소.

가. 현 6조 2항은 무리

(1) 현 6조 2항이 타국과의 조약에에 유례가 없음은 기술
하였거니와 도시 극빈자, 재해지역을 위한 구호적
특수요율등 사회정책상의 특수요율, 경제정책상의
특수요율등 예외적인 재정보조적 특수요율을 정하여야

할 필요는 배제할수 없을 것이며, 그러한 경우 주둔국도 재정보조대상이 되어야 한다고는 사료되지 않으며, 잘못하면 내정간섭을 유발할 가능성마저 없지않음.

(2) no less favorable than any other user 라는 어구는 문자 그대로 해석할수 없으며, other users of similar category under similar circumstances 라는 묵시적 양해가 없는경우 도저히 상식으로 납득 할수 없는 극단적인 경우가 발생함은 예컨데 유아의 경우 철도는 무료, 항공기는 1할인바, 미군이탁하여 무료 또는 1할 운임을 주장하지 못함은 명백한것으로 알수있다. 또 대부분의 공공요금은 가격정책상 목적 및 용도별, 이용량, 이용조건에 따라 상이하는 정액요율, 체감요율 제도를 병용하고있어, 타당한 차별과 최혜대우간의 한계선을 확정하기는 기술적, 이론적으로 극히 곤란하며, 분쟁의 요인이 될것임.

ㄴ. 6조 2항의 priorities, conditions and rates or tariffs 가 개별적으로 no less favorable 하여야 하느냐, 그것이 전체적으로 no less fovorabl한편 가하느냐의 문제

개별적으로 최선이어야 한다고 해석하는것이 미측에 유리한것은 자명하며, 미측은 그러한 해석을 취한다는 발언이 많았으나 우리측은 그것을 수락할수 없다고 사료되며, 선례로서는 철도요금의 경우 화물선 운임에

있어 일부 특혜요율이 설정되어 있었으나(수출물가, 연료,
광석등) 이에는 이의를 제기치 않었으며. 그 이유는 미측이
우선권, 사용조건 등에 여러가지 혜택을 입고 있으므로
상세하여 전체적으로 no less favorable 하다고 인정
한다는 것이었음. 만일, package standard 를
채택한다면, 전기 (수도의 경우도 동일) 의 경우, 상시송전
을 위한 별도 송전선 설치, 신규송전 시설 등 한전이 막대한
추가경비를 부담하고 있다는 사실이 고려에 들어가야 할것임.

다. 인상요율은 미군에 대한 고의적인 부당한 차별이 아님.
6조 2항 교섭기록에 의하면 아측은 최후까지 미.일 협정 유형
(정부 각부 또는 정부기관, 군대와 동등대우) 을 주장한데
대하여 미측이 현 자구를 주장한것은 과거 경험에 의하면
어데까지가 정부기관인가의 정의에 있어 분쟁이 있었으므로
이를 방지하여야 하며, 미측의 목표는 요컨대, 요율조작에
의하여 부당하게 차별대우를 받은것을 방지하는데 있다는 취지의
설명을 하였는바, 다음과 같은 사실로 된 전기요금이 고의적이며
부당한 대미군 차별이 아님은 명백함.

(1) 정부 각부 및 국군요율에 비하여 동일요율에서 대미군 요율
  은 소비세 부분이 공제되고 있다.

(2) 미군 부대에 대하여는 단독 송전선, 신규송전선 시설등으로
  최우선 배전을 하고 있으며, 이를 위하여 막대한 비용을
  부담하고 있다.

(3) 미측이 문제시하고 있는 특수산업용 배전은 한전의

전 배전량의 0.3%에 불과하며, 전적으로 예외적 요율이다.

타. 미측 입장의 일관성 결여

(1) 철도요금의 경우에는 특수요율을 문제시하지 않으면서

전기, 수도요금에서만 문제를 제기함은 이해키 곤난

하며, 미측은 그 이유를 명시하여야 할 것이다.

(2) 전기요금에 있어서도 상수도용 및 도서지역 특수요금은

문제시 하지 않으면서 유독 수출산업에 관하여서만

역점을 두고 있는것도 이론적 근거를 제시하여야 할것이다.

이러한 일관성의 결여는 관계금액의 중요성에 따라

문제를 국한하고 있을 것이라는 해명이 가능하나, 반면

에는 미측의 법적 책임 온운의 허구성을 말하는 것이고,

또 미측의 이의 제기의 자의성을 말하는 것으로서

우리측의 사전대책의 방향을 상실케 하고 있음을 지적

하여야 할 것임.

마. 미측 반응의 절차상의 무리

(1) 미측이 합의의사록 1 소정협의 절차와 6조 2항 규정을

결합하여 신요율 지불을 보류하고 있는 것은 "협의" 가

"동의" 또는 거부권을 내포하지 않는다는 교섭기록의

명문에 불구하고 "협의"를 사실상의 거부권 또는 정지권

으로 변질시키고 있는 것으로 유감이라 하여야 할것이다.

(2) 67. 11. 1. 요율개정 이전에도 현재 미측이 이의를
제기하고 있는 특혜요율은 존재하였으며, 미측도
그 사실을 알고 있는바, 미측 6조 2항의 위반을 이유로
신요율 적용을 거부한다면 당연히 협정발효 직후부터
이를 제기하고 또 11. 1. 이전 요금에 대하여 소급
할인 주장하여야 타당할 것인바, 그러지 않고 구요율을
계속 지불하고 있음은 논리적 모순임.   끝

첨부 : 1. 각국 협정 공공용역항 발췌.
      2. 개정 전기요율표.

278

전기요금 대 미군 적용에 관한 문제 요약

1. 분쟁점 및 쌍방 입장

  가. 분쟁점

    67. 11. 1. 인상전기 요금이 시행되었는바, 신요율표에는
    농사용, 상수도 양수용, 도서지역,및 특수산업용에 대한
    특혜요율 또는 할인요율이 정하여 지고 있으며(별첨 요율표
    참조) 미측은 특히 특수산업용(수출산업) 할인제를 주목하고
    협정 6조 2항의 priorities, conditions and rates or
    tariffs no less favorable than any other user
    에 위반한다 하여 6조 합의 의사록 1항 소정의 협의절차에서
    이의를 제기 상금 구요율에 의한 사용료를 지불하고 있음.
    단, 합의된 협의절차에 의하면 협의절차 완료시 신요율
    발효시부터 소급하여 신요율을 적용 납부하기로 되어 있고,
    주한 미군 사령관은 신요율에 의한 지불 소요자금의 영달을
    이미 수령하여 보관중이라고 문서로 언명한바 있음.

  나. 미측 주장

    (1) 미측은 전기 4종의 특혜 요율중 특히 수출산업에 대한
      할인(15%, 20%, 30%)에 대하여 의의를 제기하고, 6조 1항
      any other user 에는 아무런 제한어구가 없으므로

미군이 최저요율의 적용을 받아야 하며, 따라서 전기
할인제를 적용한다고 주장, 미군도 외화도 지불하고
있으며, 이점에서 수출산업과 성질이 같다고 지적하였음.

(2) 미측은 요율수준의 고하를 문제시하고 있는 것이 아니고
최혜대우를 받어야 한다는 엄측 준수를 요구한다.

(3) 한국정부가 정책상 보조금 지급을 결정하는 권한을 행사
하는 것은 미국이 관여할바 아니나, 보조금이라면 그
취지가 명시되는 방법, 예컨대 국고금 지불, 세금 공제
등의 방식을 취하여야 하며, 요율을 할인하는 경우에는
미측도 동일할인을 받어야 한다.

(4) 현 협정하에서는 신요율표를 인정 지불하는 경우, 법적
책임을 불면한다.

다. 한국측 주장

(1) 특수산업에 대한 할인은 별도 요율이 아니고 내용적으로는
보조금 지불의 성격이며, 따라서 6조 1항과는 관계가
없다.

(2) 수출산업에 대한 할인은 외화획득이 주목적이 아니며,
유치산업보조에 의한 국제경쟁력 강화를 목적으로 하는
것이다.

(3) 4종의 특수요율은 목적별, 용도별이므로 미군에 대하여
차별대우가 아니며, 미군도 소정목적으로 전기를 사용하는
경우에는 동 요율을 적용하는 것이다.

280

2. 대 책

공공요율문제 전반에 관하여 다음 두개의 단기, 및 장기대책
을 강구하여야 할것으로 사료됨.

가. 당면대책 - 협의절차의 수속완료에 의한 신요율에 의한 미납
요금의 징수.전기요금이 인상시행된지 1년이 경과한 오늘날
까지 미해결(전기요금외에 상수도 요금도 유사한 이유로
협의절차 미완) 상태에 있으므로 더 이상 방치하는 경우 정치
문제화하여 양국 우호관계에 영향을 미칠 우려가 있으며
따라서 조속해결이 필요함.

최종 타개책으로 협지당국의 법적 책임문제를 고려하여 요율
체계의 실질내용에는 변경없이 보조금이라는 성격을 명시하는
형태도 문서작성하여 미 본국정부의 양해를 얻기도 하고, 그
문서형태를 성안하기 위하여 7월 30일 우리측 초안을 수교
한바 상금 반응이 없으나, 현 협정 자구 또는 미측 해석
테두리내에서는 이것이 최선안으로 사료되므로 적극 추진을
노력함이 가하다고 사료됨.

나. 장기대책 - 협정 6조 2항의 개정 또는 해석에 관한 공식
양해 규정
(例示)
별첨 협정에 집에서도 보는바와 같이 미국이 체결한 군대지위
협정은 ~~전기만두가~~ 무규정, 내국민 대우, 동일여건 여타 사용자와
의 동등이상 대우, 주둔국 정부기관, 특히 군대와의 동등 대우,

281

들 규정하고 있는데 반하여 유독 한국만이 최혜대우를
규정하고 있어 분쟁이 야기되었는바, 한국만이 차별대우를
받어야 할 특수여건이 없으므로 일반유형 채택을 목적으로 한
협정개정을 교섭, 장차의 분쟁 재발 가능성을 제거함이
가장 유리할 것으로 사료됨.

전기 개정교섭이 불가능하거나 부적당하다고 판명되는 경우
에는 후술하는 바와 같이 협 6조 2항 **any other user**
운운의 자구는 표면상 명백하면서도 현실적으로는 문자 그대로
의 시행이 불가능한 것으로서 결국 "온당한 또는 합리적인
해석" (**reasonable interpretation**)이라는 부차적
척도의 병용이 불가피하며, 이러한 이유로 하여 미측의 해석
에도 일관성이 결여되고 있는바, 해석에 관한 공식 양해가
채택되지 않을경우 동 협정의 실질내용이 안정성을 결여하여
요율기타 조건변경 이 없을때 마다 불필요한 분쟁이 발생할 가능성을
내포하고 있으며, 따라서 몇개의 양해사항을 명문화 하는
교섭이 필요하다고 사료됨.

3. 문제에 관련되는 제요소
   가. 협 6조 2항은 무리
   (1) 협 6조 2항이 타국과의 조약에에 유례가 없음은 기술
       하였거니와 도시 극빈자, 재해지역을 위한 구호적
       특수요율등 사회정책상의 특수요율, 경제정책상의
       특수요율등 예외적인 재정보조적 특수요율을 정하여야

할 필요는 배제할수 없을 것이며, 그러한 경우 주둔국도
재정보조대상이 되어야 한다고는 사료되지 않으며,
잘못하면 내정간섭을 유발할 가능성마저 없지않음.

(2) no less favorable than any other user
라는 어구는 문자 그대로 해석할수 없으며,

other users of similar category under similar
circumstances 라는 묵시적 양해가 없는경우 도저히 상식으로 납득
할수 없는 극단적인 경우가 발생함은 예컨데 유아의
경우 철도는 무료, 항공기는 1할인바, 미군이라하여
무료 또는 1할 운임을 주장하지 못함은 명백한것으로
알수있다. 또 대부분의 공공요금은 가격정책상 목적
및 용도별, 이용량, 이용조건에 따라 상이하는
정액요율, 체감요율 제도를 병용하고있어, 타당한
차별과 최혜대우간의 한계선을 확정하기는 기술적,
이론적으로 극히 곤란하며, 분쟁의 요인이 될것임.

ㄴ. 6조 2항의 priorities, conditions, and rates or
tariffs 가 개별적으로 no less favorable하여야
하느냐, 그것이 전체적으로no less favorable하면 .
가하느냐의 문제
개별적으로 최선이어야 한다고 해석하는것이 미측에
유리한것은 자명하며, 미측은 그러한 해석을 취한다는
발언이 많았으나 우리측은 그것을 수락할수 없다고
사료되며, 선례로서는 철도요금의 경우 화물선 운임에

있어 일부 특혜요율이 설정되어 있었으나(수출물가, 연료, 광석등) 이에는 이의를 제기치 않았으며, 그 이유는 미측이 우선권, 사용조건 등에 여러가지 혜택을 입고 있으므로 상쇄하여 전체적으로 no less favorable 하다고 인정 한다는 것이었음. 만일, package standard 를 채택한다면, 전기 (수도의 경우도 동일) 의 경우, 상시송전 을 위한 별도 송전선 설치, 신규송전 시설 등 한전이 막대한 추가경비를 부담하고 있다는 사실이 고려에 들어가야 할것임.

다. 인상요율은 미군에 대한 고의적인 부당한 차별이 아님.
6조 2항 교섭기록에 의하면 아측은 최후까지 미.입협정 유형 (정부 각부 또는 정부기관, 군대와 동등대우) 을 주장한데 대하여 미측이 현 자구를 주장한것은 과거 경험에 의하면 어데까지가 정부기관인가의 정의에 있어 분쟁이 있었으므로 이를 방지하여야 하며, 미측의 목표는 요컨데, 요율조작에 의하여 부당하게 차별대우를 받은것을 방지하는데 있다는 취지의 설명을 하였는바, 다음과 같은 사실로 현 전기요금이 고의적이며 부당한 대미군 차별이 아님은 명백함.

(1) 정부 각부 및 국군요율에 비하여 동일요율에서 대미군 요율 은 소비세 부분이 공제되고 있다.

(2) 미군 부대에 대하여는 단독 송전선, 신규송전선 시설등으로 최우선 배전을 하고 있으며, 이를 위하여 막대한 비용을 부담하고 있다.

284

(3) 미측이 문제시하고 있는 특수산업용 배전은 한전의
전 배전량의 0.3%에 불과하며, 전적으로 예외적 요율이다.

타. 미측 입장의 일관성 결여

(1) 철도요금의 경우에는 특수요율을 문제시하지 않으면서
전기, 수도요금에서만 문제를 제기함은 이해키 곤란
하며, 미측은 그 이유를 명시하여야 할 것이다.

(2) 전기요금에 있어서도 상수도용 및 도서지역 특수요금은
문제시 하지 않으면서 유독 수출산업에 관하여서만
역점을 두고 있는것도 이론적 근거를 제시하여야 할것이다.
이러한 일관성의 결여는 관계금액의 중요성에 따라
문제를 국한하고 있을 것이라는 해명이 가능하나, 반면
에는 미측의 법적 책임 운운의 허구성을 말하는 것이고,
또 미측의 이의 제기의 자의성을 말하는 것으로서
우리측의 사전대책의 방향을 상실케 하고 있음을 지적
하여야 할 것임.

마. 미측 반응의 절차상의 무리

(1) 미측이 합의의사록 1 소정협의 절차와 6조 2항 규정을
결합하여 신요율 지불을 보류하고 있는 것은 "협의" 가
"동의" 또는 거부권을 내포하지 않는다는 교섭기록의
명문에 불구하고 "협의"를 사십상의 거부권 또는 정지권
으로 변질시키고 있는 것으로 유감이다 하여야 할것이다.

(2) 67. 11. 1. 요율개정 이전에도 현재 미측이 이의를
제기하고 있는 특혜요율은 존재하였으며, 미측도
그 사실을 알고 있는바, 미측 6조 2항의 위반을 이유로
신요율 적용을 거부한다면 당연히 협정발효 직후부터
이를 제기하고 또도 11. 1. 이전 요금에 대하여 소급
할인 주장하여야 타당할 것인바, 그러지 않고 구요율을
계속 지불하고 있음은 논리적 모순임.   끝

첨부 :   1. 각국 협정 공공용역항 발췌.
         2. 개정 전기요율표.

236

공공 요율 문제 해결을 위한 세가지 방안   (11월 1일)

1. 현 전기 요율표의 특수 규정의 수정

지난 7.30 한국측이 제의한 특수사용자에대한 보조금조로 전기요율을 감액
한다는 제 2항을 수정(별첨참조)하는것을 내용으로하는 서한을 윤국장이 프리드만
중장에게 발송하여 미국대사및 USAID 처장의 동의를 밥도록 하는것.

2. 보조금 지불규정을 요율표에서 삭제하고 별도 규정

우선 한국측에서 특수사용자에 대한 보조금을 공공요율표와 관계없이 별도
규정지불하겠다고하고 그 시행절차는 행정부처간의 조정을 필요로하고 복잡한
수속을 밟아야 함으로 추후 재정 시행한다고 약속함. 이 약속과 동시에 미측은
체불된 요율을 즉시 지불함.

3. 고위층을 통한 미대사와의 해결책 모색

한 고위층을 (국무총리 또는 외무장관)을 통하여 미국대사에게 정책적으로
해결하도록 강력히 압력을 가하는것.

SPECIAL PROVISIONS FOR SUBSIDY

1. Special subsidy may be provided for the following catagories of customers as may be separately determined by the Ministry of Commerce and Industry:

    a. Special Industry

    b. Manicipal Water Service

  ·c. Island Area

2. The subsidy for the special industry will be in accordance with the percentage of utlities purchersed and used in pursuant of export.

288

외 무 부

종 별

번 호 : WUS-0285 일 시 : 151005

수 신 : 주 미 대 사

발 신 : 장 관

2.15. 발송 파우치로 주한 미군 공공요금 문제에 관한 공문 미이
731 - 11444를 발송하였는바, 접수 즉시로 긴급 처리하여 그 결과를 보고
바람. (미이) 끝.

북미2과	2월15일	안	담당	과장	구장
		재			

발신시간 :

최종결재	
지참자	

접 수	담 당	주 무	과 장

289

외 무 부

종 별

번 호 : WUS-0316 일 시 : 081700

수 신 : 주미대사

발 신 : 장 관

연 : 미이 731-11444 (68. 2. 14.) 및 WUS-0285

연호로 지시한 주한미군 공공요금 청산건의 조속한 처리와 결과보고를
바라며, 최종결론도달까지 시간을 요한다면 우선 중간 보고를 바람. (미이)

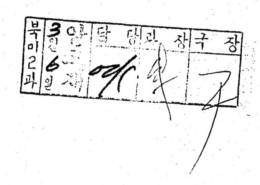

발신시간 :

최종결재	
지참자	

접 수	담 당	주 무	과 장

298

SOFA 한.미국 합동위원회 공공용역 분과위원회, 1968-69 301

외 무 부

대 외 비
종 별

착신전보

번호 : USW -0360 일시 : 111800

수신 : 외무부장관

발신 : 주미 대사

대 : 미이 731-11444, WUS -0316

주한 미군 공공요금에 관한 대미교섭:

1. 대호 지시에 관하여 국무성관계관과 접촉한바를 다음과같이 보고함.

가. 국무성에서는 지난 2월하순 주한 미대사관이 청훈한데대하여 지시를 하달하였다함.
동지시는 주한 미대사관이 국무성에 청훈한 건의를 승인하는 내용으로 본부에서 그간
누차에 걸쳐 미측에게 제시한 안과 그설명을 토의의 근거로한다는것이 포함되어있다함.
확실한 내용에 대하여는 언급하지않으나 전기 요금에 대하여는 아측 제안을 수락할것
으로보이나 인천의 수도요금에 대하여는 아국측의 양보를 고집할것이라는 인상을 받
았음.

나. 이러한 지시를 근거로 미측에서 차기 합동위원회 개최시 미측 태도를 아측에게 제시
하기로되어있다함.

다. 미국정부 내에서는 그간 본건을 중심으로 국무성관계관(한국과 및 법무관실등)과
국방성관계관간에 협의가 있었으며 전기요금에 관한한 한국의 수출진흥을 진작시켜야
한다는 견지하에 수출업자에 대한 특혜적인 보조를 미군에게도 적용시켜야한다는 주장을
미측이 고집하지않아야한다는 결론에 도달한것으로보임.

라. 어떤 사용자보다 불리하지않은 이란 용구에 대하여 국무성 에서는 "일반대중"을
일반적으로 기초로 삼고있으며 정부나 군대가 우대를 받을경우 그를 적용하여 주어야
한다는 평범한 해석을 가지고있으며 특수 사정하에 특정인에게 의식적으로 적요하는
요금을 적용시켜야한다는 극단적인 법해석을 하지않고있는것으로봄.

장관실	총무과	정문국	청와대	경기원	문교부	교통부	조달청		담당	검열	주부	과장
차관실	아주국	외연원	총리실	내무부	농림부	체신부	노동청					
차관보	구미국 O	외정신	중 정	재무부	상공부	문공부	수산청					
기관실	방교국	대사		법무부	건설부	총무처						
의전실	통상국			국방부	보사부	과학기						

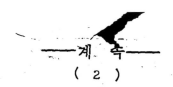

— 계 속 —
(2)

2. 이상에 추가하여 다시 교섭 할 사항이 있으면 지시 하여 주시기 바람(미이)

6P 3 26

292

기 안 용 지

분류기호 문서번호	미이723-	(전화번호)	전결규정 조 항 국 장 전결사항	
처리기한		기 안 자	결 재 자	
시행일자		북미2과		
보존년한		오명두 69. 3. 13.		
보 조 기 관	북미2과장			
협 조				
긴 유 신	경제기획원장관 기획국장	검열 1969.3.13. 통제관	1969. 3. 13 외무부	
수 참 조				
제 목	주한미군에 대한 공공요율			

1. 1967년 년말에서 68년 년초에 걸처 인상된

일련의 공공요율중 대미군사용에 있어 상급 결말을 보지

못한 전기요금 및 인천 상수도 요금에 관하여 주미대사에게

미국무성 당국과 교섭을 지시한바 별첨사본과 같은 전문

보고가 있었아오니 귀부에서 본건 처리 방침 수립에 있어

참고 하시기 바랍니다.

2. 동 전문 보고의 취지는 다음과 같습니다.

가. 국무성에서는 2월 하순 본건에 관하여 주한

미대사관에 지시를 시달하였다하며, 동 지시는 주한미대사관이

청훈한 건의를 승인하는 내용으로 본부에서 누차에 걸처

공통서식 1-2-1 (갑)　　　　　/ 계 속 /　　　　　(18진치) (2급인쇄용지 74g/㎡)
293 (1967. 4. 4. 승인)　　　　　　　　　　　294 (조남성 300,000매 인쇄)

미측에게 제시한 안과 설명을 토의의 근거로 한다는 것이
포함되어 있다고 함.

　　나.　확실한 내용에 대하여는 언급하지 않으나 전기 요금에
관하여는 아측 제안을 수락할 것으로 보이나 인천의 수도 요금에
대하여는 아국측의 양보를 고집할 것이라는 인상을 받았음.

　　다.　본건에 관하여 국무성, 국방성 관계관의 협의가
있었으며 전기 요금에 관한한 한국의 수출진흥을 진작 시켜야
한다는 건지에서 수출업자에 대한 특혜적인 보조를 미군에게도
적용시켜야 한다는 주장을 미측이 고집하지 않아야 한다는 결론에도
달한 것으로 보임.

　　라.　"어떤 사용자보다 불리하지 않은" 이란 용어에
대하여 국무성에서는 "일반대중"을 일반적으로 기초를 삼고 있으며
정부 군대가 우대를 받을 경우 그를 적용하여 주어야 한다는
평범한 해석을 가지고 있으며 특수 사정하에 특정인에게 임시적
으로 적용하는 요금을 적용시켜야 한다는 극단적인 법해석을 하지
않고 있다는 것으로 보임.

첨부 :　WSW-0360　　　전문 사본 1통.　끝.

외   무   부

미이 723-   1969. 3. 13.

수신 : 경제기획원장관

참조 : 기획국장

제목 : 주한미군에 대한 공공요율

　　1. 1967년 년말에서 68년 년초에 걸쳐 인상된 일련의
공공요율중 대미군사용에 있어 상급 검밥을 보지 못한 전기
요금 및 인천 상수도 요금에 관하여 주미대사에게 미국무성
당국과 교섭을 지시한바 별첨사본과 같은 전문 보고가 있었아
오니 귀부에서 본건 처리 방침 수립에 있어 참고 하시기 바랍니다.

　　2. 동 전문 보고의 취지는 다음과 같습니다.

　　가. 국무성에서는 2월 하순 본건에 관하여 주한 미
대사관에 지시를 시달하였다하며, 동 지시는 주한미대사관이
청훈한 건의를 승인하는 내용으로 본부에서 누차에 걸쳐 미측에게
지시한 안과 설명을 토의의 근거로 한다는 것이 포함되어 있다고 함.

　　나. 확실한 내용에 대하여는 언급하지 않으나 전기 요금에
관하여는 아측 제안을 수락할 것으로 보이나 인천의 수도 요금에
대하여는 아국측의 양보를 고집할 것이라는 인상을 받았음.

다. 본건에 관하여 국무성, 국방성 관계관의 협의가
있었으며 런기 요금에 관한한 한국의 수출진흥을 진작시켜야
한다는 건지에서 수출업자에 대한 특혜적인 보조를 미군에게도
적용시켜야 한다는 주장을 미측이 고집하지 않아야 한다는 결론
에도 달한 것으로 보임.

마. "어떤 사용자보다 불리하지 않은" 이란 용어에
대하여 국무성에서는 "일반대중"을 일반적으로 기초를 삼고
있으며 정부나 군대가 우대를 받을 경우 그를 적용하여 주어야
한다는 평범한 해석을 가지고 있으며 묵수 사정하여 특정인에게
임시적으로 적용하는 요금은 적용시켜야 한다는 구단적인 법해석을
하지 않고 있다는 것으로 보임.

첨부 : WSW-0360   건문 사본 1통. 끝.

외 무 부 장 관

EXTRACTS OF SOFA'S ON UTILITIES AND SERVICES

Japan (June 23, 1960)

Article VII

The United States armed forces shall have the use
of all public utilities and services belonging to, or
controlled or regulated by the Government of Japan, and
shall enjoy priorities in such use, under conditions no
less favorable than those that may be applicable from
time to time the ministries and agencies of the Government
of Japan.

Republic of China - no provisions (Aug. 31, 1965)

Philippines

Article VII   Use of Public Services

It is mutually agreed that the United States may
employ and use for United States military forces any and
all public utilities, other services and facilities,

297

airfields, ports, harbors, roads, highways, railroads,
bridges, viaducts, cannals, lakes, rivers and streams in
the Philippines under conditions no less favorable than
those that may be applicable from time to time to the
military forces of the Philippines.

Australia (May 9, 1963)

Article XXIII   paragraph (1)

The United States Forces and all persons associated
with activities agreed upon by the two Governments may
use the public services and facilities owned, controlled
or regulated by the Australian Government or its instrumentalities.
The terms of use, including charges, shall be no less
favorable than those available to other users in like
circumstances unless otherwise agreed.

Dominican Republic (March 19, 1957)

Article XXVI

The Government of the United States of America shall
have the right to employ and use, in order to carry out
the purposes of this Agreement, all public services, including
any water rights owned or controlled by the Dominican Republic,

298

subject to the tariffs established by the Dominican laws
and regulations. Utilities and other facilities, bays,
roads, highways, bridges and similar channels of transportation
belonging, controlled or regulated by the Government of
the Dominican Republic shall be used under such terms and
conditions as shall be mutually agreed upon by the two
Governments.

Nicaragua (Sept. 5, 1958)

No provisions

West Indies (Feb. 10, 1961)

Article VII

Public Services and Facilities

(1) The United States Forces, United States contractors
and the members of the United States Forces and contractor
personnel may use the public services and facilities
belonging to or controlled or regulated by the Federal
Government or the Government of the Territory. The terms
of use, including charges, shall be no less favorable
than those available to other users unless otherwise agreed ...

299

Ethiopia (May 22, 1953)

        The Imperial Ethiopian Government grants to the
Government of the United States the right to employ and
use public and commercial utilities, services, transportation
and communication facilities in Ethiopia in connection with
operations under this Agreement. The Government of the
United States shall pay for any employment or usage of such
facilities at the most favorable rates obtained by other
public users who employ and use such facilities.

Libya (Sept. 9, 1954)

                        Article V

                Public Services and Facilities

        Upon the request of the Government of the United
States of America and provided that the Government of the
United Kingdom of Libya will be duly safeguarded, the
public services and facilities inLibya shall be made
available as far as practicable for the use of the Government
of the United States of America and members of the United
States forces. The charges therefor shall be the same as
those paid by other users, unless otherwise agreed.

NATO (June 19, 1951)

Article IX

1. Members of a force or of a civilian component and their dependents may purchase locally goods necessary for their own consumption, and such service as they need, under the same conditions as the nationals of the receiving State.

3. Subject to agreements already in force or which may hereafter be made between the authorized representatives of the sending and receiving States, the authorities of the receiving State shall assume sole responsibility for making suitable arrangements to make available a force or a civilian component the buildings and grounds which it requires, as well as facilities and services connected therewith. These agreements and arrangements shall be, as far as possible, in accordance with the regulations governing the accommodation and billeting of similar personnel of the receiving State. In the absense of a specific contract to the contrary, the laws of the receiving State shall determine the rights and obligations arising out of the occupation or use of the buildings, grounds, facilities or services.

301

Germany (Aug. 3, 1959)

Article 47

1. The Federal Republic shall accord to a force or
a civilian component treatment in the matter of procurement
of goods and services not less favorable than is accorded
to the German Armed Forces.

Greece (Sept. 7, 1956)

NATO Agr.

302

상　공　부

동전 1321-/13ㄹ (73-9375)　　　1969.8.28

수신　외무부장관

제목　한미합동위원회　협의　요정

　　　1.현행　한국전력주식회사　전기요금중　특수산업용
전기요금　할인규정을　별첨과같이　개정　실시코저하는바
　　　2.이에　관련하여　한미행정협정　합의　의사록
제6조제1항에　의한　협의를　요정하였더니　별첨과같이
경제기획원으로　부터　회신이　있기　이에　대한　귀견을
조속　통보하여　주시기　바랍니다

첨부 : 1.2급무회의　안건　　　　　　1부
　　　　2.경제기획원　공한　사본　1부.끝

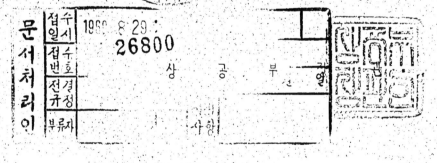

북미2과

2.12.1 23

경 제 기 획 원

물정 331.24-199   (72-9714)   1969. 8. 19

수신 상공부장관
제목 한미합동위원회 협의요청

　　　1. 동전 1321-1015 (69.8.6)에 대한 응신입니다

　　　2. 물정 331.24-187 (69.7.31)로 이미 통보한바와
같이 본건은 한미행정 협정 6조 2항 및 합의의사록
6조 1항에 의하여 미군에 적용되는 것이 아니므로 원칙적
으로 한미간 협의가 불필요한 사항입니다

　　　3. 다만 비공식적으로 미군측 실무자와 접촉한결과
본건에 대해 미군측에서 문제를 제기할 가능성이 있을
것으로 보이나 이경우 이미 수출산업요율을 미군에 적용
하도록 합의할 당시 상수도에 대하여는 46.7 프로의 할인을
하고 있던점에 비추어 보아 원래 문제된점이 다시 제기
되는 것에 불과한 것입니다. 끝

　　　　　　경 제 기 획 원 장 관

304

의안번호	제 호
의 결 년 월 일	1969. . . (제 회)

의결사항

특수산업용전기요금할인의 건(안)

제 출 자	국무위원 김정렴 (상공부장관)
제출년월일	1969. 7. 8.

305

1. 의결주문

한국전력주식회사 전기요금(특수산업용 전기요금 할인)을 별안과 같이 개정 실시할 것을 의결한다.

2. 제안이유

가. 현행 전기요금 할인제도는 정부의 산업정책상 실시하고 있으나 국제경쟁산업에 대하여는 보다 다각적인 정부 지원책을 필요로 하고 있음.

나. 따라서 국제경쟁산업중 전력비 비중이 과중한 업종에 대하여는 현행 할인율을 확대 적용함.

3. 주요골자

가. 할인율 개정대상

업 종	개정할인율	현 행	할인율개정기준
제철, 제강	최저 20%	15%	선진국의 동일업종에 사용되는 전기요금과

~1~

306

업 종	개정할인율	현 행	할인율개정기준
			대등할 수 있는 수준
알미늄 제련	최저 25%	20%	
P.V.C용 카바이트	50%	30%	P.V.C 수입원료와 경쟁할 수 있는 수준

나. 기타 특수산업용 할인은 현행대로 적용함.

다. 케도사업용 할인규정은 적용대상이 없으므로

   삭제함.

라. 개정요금 적용은

   1969년 원분 요금조정부터 적용함

4. 참고사항

가. 관계법령

   별첨

나. 예산조치

~2~

3 07

별도조치 필요없음.

다. 합 의

제38차 공공료금심사위원회에서 원안대로
의결됨.

단, 시행월자는 상공부장관이 대통령의 재가
를 얻어 별도 정하는 일자로 함.

라. 참 고 자 료

(1) 관계법령조문 (별첨 1)

(2) 전기요금할인추가액 (별첨 2)

(3) 현행전기요금할인대상 (별첨 3)

(4) 외국전기요금비교표 (별첨 4)

~3~

308

전기요금개정 (안)

1. 전기요금표 1 ~ (7) 특수산업요금을 아래와 같이 개정한다.

(7) 특수산업요금

　　200KW 이하의 수출산업, 제철, 제강업, 알미늄제련업, P.V.C 제조업과 상공부장관이 정하는 전력비가 총제조 원가의 20% 이상이 되는 업종에 대하여는 수용가별로 다음과 같이 요금을 할인 합니다.

　　총제조원가에 대한 전력비의 비중산정과 요금할인 요령은 상공부장관이 정합니다.

가. 200KW 이하의 수출산업은 30%

나. P.V.C 제조업체가 이에 소요되는 자가 카바이트 생산에 사용하는 전력은 50%

다. 제철·제강업은 최저 20% (선철 철강인고트 생산에 한함)

~4~

309

라. 알미늄 제련업은 최저   25 %

마. 전력비가 총제조 원가의

　　① 20% 이상 30% 미만은   15 %

　　② 30% 〃　40%　〃   20 %

　　③ 40 %　〃　50 %　〃   25 %

　　④ 50 % 이상은   30 %

2.　1～(10) 전기제도 사업용 전력요금청을 삭제 함

3.　Ⅱ 요금의 적용

　　1969 년　　　월분 요금조정부터 적용합니다

~5~

310

대 비 표

현 행	개 정 안
(7) 특수산업요금 200KW 이하의 수출산업 과 전력비가 총제조원가 의 20% 이상인 업종에 대하여는 상공부장관이 정하는 바에 의하여 다음 과 같이 요금을 할인합 니다.	(7) 특수산업요금 · 200KW 이하의 수출산업 제철. 제강업. 알미늄제련 업. P.V.C제조업과 상공 부장관이 정하는 전력비 가 총제조원가의 20% 이상이 되는 업종에 대 하여는 수용가별로 다음 과 같이 요금을 할인합 니다. 총제조원가에 대한 전력비의 비중산정과 요 금할인 요령은 상공부장 관이 정합니다

~6~

211

현 행	개 정 안
가. 200KW 이하의 수출산 업은 30%	가. 좌 동
〈신설〉	나. P.V.C 제조업체가 이에 소요되는 자가 카바이드 생산에 사용하는 전력은 50%
〈신설〉	다. 제철, 제강업은 최저 20% (선철, 철강인고트 생산에 한함)
〈신설〉	라. 알미늄제련업은 최저 25%
나. 전력비가 총제조원가의	마. 전력비가 총제조원가의
① 20% 이상 30% 미만은 15%	① 좌 동

~7~

312

현 행	개 정 안
② 30% 이상 40% 미만은 20%	
③ 40% 〃 50% 〃 25%	
④ 50% 이상은 30%	
(10) 전기궤도사업용 전력요금 일반요금의 46.7% 를 할인 합니다 단 전기궤도사업용 전력요금에 대하여는 1968년 1월 1일부터 적용합니다	(10) 삭 제
Ⅱ 요금의 적용 1967 년 11월 1일부터 본요금을 적용합니다	Ⅱ 요금의 적용 1967년 월분 요금 조정부터 적용합니다

313

참 고 자 료

~9~

314

(별첨 1)

관계법령조문

(1) 전기사업법

제19조 (전기요금 기타 공급조건의 허가) 전기사업자는 전기요금 기타의 공급조건에 관하여 상공부장관의 허가를 얻어야 한다. 이를 변경할때 또한 같다. 단, 한국전력회사법에 의한 한국전력회사의 전기요금에 관하여는 예산회계법 제3조에 의한다.

(2) 예산회계법

제3조 (공공요금의 결정) ① 국가독점사업의 전매가격과 사업요금은 공공요금 심사위원회와 국무회의의 심의를 거쳐 대통령의 승인을 얻어야 한다. ② 전항의 공공요금 심사위원회의 조직과 운영에 관한 사항은 법률로써 정한다.

~10~

315

(3) 공공요금 심사위원회 설치법

제2조 (정의) 본법에서 공공요금이라 함은 법률 또는 사실상 국가가 독점하는 사업의 전매가격과 사업요금을 말하며 그 사업의 종목은 각령으로 정한다.

(4) 공공요금 심사위원회 설치법시행령

제2조 (사업의 종목) 법제2조의 규정에 의한 사업종목은 다음과 같다.

1. 철 도
2. 전 기
3. 석탄 및 비료
4. 제조연초
5. 우편 전신 전화 우편환 및 우편대체저금

~11~

316

(별첨 2)

전기요금할인추가액

업 종	할인추가액	비 교 (총할인액)
제철. 제강	222,080 천원	(356,308)
알미늄 제련	53,000 "	(265,000)
P.V.C 용 카바이트	28,800 "	(72,000)
계	303,880 천원	(693,308)

~12~

317

현행전기요금할인대상

업 종 별	전력비 비중	할 인 율
1. 수출산업체	—	30 %
2. 전력비 할인		
가. 카바이트제조업	56.01 ~ 48.26 %	30 ~ 25
나. 가성소다 〃	51.62 ~ 27.75	30 ~ 15
다. 제철, 제강	21.66 ~ 20.02	15
라. 금속광업	22.10 ~ 20.51	15
마. 화학비료	50.11 ~ 30.27	30 ~ 20
바. 제빙업	37.89 ~ 20.61	20 ~ 15
사. 알미늄제련	40.00 ~ 30.000 (추정)	20
3. 상 수 도	—	46.7

~13~

318

외국전기요금비교표

국 별	제 강	알 미 늄	P. V. C용 카 바 이 트
한국 (세포함)	4.80	4.26	4.31
한 국	4.18	3.71	3.24
일본 (구 주)	3.94	3.60	3.60
영 국	3.81	3.37	3.37
한국(면세＋20%)	3.34 (3.84)	-	-
〃 (면세＋25%)	-	2.78 (3.20)	-
〃 (면세＋50%)	-	-	1.82 (2.45)
일본 (동 경)	2.62	2.45	

※ （ ） 내는 세포함

~14~

319

기안용지

분류기호 문서번호	미이-	(전화번호)	전결규정	조 항
			국 장	전결사항
처리기한		기 안 자	결 재 자	
시행일자		북미2과		
보존년한		박양천		
		69.9. 2.		
보조기관	북미2과장	OK		
협 조				
수신 유신	상공부 장관	통제 검열 1969.9.2 통제관	두부	
제 목	한.미합동위원회 협의 문제 회답			

1. 동전 1321- 1132(69.8.28.) 의 회신 입니다.

2. 귀부의 특수산업 전기요금 할인규정의 개정에 대하여 주한미군 당국은 한.미군대지위협정 제6조 2항과 제6조 1항에 대한 합의 의사록 1항에 의거하여 문제를 제기할 가능성은 있으나

3. 상기 할인규정의 개정에 앞서 미국측과의 사전 협의는 불필요 한것으로 판단됩니다.

4. 미국측의 문제 제기에 대비하여 관계부처간에 사전협의를 통해 한국 정부 입장을 미리 준비하는것이 가할것임을 아울러 첨언 합니다. 끝.

321

동동서식 1-2-1 (삽)
1967. 4. 4. 승인

(18절지) (2급인쇄용지 74g/m²)
(조달청) (100,000대 인쇄)

320

외   무   부

미이-   1959. 9. 2.

수신: 상공부 장관

제목: 한.미합동위원회 협의 문제 회답

    1. 등전 1321-1132(69. 8. 28.)의 회신입니다.

    2. 귀부의 특수산업 전기요금 할인규정의 개정에 대하여
주한미군 당국은 한.미군대지위협정 제6조 2항과 제5조 1항에
대한 합의 의사록 1항에 의거하여 문제를 제기할 가능성은
있으나

    3. 상기 할인규정의 개정에 앞서 미국측과의 사전 협의는
불필요한것으로 판단됩니다.

    4. 미국측의 문제 제기에 대비하여 관계 부처간에 사전
협의를 통해 한국 정부 입장을 미리 준비하는것이 가합것임을
아울러 첨언합니다.   끝

                외   무   부   장

특수산업용 전기 요금 할인안에 관한 분석집

1. 한.미군 대지위협정 제6조2항은 미군의 공공용어 사용에 있어
   최혜요율적용을 규정하고 있으며 (주1), 동 조 합의의사록 1항은
   요율변경에 있어 미군과의 사전 협의를 규정(주2)하고 있고 이에
   따라 합동위원회는 협의 절차를 정한바 있음.

2. 1967년 11월 인상된 전기요율의 대미군적용은 각종 할인요율
   중 최저요율을 적용하여야 한다는 미측 주장으로 인하여 1년반이나
   보류된후 수출제조업자할인 조항(계약용량 200킬로와트이하 30%할인)
   적용선에서 타협되었고, 1968년 2월 인상된 인천수도요금은 상급
   인상요율을 징수하지 못하고 있는 실정임.

3. 본안이 통과되는 경우 미군도 동일할인요율적용을 주장 할 가능성이
   있는바 협정문구 해석상으로는 이를 거부할 근거가 박약함.

4. 미군에게도 동일 할인요율적용 용의가 없는 경우는 면세, 보조금
   지불등 지정 보조형식을 취함이 가할것임.

5. 그렇지 않으면 본건 미군당국으로부터 동일한 할인요율 적용을 요구
   하여 올 경우 정부측으로서도 이에 적의 응할것을 고려하여야 할것임.

322

REPUBLIC OF KOREA-UNITED STATES
UTILITIES SUBCOMMITTEE

September 11, 1969

Subject: Change in Maintenance and Repair Service
         Charge on U.S. Military Sidetracts Under Article
         VI of the Status of Forces Agreement.

To: Chairman, U.S. Utilities Subcommittee

    1. Reference: Paragraph 2 and Agreed Minute 1
of Article VI of the Status of Forces Agreement.

    2. The Government of the United States is informed
through this written consultative process that the Republic
of Korea proposes to change the following rates/tariffs
at locations indicated below:

Rate/Tariff   Location

Maintenance and Repair Service   Whole Country
Charge on U.S. Military
Sidetracts.

    3. The following data is provided.

        a. Effective date.
            August 1, 1969

        b. Rate Schedule of proposed change.
            Refer to item "d"

        c. Rate Schedule showing rates that are charged
            all classes of users.
            Refer to Attachment I.

        d. Calculation of old and new rate base.

Classification	Unit	Old Rate	New Rate
Track	per meter	496	524
Highway Crossing	per meter in breadth	2400	2923
Bridge	per meter	1103	1234
Culvert	one place	4941	5563
Drainage	one place	1854	2121

e. Reasons for revision of rates.
   Increased prices of repair parts and
   personal expenditures

4. The Government of ROK advises the Government of
the United States that the priorities, conditions and
rates or tariffs being changed are no less favorable than
those accorded any other user. The view of the Government of the United States is solicited prior to the effective date of the rate change. You may be assured that
your views will be greatly appreciated.

for Suck J. Suh, Secretary
                Chung Uai Duc
                Republic of Korea Chairman
                Utilities Subcommittee

(Attachment I)

Maintenance and Repair Service Charge on
Sidetracts

Unit: Won per year

Clissification	Unit	Rate
Track	per meter	524
Highway Crossing	per meter in breadth	2923
Bridge	per meter	1234
Culvert	one place	5563
Drainage	one place	2121

Note: Above rate is applicable to all classes
of users.

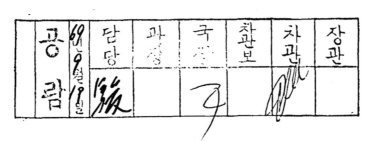

특수 산업용 전기요율 할인의 국무회의 상정

1. 상정 내용

   제철, 제강, 알미늄제련, PVC 용카바이트 제조등 전력비 비중이
   과중한 국제경쟁 산업에 대하여 정부가 정책적으로 이들 산업을 육성하기
   위하여 전기할인 요율을 각각 20%, 25%, 50%로 확대하려는 것임.

2. 국무회의 상정 보류 경위

   동 문제는 69. 7. 10. , 69. 9.4. 2차에 걸쳐 국무회의에 상정
   되었었으나 다음과 같은 외무부의 의견으로 본안이 보류되어 왔음.
   (외무부 의견)

   한. 미군대지위협정 제6조 2항은 미군의 공공용역 사용에 있어
   최혜요율 적용을 규정하고 있으며, 동조 합의 의사록 1항은 요율변경에
   있어 미군과의 사전 협의를 규정하고 있으므로 본안이 통과되는 경우
   미군도 동일 할인요율적용을 주장 할 가능성이 있으며 협정문귀 해석상
   으로는 이를 거부할 근거가 박약함. 그렇지 않을 경우 미군 당국으로
   부터 동일한 할인요율 (50%) 적용을 요구하여 올 경우 이에 적의 응할것을
   고려하여야 한다.

   * 현재 미군에 적용되는 전기 할인요율은 30% (200kw 이하의 수출산업용에
     적용되는 할인율임)

326

723.16(3)-4

3. 관계부처와의 협의

　　　외무부, 경제기획원, 상공부의 실무자들은 동 할인율적용의 한.미
행정협정상의 문제점을 검토하고 협의하였으며 이에 대하여 미군 당국이
협정문귀의 해석을 이유로 문제를 제기할 가능성은 있으나 이번 할인요율
확대는 미군에 적용될 성질의 것이 아니며 사전에 미군 당국과 협의 할
필요도 없다는 결론을 내리고, 만약 미군이 문제를 제기 할 경우에 대비
하여 관계부처가 협의, 필요한 준비를 하기로 합의하고 국무회의에
다시 상정키로 함.

4. 국무회의 재상정

　　　상공부는 69. 9. 19.의 국무회의에 본안을 재상정키로 하였으며
이번에 상정되는 안은 문제가 제기 될 가능성이 있는 요소인 PVC　용
카바이트제조의 50%할인안 (종전 30%할인)을 삭제하였음. 따라서
동안이 국무회의를 통과하고 시행된다 하드라도 미측에서 문제를 제기 할
여지가 없게되었음.

327

기 안 용 지

분류기호 문서번호	미이-	(전화번호　　　　)		전결규정	조　항
				국 장	전결사항

처리기한		기 안 자	결 재 자
시행일자		북미2과 김준모	기
보존년한		69. 9. 30.	

보 조 기 관	북미2과장	OK

협　조	
수 신 참 조	경제기획원장관 경제기획원(한.미합동위원회 공공용역분과위원회 한국측 위원장)
제　목	공공요율변경에 관한 한.미간의 사전 협의 절차

1. 사유화차의 요율변경등 공공요율변경의 경우 협정 제6조의 합의 의사록 1에 의한 사전 협의 절차에 있어 귀원은 한.미합동위원회를 거치지 않고 직접 미군당국과 협의를 개시하고 그 결과를 공공용역분과위원회 건의 형식으로 합동위원회에 상정하므로서 한.미군대지위협정의 시행 과 합동위원회 운영에 혼란을 가져왔읍니다.

2. 한.미군대지위협정에 의한 한.미합동위원회 분과위원회 "의사규칙" 1항에 의하면 "합동위원회는 분과위원회를 구성하여 기술적인 사항에 관하여 동위원회에 조언과 건의를 제공하도록 한다. 분과위원회는 합동위원회로부터 특별히 회부된 사항에 한하여서 조언과 건의를 한다" 라고 되어 있읍니다. 따라서 합동위원회가 과제로 위촉하지 아니한

공통서식 1-2-1 (갑)
1967. 4. 4. 승인
／ 제 속／
329
(조 달 청) (공급인쇄용지 74g/m²)
(400,000매 인쇄)

어떠한 문제에 관하여서도 분과위원회가 독자적으로 합동위원회에 건의할수 없읍니다.

3. 당부는 한.미합동위원회 미측 간사보부의 귀원이 1969. 9.11.자로 다시 합동위원회를 거치지 않고 미군사용 철도측선 보수요율 변경에 관한 사전협의를 미측에 제의하였다는 통보를 받았는바 이러한 귀원의 조치는 상기 분과위원회 의사규칙에 위배되는 한편 대외적으로 관계부처간의 협조가 결여되었음을 나타내는 결과를 초래하고 있음을 통보드립니다.

4. 동 미군사용철도측선 보수요율변경에 관하여서는 협정규정과 분과위원회 의사규칙에 따라 필요한 조치를 취하여 주시기 바라며 앞으로 요율변경의 사전 협의에 있어서는 반드시 합동위원회를 거쳐 과제가 위촉되어 협의를 개시하도록 협조하여 주시기 바랍니다.

5. ~~최후 소정의 절차에 의하지 아니한 분과위원회의 어떠한 건의도 합동위원회에 대한 건의로 인정하지 않을 것임을 첨언합니다.~~ 끝.

외   무   부

미이_   1969. 9. 30.

수신: 경제기획원장관

참조: 경제기획관(한.미합동위원회 공공용역분과위원회
                        한국측 위원장)

제목: 공공용역변경에 관한 한.미간의 사전 협의 절차

    1. 사유화차의 요율변경등 공공요율변경의 경우 협정 제6조
의 합의의사록 1에 의한 사전 협의 절차에 있어 귀원은 한.미합동
위원회를 거치지 않고 직접 미군 당국과 협의를 개시하고 그 결과
를 공공용역분과위원회 건의 형식으로 합동위원회에 상정하므로서
한.미군 대지위협정의 시행과 합동위원회 운영에 혼란을 가져왔읍니다.

    2. 한.미군 대지위협정에 의한 한.미합동위원회 분과위원회
"의사규칙"1항에 의하면 "합동위원회는 분과위원회를 구성하여
기술적인 사항에 관하여 동위원회에 조언과 건의를 제공하도록한다.
분과위원회는 합동위원회로부터 특별히 회부된 사항에 한하여서
조언과 건의를 한다"라고 되어있읍니다. 따라서 합동위원회가 과제
로 위촉하지 아니한한 어떠한 문제에 관하여서도 분과위원회가
독자적으로 합동위원회에 건의할수 없읍니다.

330.

3. 당부는 한.미합동위원회 미측 간사로부터 귀원이 1969.

9. 11자로 다시 합동위원회를 거치지 않고 미군사용 철도측선 보수

요율변경에 관한 사전 협의를 미측에 제의하였다는 통보를 받았는바

이러한 귀원의 조치는 상기 분과위원회 의사규칙에 위배되는 한편

대외적으로 관계 부처간의 협조가 결여되었음을 나타내는 결과를

초래하고 있음을 통보드립니다.

4. 동 미군사용철도측선 보수요율변경에 관하여서는 협정

규정과 분과위원회 의사규칙에 따라 필요한 조치를 취하여 주시기

바라며 앞으로 요율변경의 사전 협의에 있어서는 반드시 합동위원회

를 거쳐 과제가 위촉되어 협의를 개시하도록 협조하여 주시기

바랍니다. 끝

외 무 부 장 관

351

경 제 기 획 원

물 정·331.24-246 (72.9704)   1969.   10.   2
수 신·외무부장관
참 조·구미국장
제 목·공공요율 변경에 관한 한미간의 사전 협의
       절차

   1. 미이 - 17557 (69. 9. 30) 과 관련 입니다.
   2. 귀부가 지적한 바에 의하면 분과위원회는
합동위원회의 개별적인 과제 위촉에 의해서만 합동
위원회에 조언과 건의를 하도록 하고 있으므로
용역분과 위원회에서 1969. 9. 11. 합동위원회를
거치지 않고 미군 사용 철도측선 보수 요율변경에
관한 사전협의를 미측에 제의함으로서 분과위원회
의사규칙에 위배함은 물론 합동위원회 운영에 큰
혼란을 야기 하였다는 것입니다.
   3. 그러나 본 문제 처리에 있어 용역분과
위원회는 이미 합동위원회에서 한미간에 합의된
절차에 따라 한것이며 다음과 같은 점을 참고하시기
바랍니다.

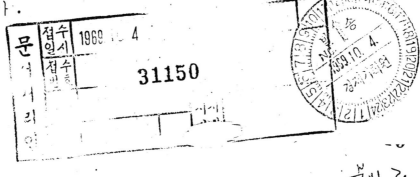

392

가. 미이 741.1 - 1555 (68. 1. 20)에 의하여 요율
변경에 관한 협의 절차를 용역분과위원회에서
협의 결정하여 합동위원회에 건의하도록 과제
부여가 있었을뿐아니라 본 문제에 관하여서는
문제의 기술적인 성격과 시간적 제약을 감안하여
"분과위원회 운영규정의 일반원칙에 예외를
설정"하여 공공용역분과위원회는 합동위원회의
명문과제 부여없이 자발적으로 문제를 취급하는
권한이 부여되었으며 이러한 원칙은 귀부가
당원에 미이 720 - 2256 (68. 1. 30)로 통보한
제20차 한미합동위원회 회의록에 의하여
확인된 것인점 .

나. 위의 과제부여에 따라 용역분과위원회의
협의 절차를 제22차 합동위원회에서 합의한바
이협의 절차에 의하여도 합동위원회의 과제부여가
불 필요한 것인점 . 끝.

경 제 기 획 원 장 관

393

경   제   기   획   원

물 정 331. 24 - 3 ㅡ4ㅡ9 (72 - 9704)   1969. 12.   26.

수 신· 외 무 부 장 관

제 목· S O F A 협정에 의한 전기 및 철도요금 변경협의

1969. 12. 27 부터 전기요금 (10% 인상) 및 철도 요금이 인
상조정 되었으므로 이를 주한 미군에 적용하기에 앞서 한미행정협
정 제 6조에 의한 협의를 한미 합동위원회 공공용역 분과위원회의
협의 절차에 의거 별첨과 같이 미국측 공공용역 분과 위원장에게
통보하였아오니 양지하시기 바랍니다.

별 첨·   1) S O F A 협정에 의한 전기요금 변경
        2) S O F A 협정에 의한 철도요율의 변경·   끝.

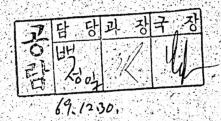

경   제   기   획   원

REPUBLIC OF KOREA-UNITED STATES
UTILITIES SUBCOMMITTEE

December 26, 1969

Subject: Change in Electric Rate Schedule applicable to
the US Armed Forces under Article VI of The
Status of Forces Agreement

To: US Chairman, Utilities Subcommittee

1. Reference: Paragraph 2 and Agreed Minute 1 of
Article VI of the Status of Forces Agreement.

2. The Government of the United States is informed
through this written consultative process that the ROK
proposes to change the following rates/tariffs at locations indicated below:

Rate/Tariffs   Location

Electric rate schedule applicable
to the US Armed Forces   Whole Country

3. The following data is provided:

a. Effective date
   27 December, 1969
b. Rate Schedule showing rates that are charged
   all classes of users.   Attached
c. Rate Schedule of proposed change.
   10% increase with no exception over the old
   rate schedule. For detailed information,
   refer to item "b".
d. Calculation of old and new rate base.
   Refer to item "b"
e. Reasons for revision of rate.
   To secure fair return and investment fund.

4. The Government of ROK advises the Government of
the United States that the priorities, conditions and
rates or tariffs being changed are no less favorable than
those accorded any other user. The view of the Government
of the United States is solicited prior to the effective
date of the rate changes. You may be assured that your
views will be greatly appreciated.

Suck Joon, Suh
Director, Office of Price Policy
Republic of Korea Chairman
Utilities Subcommittee

<u>New Electric Rate Schedule</u>

(Effective From 27, Dec. 1969)

TARIFF 1
GENERAL SERVICE A

APPLICABLE:

To residential service without limit and general service of 4kw demand or under.

TYPE OF SUPPLY:

Single or three phase supply at any one of the Company's available standard voltages, 100v or 200v.

MONTHLY BILL:

Basic Rate:

Energy Charge::

W 142.50 for the first 3 kwh
W 13.50 per kwh for the next 27 kwh
W 10,25 per kwh for the next 180 kwh   *
W 7,90 per kwh for each additional kwh
* Add 90 kwh at W10.25 block for each kw in excess of 3kw of demand

Minimum Charge : W142. 50.

TARIFF 2
GENERAL SERVICE B

APPLICABLE:

To general service of 4 kw of contracted demand and over

TYPE OF SUPPLY:

Single or three phase supply at any one of the Company's available standard voltages, 20kv 10kv 6kv 5.2kv, 3kv,200v, 100v or others.

MONTHLY BILL:

Basic Rate:

a. Demand Charge:

W160.00 per kw for the first 50 kw of contracted demand.
W127.00 per kw for the next 450 kw of contracted demand.
W 95.00 per kw for each additional kw of contracted demand.

b. Energy Charge:

W 8.25 per kwh for the first 90 kwh per kw of contracted demand.
W 5.65 per kwh for the next 90 kwh per kw of contracted demand.
W 4.07 per kwh for the next 180 kwh per kw of contracted demand.
W 2.75 per kwh for each additional kwh.

C. Minimum contracted kw of demand; 4 KW.

TARIFF 3
HIGH TENSION SERVICE

HIGH TENSION SERVICE

APPLICABLE:

To service of 100 Kw of contracted demand and over and 20 kv and over

TYPE OF SUPPLY:

Three phase supply at any one of the Company's available standard voltages 20 kv and over.

MONTHLY BILL:

Basic Rate:

a. Demand Charge:

W 132.00 per kw for the first 500 kw of contracted demand.
W 88.00 per kw for each additional kw of contracted demand

b. Energy Charge:

W 8.25 per kwh for the first 90 kwh per kw of contracted demand
W 5.37 per kwh for the next 90 kwh per kw of contracted demand
W 3.74 per kwh for the next 180 kwh per kw of contracted demand
W 2.36 per kwh for each additional kwh

c. Minimum contracted kw of demand; 1,000 KW.

HIGH STENSION SERVICE B

APPLICABLE:

To service of 150 kv and over.

TYPE OF SUPPLY:

Three phase supply at any one of the Company's available standard voltages, 150 kv and over.

MONTHLY BILL:

Basic Rate:

a. Demand Charge:
W 88.00 per kw of contracted demand.

b. Energy Charge:

W 8.25 per kwh for the first 90 kwh per kw of contracted demand.
W 5.31 per kwh for the next 90 kwh per kw of contracted demand.
W 3.66 per kwh for the next 180 kwh per kw of contracted demand.
W 2.35 per kwh for each additional kwh.

TARIFF 4
IRRIGATION SERVICE

APPLICABLE:

To service required for the operation of pumps which are used to irrigate land for the cultivation and growing of grain for food purpose Lighting necessary and incidential to the operation of pumps is permitted.

TYPE OF SUPPLY:

Same as "General Service B"

MONTHLY BILL:

Basic Rate:

Demand Charge: W 47.00 per kw for contracted demand.
Energy Charge: W 3.05 per kwh for each kwh

TARIFF 5
STREET LIGHTING SERVICE

APPLICAB LE:

To servide for operation of lighting of streets parks and similar places for the benefit and convenience of public

TYPE OF SUPPLY:

Single phase at either 100 v or 200 v

MONTHLY BILL:

Basic Rate: W 2.40 per watt for connected load
Minimum Charge: W 80.00

TARIFF 6
FLAT RATE LIGHTING SERVICE

APPLICABLE:

To lighting service (including radio substituted on set as one lamp), principally limited to 100 watts of connected load with three lamps or under One radio set shall be counted as 20 watts

- 3 -

359

TYPE OF SUPPLY:

Single phase supply at eigher 100 v or 200 v

MONTHLY BILL:

Basic Rate:

W 4.70 per watt for first 60 watts of connected load
W 3.20 per watt for additional watts of connected load

Minimum Charge: W 80.00.

SPECIAL PROVISIONS

1. SPECIAL INDUSTRY:

   a. To export industry customers with 200 kw of contracted demand
   or under
   b. To aluminium iron and steel industry customers whose power
   charges occupy more than 10% of the total production cost
   c. To industry customers whose power charges occuply more than 20%
   of the total production cost who are designated by the Minister
   of Comenerce and Industry.

DISCOUNT: Monthly bill shall be discounted as follows:

a. 30% duscount: for esport industry customer with 200 kw of contracted
demand or under.

b. 20% discount: for the aluminium, iron and steel industry customer
whose electric charges occupy 10% and over, of the
total production cost.

   25% discount: for the aluminium, iron and steel industry customer whose
electric charges occupy 30% and over, of the total production cost.

   30% discount: for the aluminium, iron and steel industry customer whose
electric charges occupy 40% and over of the total production cost.

c. 15% discount: for the industry customer whose electric charges occupy
20% and over, of the total production cost.

   20% discount: for the industry customer whose electric charges occupy
30% and over, of the total production cost.

   25% discount: for the industry customer whose electric charges occupy
40% and over, of the total production cost.

   30% discount: for the industry customer whose electric charge occupy 50%
and over, of the total production ocst.

2. MUNICIPAL WATER SERVICE:

Rate for Municipal Water Service shall be discounted by 46 7%

- 4 -

340

REPUBLIC OF KOREA-UNITED STATES
UTILITIES SUBCOMMITTEE

December 26, 1969

SUBJECT: Change in Railroad Rate Schedule applicable to the US
Armed Forces under Article VI of the Status of Forces
Agreement

TO :   US Chairman, Utilities Subcommittee

1.   Reference: Paragraph 2 and Agreed Minute 1 of Article VI
of the Status of Forces Agreement.

2.   The Government of the United States is informed through
this written consultative process that the Republic of Korea proposes
to change the following rates/tariffs at locations indicated below:

Rates/Tariffs   Location

Railroad rate schedule applicable   Whole Country
to the US Armed Forces

3.   The following data is provided:

a. Effective date.
    27 December, 1969

b. Rate schedule of proposed change.
    Refer to item "d".

c. Rate schedule showing rates that are charged all classes
    of users. (Attachment I)

d. Calculation of old and new rate.
    (Attachment II)

e. Reasons for revision of rate base.
    To secure transportation cost and investment fund.

341

4.   The Government of ROK advises the Government of the United States that the priorities, conditions and rates or tariffs being changed are no less favorable than those accorded any other user. The view of the Government of the United States is solicited prior to the effective date of the rate changes. You may be assured that your views will be greatly appreciated.

Suck Joon, Suh
Director, Office of Price Policy
Republic of Korea Chairman
Utilities Subcommittee

342

〈Attachment I〉 SCHEDULE OF RATES, FARES AND CHARGE

Item No.	Applicable Tech Spec.	Description	Unit	Rate (Won)	Remarks
I.	3.I.2.	Carload Freight			
a.		Basic Rate Using Carrier's Car	Per Car/ Per Km	58.15	All type of car.
b.		Baisc Rate Using US Owned Car	"	37.80	"
c.		Minimum Charge for Carloadof Rented and US Owned Car	per Car	2,880.00	
2.	3.1.3.	Special Train Service	Per Train	125,730.00	Basic Rate shall be same as Itm No. 1 above.
3.	3.1.4.	Demurrage	Per Car Per unit of 6 hrs.	1,006.00	6 hours or fraction there of beyond the first initial free time.
4.	3.1.5.	Diversion or Reconsign-ment	Per Car	2,016.00	No Payment shall be applied if the request is make prior to spotting for unloading
5.	3.1.6.	Cancellation of Car Ordered	Per Car	1,004.00	
6.	3.1.7.	Switching Charge	Per Car	523.00	
7.	3.1.8.	Stopoff in Transit	Per Car	939.00	
8.	3.1.9.	Equipment Rental	Per Car/ Per Day	798.00	Only when the car is in servi- ceable condition.
9.	3.1.11	Deadhead Movement of Rented or US Owne Car	Per Car/ Per Km	14.30	
~~10.~~	~~3.1.12~~				
10.	3.1.12.	Surcharge for Oversized freight	Per Car/ Per km	2.60	
11.	a.3.2.2.	Passenger Services Basic Rate	Per Car/ Per Km	118.80	
		Minimum charge	Per Car		Distance less than 50km. will be computed as 50km.
		Janitorial Svcs Including Cleaning at Origin	Per Car/ Per Day	450.00	
	b.3.2.2.a.	Minimum Charge for Special TRAIN Service	Per Car/ Per Km	118,580.00	
	c.3.2.2.b.	Basic Rate for Motor Coach/	Per Coach/ Pe Km	118.80	
		Surcharge for Motor Coach	Per/ Coach	25,920.00	
		Minimum Charge for motor coach	Per/ coach	36,460.00	

343

d.	3.2.2.c.	Surcharge for Common Express	Per Car/ Per Trip	7.200	From 1km to 200 Km km.
				14.400	From 201km to 400 Km km
				21.600	401km over.

e.	3.2.2.d.	Surcharge for Special express	Per Trip	10.800	From 1km to 200km
				21.600	From 201km to 400km
				43.200	401km over

		Surcharge for sight-seeing *express*	Per Trip	11.200	From 1km to 200km
				22.400	From 201km to 400km
				44.800	401km over

		Seat-charge sight-seeing express	Per Car/ Per Trip	56,000.00	surcharged 24.000 won for special passenger car
		special class	"	33.600	
		1st class	"	7.200	

12. 3.2.3. **Individual Travel**

a. **Rate:** Rates prescribed in the officially published KNR passenger tariff effective on the date travel ticket is purchased for class of accommodations as requested.

b. **Unused Ticket:**

Unused teckets for regular trains may be returned to station of issue for cancellation of the TR(Transportation) at any time prior to departures of the train, without charge.

Unused tickets for special express, 2d class of common express and semiexpress train and 2d coaches shall be refunded 80% of purchased rate when the ticket is returned to station of issue on the day prior to scheduled departure of train.

Unused tickets for special express, 2d class of common express and semiexpress train and 2d coaches shall be refunded 50% of purchased rate when the ticket is returned to station of issue on the days of scheduled departure but prior to actual departue of trains.

For all unused tickets returned for cancellation after train departure time, full payment will be make to the Korean National Railroad.

13. 3.2.4. **Equipment Rental**

a.		Business Car, Sleeper, Hospital Car, Dinning Car, Kitchen Car & Passenger Type Coach	Per Car/ Per Day	1,620.00
b.		Baggage and Mail Car	Per Car/ Per Day	1,290.00
c.		Passenger and Mail Combination Car	Per Car/ Per Day	1,076.00

14.	3.2.5.	Deadhead Movement of Rental or US-Owned Car	Per Car/ Per Km	28.00
15.	3.2.6.	Transportation of Sentry Dog		
a.		Less than 100km	Per Dog	369.00
b.		100.1-200km	Per Dog	621.00
c.		200.1-500km	Per Dog	854.00
d.		More than 600km	Per Dog	1,071.00
16.	3.3.2.	US Government Owned Cars		
a.		Scheduled general inspection and repair excluding painting (every 24 months)	Per Car	32,000.00
b.		Painting Only	Per Car	12,800.00

In the event, KNR can not furnish sand blasting without faults or negligence of KNR, the price shall be adjusted accordingly pursuant to KNR regulations.

17. 3.3.2. Equipment, Parts and Materials:

In the event the following parts and materials are requested to be furnished by the Korean National Railroad instead of the Government furnished material as specified in this contract the following rate shall be applied:

Wheel, chilled solid, (Including an Axle and two (2) wheels)	Set	$ 320.00
Wheel, Tired (one(1) wheel)	Ea	$ 153.00
Axle	"	$ 78.00
Coupler	"	$ 90.00
Draft Gear	"	$ 90.00
Triple Valve	"	$ 70.00
Bolster Spring	"	$$ 93.00
Side Frame	"	$ 110.00
Brake Beam	"	$ 23.00
Bolster	"	$ 120.00

17. (Contd'd)

Paint: Black	kg	$ 1.40
Red Lead	"	$ 1.40
White	"	$ 1.40
Silver	"	$ 1.40
Thinner	"	$ 1.40

345

(Attachment II)

CALCULATION OF OLD AND NEW RATE BASE

Description	Unit	Old Rate (won)	New Rate (won)	Remarks
Passenger Services Basic Rate	Per Car/ Per km	175.00	118.80	
Minimum Charge for Passenger Services (new charge)		—	5,940.00	Distance less than 50 Km will be computed as 50 km
Basic Rate for Motor Coach	Per Coach/ Per km	156.16	118.80	
Surcharge for Motor Coach	Per Coach	19,200.00	25,920.00	
Minimum Charge for Motor Coach	Per Coach	27,008.00	36,460.00	
Minimum Charge for Special Train Service	Per Train	87,840.00	118,580.00	
Surcharge for Kwan Kwang Ho (Sightseeing Express) (new charge)	Per Car/ Per Trip	—	To 200km; 11,200.00 To 400km; 22,400.00 From 401km and over 44,800.00	
Surcharge for Special Express	Per Car/ Per Trip	43,200.00	To 200km; 10,800.00 To 400km; 21,600.00 From 401km and over 43,200.00	
Surcharge for Common Express	Per Car/ Per Trip	21,600.00	To 200km; 7,200.00 To 400km; 14,400.00 From 401km and over 21,600.00	

346

Description	Unit	Old Rate (won)	New Rate (won)	Remarks
Surcharge for Super Express	Per Car/ Per Trip	86,400.00	Obsolete	
Surcharge for Semi-Common Express	Per Car/ Per Trip	10,800.00	Obsolete	
Charge for Seat Reserved (new charge)				
a. Kwan Kwang Ho	Per Car	-	56,000.00	24,000.00 will be added for special room
b. The first class	Per Car	-	33,600.00	
c. The second class	Per Car	-	7,200.00	
Equipment Rental				
a. Business Car, Sleeper, Hospital Car, Dining Car & Passenger Type Coach	Per Car/ Per Day	1,196.00	1,620.00	
b. Baggage and Mail Car	Per Car/ Per Day	956.90	1,290.00	
c. Passenger and Mail Combination Car	Per Car/	1,676.00	1,290.00	
Deadhead Movement of Rental or US Owned Car	Per Car/ Per km	20.05	28.00	

외교문서 비밀해제: 주한미군지위협정(SOFA) 34
주한미군지위협정(SOFA) 공공용역 합동위원회 1

초판인쇄 2024년 03월 15일
초판발행 2024년 03월 15일

지은이 한국학술정보(주)
펴낸이 채종준
펴낸곳 한국학술정보(주)
주 소 경기도 파주시 회동길 230(문발동)
전 화 031-908-3181(대표)
팩 스 031-908-3189
홈페이지 http://ebook.kstudy.com
E-mail 출판사업부 publish@kstudy.com
등 록 제일산-115호(2000. 6. 19)

ISBN 979-11-7217-045-5 94340
       979-11-7217-011-0 94340 (set)